P9-DUN-025

DATE DUE

DE 16 '94		
AP 24 '05		
AG 1 '96		
OC 22 '96		
DE 2 '00		
NO 7 '01		
NO 26 '01		
NO 18 '03		
DE 8 '04		
JY 28 '05		

DEMCO 38-296

How to PRODUCE Effective TV Commercials

Hooper White

Third Edition

NTC Business Books
a division of *NTC Publishing Group* • Lincolnwood, Illinois USA

Library of Congress Cataloging-in-Publication Data

White. Hooper.
    How to produce effective TV commercials / Hooper White. — 3rd ed.
      p.   cm.
    Includes index.
    ISBN 0-8442-3017-0
    1. Television advertising.   I. Title.
HF6146 . T42N46   1994
659 . 14 ' 3—dc20   93-8009
                                                              CIP

Published by NTC Business Books, a division of NTC Publishing Group
4255 West Touhy Avenue
Lincolnwood (Chicago), Illinois 60646–1975, U.S.A.
© 1994 by Hooper White. All rights reserved.
No part of this book may be reproduced, stored in a retrieval system,
or transmitted in any form or by any means,
electronic, mechanical, photocopying, recording or otherwise,
without the prior permission of NTC Publishing Group.
Manufactured in the United States of America.

  4 5 6 7 8 9 0 VP 9 8 7 6 5 4 3 2 1

To Maris, my wife, my severest critic,
and my best friend.

CONTENTS

FOREWORD

By Leonard S. Matthews, Former President,
American Association of Advertising Agencies

I first met Hooper White in 1959, when he joined Leo Burnett to develop a television commercial production office for that agency in New York City. I was in charge of the Media Department at Leo Burnett and later became its president.

I would drop into Hooper's office at 8:30 in the morning, a good Chicago hour, but a very lonely one in New York. We would chat about our business in general, and his part of it in particular. I was interested in getting more information about commercial production so that I would be better prepared to judge the commercials as he sent them to us back in Chicago, where the agency was and is headquartered.

I was impressed by Hooper's enthusiasm for his work in the relatively new advertising medium, television. Hooper would describe all sorts of unusual things; for example, "blue dupes," "keystoning," and "out of sync." As a result, I was better prepared for commercial screenings in Chicago.

In the years Hooper worked with me at Burnett, he was involved in the production of commercials for Marlboro, Virginia Slims, Kentucky Fried Chicken, Camay, Nestle's products, Heinz Ketchup, and many more blue-ribbon advertisers. During that time, Burnett's involvement in television as an advertising medium rose from 40 percent to 70 percent—and Burnett's billings rose from $90 million to more than $800 million. Eventually, the agency became the fourth largest in the world.

One of the interesting aspects of our business is that each advertising agency does things slightly differently. This applies particularly to commercial production, but no matter how an agency handles production, somewhere in the middle of the team is the producer, with varying duties and responsibilities. Hooper White has seen all the variations, and worked through a number of them at Leo Burnett before starting his own company in 1976.

Hooper White is one man writing one book and, as with most books, a great deal of the information is drawn from the author's own personal experience. He strives to bridge the gap between his experience in the field and how other people create and produce. Because he was around when it all started back in the late 1940s, I think he has an edge that will make this book all the more worthwhile.

Good creative advertising people as well as good commercial producers are a combination of all sorts of things. They are involved in music, art, writing, business procedures, budgets, time schedules, but most of all in advertising. Hooper White exemplifies this combination to the nth degree. I believe he is amply qualified to write this in-depth study, not only because of his past experience, but also because of his ongoing involvement in the creation and production of television advertising.

I recommend this book highly to everyone in advertising: neophyte or professional, agency or client, student or practitioner. You'll find it interesting even if you only watch television.

ACKNOWLEDGMENTS

I want to say thank you to the many people who have helped me during the writing and researching of this third edition. For taking the time to read specific chapters on their craft, I am indebted to Rick Ledyard, Robert Greenberg, Jim Martin, Dale Freres, Tom Kennedy, Henry Sandbank, and John Hughes. For additional help over the years, some of it inadvertent, I am indebted to Mort Goldsholl, Al Lapides, Bill Young, Ken Nordine, Dick Marx, Albert Maysles and the late David Maysles, Bob Kurtz, Bob Peluce, Dick Orkin, Steve Allen, Bert Berdis, Art Bellaire, Jack Graham, Stu Hagmann, David Impastato, Dick Kerns, Rick Thompson, Joel Hochberg, Bob Abel, Sandy Martin, and Lori White. Posthumously, this book owes a great deal to Leo Burnett, Sid Bernstein, and Cleo Hovel.

Throughout this book I have changed the nomenclature of certain jobs from their former sexist terms: camera man is now referred to as camera person—script girl is now referred to as script clerk, and so on. In truth, the industry is changing with the rest of life, and sexist roles and names are fading away. Many home economists and script clerks are men, and many directors and camera operators are women. Which is as it should be.

PROLOGUE

When I was in college, I wanted to write for a newspaper. Not just any newspaper. A big city daily, preferably in the sports department. Little did I know that instead I would spend my life in an industry that didn't even exist at that time.

When I graduated from North Central College, a wonderful, small liberal arts college in Naperville, Illinois, I had been editor of the college newspaper for two years and also had a bona fide rejection slip from *The New Yorker* with Harold Ross's name stamped on it. Armed with these formidable credentials, I went to see the managing editors of the Chicago newspapers; the *Chicago Tribune*, the *Chicago Herald and Examiner*, and the *Chicago Daily News*. I offered them my great abilities and was met with a uniform "Thanks, but no thanks."

Slowly, it dawned on me that I really wasn't ready for such a step, so maybe I'd better try somthing else. I wrote letters to every radio station in Illinois, filling each with the joyous news of my availability. I received one reply—from the program director of WTMV, East St. Louis, Illinois (not to be confused in any way with the great city of St. Louis, just across the Eads Bridge). With gratitude, I accepted the job, at $20 a week.

My job was to be Everyman: announce all live commercials during an eight-hour shift, answer phones after regular office hours, and write local radio commercials—including those for "Suzy and Her Sons of the Ozarks," sponsored by Uncle Dick Slack of the Slack Furniture Company. (One of our announcers almost put us off the air with a transposition of our client's name as he introduced this country group.)

From these bucolic beginnings, I followed the stream of broadcast as it became "big-time network." I worked for the CBS owned-and-operated WBBM radio as a director for eight years. Then the broadcast stream went over a waterfall, and pictures were introduced to the sounds of radio. Television lit up the homes of America.

Through the coincidence of time and place, I was around when television started and became the commercial producer for the "Wednesday Night Fights," followed by several years as a TV producer with the Chicago office of J. Walter Thompson.

After almost 19 years with the Leo Burnett agency—both in New York and hometown Chicago—I decided to strike out on my own. I really wondered whether I knew anything about the business, after producing commercials for Burnett all over the world. My wife and I formed the Hooper White Company, a two-person Delaware Corporation complete with phone, fax, and two small computers, headquartered on the back porch of my home in Barrington Hills, Illinois.

I began to write a full-page monthly column titled "The Art of Commercial Production" for the advertising bible, *Advertising Age*, and the next thing I knew, several large companies hired me to consult with them on the production of their TV commercials. I also wrote the first edition of "How to Produce Effective TV Commercials." You are now reading the third edition.

I know of no other communications force that developed as quickly as television. From the early days of black-and-white reception, through the introduction of color, we now are witnessing a veritable explosion in TV communication. Where we originally had only a few channels, we now have more than 50—with the possibility of as many as 500 channels just over the horizon. With this proliferation of channels has come a flood of electronic wonders offering interactive communication on a global scale.

The biggest time-bite I ever attempted to chew was to write this book. I truly thought, when I wrote the first edition in 1982, that I could rest on my word processor while the book was digested for at least ten years. Wrong. That edition was out of date by 1988, so I wrote the second edition. Now, thought I, for a well-deserved rest from writing. Wrong again.

That second edition reads today like the specs for the Edsel automobile, all because of the introduction of one word in the production process . . . digital.

From the moment in the late '80s when both sight and sound could be turned into the 0s and 1s of the computer, all the old rules of commercial production became history. No longer is there a need to go to an Optical House to add dissolves and titles. As a matter of fact, we now have one-stop editing and finishing, with elapsed post-production time reduced from a few weeks to a few days, or even a few hours.

But that's only one of the latter-day phenomena. The folks who produce commercials now come from many seemingly unassociated paths . . . mathematicians, computer wizards, philosophers, men and women with degrees in architecture and environmental design. It's a wonderful new approach to producing commercials, realized in the ever-changing world of computer programming. And these new eyes are looking at producing commercials in a new way, as they originate new combinations of sight and sound.

Another shift in the production process has been in the leadership of the creative team. Once the agency producers' perogative, the mantle moved on to the shoulders of the writer as the originator of the "idea" for the commercial. But now, as the "look" of the commercial becomes more important than the words heard in the soundtrack, the art director steps into the leadership role. As in the past, each agency administers production roles in its own manner, but in general the lines between writer, producer, and art director have become more blurred. In many agencies the entire creative/production process has become a flow—a community effort from beginning to end.

If I were to define the audience for whom I am writing this third edition, I would first of all include students looking toward a career in advertising or in the making of commercials. It is my hope that this book will help explain the varying roles involved in the production process. Then, I would hope this book would provide information for the many people in the advertising and promotion process not directly connected with the various stages of producing broadcast advertising. If I perform my author's role well, this book should remove a great deal of the mystery from the methods used in making commercials.

This book is also intended to assist brand managers in today's market-oriented business world. Quite often, the various stages in the development of a commercial have not been fully understood by the very people who are footing the bill. I hope this book will take some of the mystery from the commercial-making process.

One of the ever-present mysteries involves money: Why do commercials cost so much? Is there a direct relationship between production cost and commercial effectiveness? The answer is "not really," and I hope this book will help clarify that enigmatic answer. To put the answer in as few words as possible, commercial production cost is typed into the commercial by the writer, and drawn into the commercial by the art director. And that is what this book is all about. I will attempt to prove that Big Ideas do not have a direct relationship to production cost.

Because production has become an expensive procedure, I feel the more complete the information is, the better the end product will be—and hopefully, production dollars will be saved with this knowledge. As the technology becomes even more sophisticated, it becomes even more important for those paying the bills to be aware of what those producing the commercials are asking them to pay for.

To these propositions, then, I set my course. I hope this book opens up new vistas and that we arrive together at the same destination; a better understanding of how to create and produce one of the most potent selling tools ever forged—the television commercial.

1 TV COMMERCIAL PRODUCTION TODAY

I once compared producing a TV commercial to writing a story on a block of ice. Very few commercials stick around very long; they melt quickly into the past. Therefore, one of the major challenges of producing commercials is to produce a message that will continue to influence the marketplace for more than two or three 13-week cycles.

Although the methods of originating ideas and producing TV commercials have changed since commercial television began in the late 1940s, the major challenge is still with us: What can I produce within the discipline of a few seconds of airtime that will make a difference in the marketplace?

Change Affecting TV Commercials

Although this ultimate goal remains the same, the producers of TV commercials in the 1990s must contend with several new trends. The length of TV commercials has become a game of extremes—either very short or very long—bringing about a whole new set of rules. The choice of outlets for the final product has become nearly limitless because of expanding cable networks and new media offerings from telephone companies. The new emphasis among advertisers upon sales promotion has created new conflicts both in carrying out the sales strategy and in monitoring the ever-important "bottom line." Let's look at these changes in more detail.

Today's TV commercial has become both shorter and longer than in the past. On the one hand, the 60-second commercial gave way to the 30-second commercial, and now 10- and 15-second commercials are also in vogue. On the other hand, "infomercials," which last as long as 30 minutes, have helped sell everything from self-help programs to Ross Perot's bid for the presidency in 1992. Perot's 30-minute political commercials, which featured Perot discussing in detail his concerns about the economy, were pivotal in garnering almost 20 percent of the presidential vote that year, even though he wasn't affiliated with either major party.

Along with extremes in the length of TV commercials, there is an extreme expansion of choices of where to place the final product.

There is no end in sight of the proliferation of TV channels, whose programming is aimed at ever-narrowing demographic segments of the population. The increasing influence of alternative informational outlets is eroding the previously concentrated power of commercials shown on the Big Three traditional networks: ABC, CBS, and NBC.

The last decade of the 20th century will see new entertainment and information sources pouring into the home via telephone wires, rather than by broadcast or cable channels. The advent of such marketing from the nation's telephone companies will have a direct effect on the type of commercials to be produced for American products and services.

These new forms of media, linked to personal computers in people's homes, will allow for immediate response to advertising messages. This interaction will produce increasingly individualized marketing data. The availability of this information will in turn create pressure for commercials to appeal not to a broadly defined demographic segment of the population, but to "micro-markets" of people with idiosyncratic needs, desires, and interests.

A change outside the area of traditional advertising has revolutionized the ground rules for production of TV commercials. The operative word with many advertisers these days is *promotions*. Instead of channeling the advertising dollar directly into the measured media, an increasing percentage of that dollar is going into sales promotions.

One side effect of this dollar diversion has been the advertiser's closer scrutiny of the cost of producing commercials. At a time when expensive computerized effects are available for commercial production, advertising agencies are being urged to produce their TV commercials for less money so more of the advertising dollar can be divided into these new avenues of sales and promotion.

Who Are Today's Advertising Agency Production Teams?

Along with these external changes, television commercial production is experiencing upheaval from within. In the beginning, the advertising agency producer ran the show in TV commercial production. The producer hired and supervised the production company, the director, and the editor. Final decisions on the set or location were the province of the agency producer.

That power gradually was assumed by the advertising agency writer. The rationale went like this: The commercial idea has come from the mind of the writer. The final responsibility for the success or failure of that idea thus lies in the hands of the writer. Therefore, the writer should be completely in charge of the production of the commercial.

Under this revised leadership, the agency producer was relegated to handling the budgets and schedules of commercial production. Although this change in leadership varied from one agency to another, this was the general trend in commercial production.

The next bend in the flow of the production river found the agency art director rising to prominence in the production of TV commercials. The reason for the rising power of the art director was the rising importance of visuals in relation to verbal copy in TV commercials. There are two main reasons why many of today's commercial ideas are based on visual expression, rather than on written copy:

1. Many new production techniques, aided and abetted by computers, rely on visual expression.
2. With global advertising as a future target, the nonverbal possibilities of visually oriented commercials become more important.

Therefore, the leadership in commercial production is changing again. Starting with the producer as leader, then the writer as leader, the trend is now definitely toward the art director as leader. These changes within the agency administration of commercial production have been the result of (1) the continuing sophistication of the modes of commercial production and (2) the flow of tomorrow's commercials toward more universally understood nonverbal communications.

Changes within Companies That Shoot Commercials

In general, advertising agencies don't actually shoot and edit commercials. They supervise these duties, which are performed by independent production and finishing facilities. The roles of these companies have also changed and will continue to change in the future. Whereas at one time the film production company was also responsible for editing and finishing, that is no longer the case.

Production companies are now owned and operated by directors, whose main responsibility is to plan and shoot the commercials. When the dailies have been viewed, the film and/or tape is transferred from the production company and becomes the responsibility of editorial and finishing facilities independent of the production company. In many instances, the editing and finishing of the commercial is a one-stop operation. Sometimes all three duties (production, editing, and finishing) are completed within one company, but that is the exception rather than the rule.

Putting the Selling Idea at the Center of Production

The continuing development of computerized editing and finishing techniques will undoubtedly point to further changes in the commercial production process. But one hard fact remains: A good, hard-selling, memorable commercial is not one of sophisticated form alone. It relies on content, and content is the IDEA brought to its production by the advertising agency.

The marketplace is surfeited with visual effects, to the point where there is no longer any surprise value in visual virtuosity. The main moving force of a good commercial still resides in its original idea, which may be produced very simply indeed. And that idea must come from the advertising agency, no matter who is leading the team in the production of the idea.

At the risk of being called a traditionalist in a changing society, let me quote David Ogilvy, whose pronouncements are timeless:

> We go through periods where the advertising business goes mad. It starts producing self-conscious, award-winning, obscure, incomprehensible, arty advertising. You go through one of those periods and generally they win all the awards. Then it passes, and the business goes back to producing advertising whose purpose it is to sell.[1]

There are advertising agencies in this changing world that are dedicated to that premise. And their considered understanding of the commercial production process will aid them in achieving their sales goal.

This book will take the reader through the wonderful maze of commercial production and its infinite possibilities of visual and auditory expression. But the reader will bring the most necessary ingredient to this book: the individual selling ideas that have made commercial television production such a potent force.

---

[1] David Ogilvy, speech in New York City, 1992.

2 WHO CREATES TV COMMERCIALS?

In its comparatively short history, television has become the dominant communications, news, entertainment, and advertising vehicle in the United States. Evening televised newscasts have almost completely replaced the evening newspaper, and morning newspapers have become supplemental forces to the presence of the glowing tube.

Presidential candidates are chosen by the strength of their TV appearances. Politicians fight for the opportunity to appear in televised "sound bites," which may last only a few seconds but will be seen and heard instantly by millions of potential voters.

In the world of advertising, television has single-handedly introduced and sold thousands of new products through the persuasiveness of commercials that are seen and heard in millions of homes. The dominance of television in American life has caused a restructuring of advertising agency creative, research, media, and account departments to service this medium, which is still a comparative youngster. Television continues to provide large, full-service advertising agencies with up to 70 percent of their media income.

The influence and reach of television now extends into homes around the world, and global communication is not only a possibility but an expanding reality. Truly, the "global village" Marshall McLuhan foresaw half a century ago is at hand.

The Impact of New Technologies on Commercial Production

This most powerful of all communications media is less than 50 years old, but as it continues to expand into local-access cable channels and interactive person-to-person possibilities, the potency of television continues to increase. As these new applications of television become available to the public, the way in which advertising is created and produced continues to change. Alternative communications technologies include the use of remote-control satellites, 800 phone numbers, broadcast faxes, computer networks, and electronic menus detailing consumers' video choices and purchasing decisions dialed directly into their TV sets or personal computers over telephone lines. We will discuss the origination of such advertising messages and the modes of disseminating them in Chapter 15.

How TV Advertising Is Created and Produced

To fully understand the impact of the electronic media on the continuously changing advertising business, it is necessary to know a little about the duties of everyone involved in TV commercial production in a full-service advertising agency.

I must qualify what I am about to describe. Because this book deals with the creation and production of advertising for the electronic media, my description of the various departments is truncated. I will focus on the way the departments relate to and are involved with producing TV commercials.

ACCOUNT MANAGEMENT

Account management is the business side of the advertising agency. It is made up of men and women who administer the many client-directed activities within the agency. It is the account managers who first perceive the advertising needs of the agency's clients. They in turn convey these needs to the creative department. They are also responsible for making sure that the agency makes a profit from its work. Sometimes a push-pull relationship exists between account people and creative people because of their differing functions and approaches to satisfying the advertiser's sales and image needs.

For instance, account management is responsible for the overall coordination of the advertiser's business, while the creative folks are charged with dreaming up commercial ideas that can produce awareness and, eventually, sales of products and services. Often, account management will say to the creatives: "That idea is too expensive—such a commercial won't fit into the client's budget." To which the creatives may well reply: "If it generates the awareness we believe it will, they MUST have this commercial, and the cost will become secondary to the success of the commercial in the marketplace." Thus, the conflict between business and creative ideas. But the two departments need each other, and the most successful advertising agencies are those that recognize this need.

THE RESEARCH DEPARTMENT

Full-service agencies often have large research departments. These departments are staffed with experts who are specially trained in the techniques of testing ideas for commercials. With their expertise, they can help define the type of advertising that will appeal to a particular market.

Their duties start with pretesting advertising approaches. This is often done by inviting focus groups to look at storyboards, or test commercials, and to give their opinions on what they see. Focus groups are carefully chosen to represent the specific market segment at which the commercial will be aimed. If the focus group finds the idea to be interesting, their remarks will help guide the final commercial plan, which will be presented to the client for production.

Researchers also posttest commercials. After the commercial has run a specified number of times, a second focus group will be shown the commercial to determine whether it is conveying the message intended by the agency and the client. Posttesting a commercial evaluates the viewer's opinions of the commercial itself. As a result of these opinions, entire campaigns can be expanded, canceled, or amended

Potential Conflict with Creatives

Some creative people find researchers to be helpful in planning and evaluating their advertising efforts, but others consider them restrictive in the creative effort. This is another source of conflict within the structure of an advertising agency.

Most criticism of research department opinions by the creative department has to do with pretesting advertising ideas for commercials. Many writers and art directors who are seeking new ways to present a product or service to the buying public believe that research only shows you where you've been—not where you hope to go with new ideas. In their opinion, this means that many new and original ideas can be nipped in the bud before the commercial is produced, because the pretesting doesn't necessarily recognize the validity of new and original thinking.

The Evolution of Account Planners

This viewpoint is being countered by an alliance in some advertising agencies between account management and the research department. Account planners have been used in British agencies for several years, and they have been introduced into some American agencies. An account planner takes cold, hard research and adds a human dimension. Unlike a traditional market research department, which deposits its stacks of crunched numbers and focus-group feedback at the feet of account and creative teams, planners interpret the data. And that's the big change—their interpretation of research.

Suffice it to say that a great part of today's advertising is guided by the efforts of various research organizations, either inside or outside the advertising agency.

THE MEDIA DEPARTMENT

The media department is responsible for placing the advertising in the various media. Working closely with the pivotal department on the business side—account management—the media people contract for the broadcast time into which commercials are placed. They choose the time of day, the programs on which the commercials will be played, the location, and the number of times each commercial will be aired. They also decide whether to buy network time or to place the commercials on separate local stations.

After the target market has been selected, it is the function of the media department to use its media-buying power to zero in on that market. An efficient media department employs the client's dollars to their fullest selling potential. The best media departments are those that work closely with the creative department in order to maximize the placement of commercials with the specific buying audience being addressed by the commercial itself. In small advertising agencies, media buying and market research are usually supplied by outside sources.

THE SALES PROMOTION DEPARTMENT

A curious combination of events has had a lasting effect on the production of TV commercials. First, the introduction of cable television has multiplied the number of available channels. This has weakened the effectiveness of network television and also the potency of commercials played on network programming. Along with these combined forces (the introduction of alternative viewing channels and weaker programming by the traditional TV networks), a new and increasingly important selling approach has emerged.

The approach originates in the sales promotion department. In the past, TV advertising consisted of seeking long-term brand loyalty through commercials. Sales promotion, in contrast, strives to give the consumer a short-term incentive to purchase a product. This approach often increases immediate sales through various types of money-saving promotions, but too often at the price of weakening long-term brand loyalty.

This has put an increased burden on the production of TV commercials. The commercial must now sharpen its visual and auditory approach to support brand loyalty, while "cents-off" sales promotions are fighting for immediate sales.

It used to be that large agencies looked down their noses at promotions, believing that such efforts were below their creative ability and brought in very little revenue to the agency. They expressed this feeling by saying things like, "We don't do matchbook covers." That is no longer true, as advertisers opt to promote their products and services through a widening variety of promotional opportunities. Willingly or not, the agencies have joined the surge in sales promotion.

The diversity of sales approaches has increasingly taken available client dollars away from what has traditionally been called advertising. It has also caused advertisers to take a more cautious view of the cost to produce TV commercials—dollars that might otherwise go into sales promotions.

The wise advertising agency of the present and future makes promotion a contributor rather than a competitor for commercial production dollars and adds sales promotion to traditional advertising approaches. For instance, when it comes to TV commercial production, the need for promotional vehicles has spawned the *infomercial*, a type of commercial-program that devotes as much as half an hour to promoting a product or service in a combination of programming and selling. Many commercials now try to achieve both aims in the same selling effort, insisting on brand loyalty while at the same time promoting a sales incentive for immediate purchase.

THE CREATIVE DEPARTMENT

Staffed by writers, art directors, and producers, the creative department creates and produces the advertising. This book focuses on their efforts in one medium—television. We will primarily be concerned with the creative department in this book, because it carries through from the beginning to the end of the TV commercial—from ideas to commercials ready to be telecast. Let's look at each of the three groups within an advertising agency creative department.

Writers

The dominant group in most agency creative departments is the writers. Although they may use as few as 10 words in a 30-second commercial, the writers usually originate the selling idea, and they express that idea in as few words as possible. Many potent commercials rely on the writer's ability to (a) create a selling idea for a commercial and (b) express that idea in a few words.

In most advertising agencies, the creative director is a writer who also has the leadership ability to inspire the creative team and the innate capacity to sort out good ideas from "also-rans."

Art Directors

In the past, the art director took orders from the writer, who wanted the idea "illustrated." This was done by the art director in the form of a storyboard or another type of visualization, such as an animatic (illustrations videotaped to a sound track to emulate the final commercial).

Now, however, as the strength of the visual over the spoken word becomes more apparent in TV advertising, many creative directors, who were originally art directors, possess the combined ability to originate new ideas of their own visually and also to lead other members of the creative department to originate new commercial campaigns.

Additionally, many of the creative people who are in charge of the agency effort in actual production have an art director's background, rather than that of a writer.

Producers

The role of commercial producer varies among agencies. In my experience with both J Walter Thompson and Leo Burnett, the producer was an integral part of the creative production team. In many instances, the choice of directors and production companies to work with the advertising agency in producing commercials was ultimately the responsibility of the producer.

This is not the case in many advertising agencies. As writers and art directors become more involved in the creative production process, their separate or combined opinions have become the determining factor in the choice of directors, editors, composers, etc. Their final responsibility for the success of their original idea now extends into the entire production process as well.

This is a good thing, as long as the person in charge from the agency has a full knowledge of such elements as cost and production timing. If not, this type of leadership can cause serious problems for the agency and client.

If the producer is in charge on the set, he or she is the person through whom all agency and client questions should be funneled. The pecking order in production should be well established, and the agency person in charge should be truly that.

When No Advertising Agency Is Involved

We have discussed the five basic departments of a full-service advertising agency. Be aware that many clients, large and small, do not necessarily have such advertising agency assistance. Many small advertisers have minuscule budgets, and they work directly with free-lance writers and/or art directors. The production is handled directly with either a production company or a TV station (if it is only to be telecast in one market).

IN-HOUSE ADVERTISING DEPARTMENTS

In-house means an advertising department within the structure of the client organization rather than an external, full-service advertising agency. Many large advertisers direct most of their advertising and promotion dollars "to the trade." They direct their messages to their distributors or other businesses, rather than to the ultimate consumer. So when they decide to produce commercials aimed at the consumer market, their agencies or in-house departments are not geared for such duties.

FREE-LANCERS

When such a large company decides to do a TV commercial campaign, they generally go outside their organization to hire personnel on a free-lance basis. I was asked to put together such a "boutique" operation for National Cash Register when they wanted to change the public's perception of the company from a manufacturer of cash registers to "NCR Corporation," a company involved in the computer industry. I hired a free-lance writer and art director and put together all the storyboards and scripts we needed for NCR's approval. I then became the producer of the campaign. This was a free-lance assignment, outside the National Cash Register corporate structure.

In Summary

An advertising agency is divided into the business side (account management, research, media) and the creative side (writers, art directors, producers). Each of the five basic departments within a full-service advertising agency requires people with different skills.

In smaller agencies, many of these skills must be developed in one person: The person who creates the advertising may also be the account executive who presents it to the client.

This book will deal basically with the efforts, duties, and advertising results of the creative department in a full-service advertising agency in the specific area of the TV commercial. Although this book will be concerned primarily with the creative side, you should note how each of the other departments adds its influence and expertise to the final effectiveness of the advertising.

As new modes of communication continue to proliferate, the types of commercials to be produced will expand as well. More and more TV commercials on the three major networks will be 15 seconds long, instead of 30 seconds. At the same time, commercials on the so-called "alternative" cable channels will become not only longer, but also interactive with the viewing audience. These variations will increase as the nation's telephone companies become commercial carriers. The demand for commercial production versatility continues to increase, and the whole area of televised selling will become more versatile as well.

3 Working with Ideas

The IDEA is the most elusive, intangible, and important product of an advertising agency. The idea is the core of the selling tool called a TV commercial. It has been described in different ways by different people. Rosser Reeves of Ted Bates & Co. referred to an idea as a Unique Selling Proposition (USP). Leo Burnett called finding and identifying an idea as "the search for the inherent drama of the product." However the idea is described, campaigns succeed or fail on the strength or weakness of the idea.

However, having the right idea for a commercial is not necessarily the end of the rainbow. How the idea is expressed can sharpen or blunt its effectiveness. And this is the importance of commercial production. A badly produced commercial can result in a failed campaign.

The creative department of a full-service advertising agency is dedicated to finding and nurturing ideas. That's why it is called the *creative* department: It is staffed with well-paid men and women dedicated to locating attention-getting ideas and turning them into ads and commercials that will help sell products and promote services.

The idea is mainly the product of the creative department. However, other departments help to develop, nurture, and present the idea to the buying public. Account management relays the objectives (and budgets) of the advertiser to the creative department. The research department identifies the product's or service's market position as compared to its competitors. In so doing, research helps to position the idea for maximum effectiveness. This lays the groundwork for developing ideas that will strengthen market share or reposition a product or service for maximum sales impact.

It is now the duty of the media department to take the finished commercial and place it on TV channels that will deliver it to the target audience at the optimum time and frequency. The research department provides information to help in this selection. But the first and final burden falls on the creative department, which must originate the idea and bring it to the light of day.

Where Do Ideas Originate?

Many ideas for TV commercials have already been expressed in print. In such cases, commercials become extensions of basic ideas already presented to the marketplace in newspapers, magazines, billboards, or other modes of print exposure. It is the addition of sound and movement to a print-originated idea that may sharpen acceptance through the use of television.

Other ideas originate from taking a new look at the product and finding some dramatic difference that can best be explained on television. Such ideas, which exploit the use of the added dimensions of movement and sound, immediately dictate the necessity of producing commercials instead of print ads. In such cases, print may become only a backup for the use of television.

The TV commercial is a unique advertising medium. No other medium has the power of this combination of sight and sound. Real or illusionary, these moving pictures and sounds can command attention, evoke emotion, and motivate response in ways no other medium can. This makes the TV commercial a potent selling tool.

Eleven Ways to Express TV Commercial Ideas

There are various options open to the creative department in deciding how to produce a commercial. A choice can be made to film or videotape a live-action commercial. Options for live action include choices of casting, lighting, types of editing, the use of music or sound effects (or even silence instead of sound), and still photography instead of motion-picture footage. If animation is chosen over live action, a whole new set of options emerges, such as computer-generated images, claymation, or live animation.

Most of these choices are only available in this one medium—television. The choices include the following eleven techniques, many of which can be used in combination:

1. Stand-up presenters
2. Personality testimonials
3. "Real people" reactions and opinions
4. Slice-of-life episodes
5. Animation
6. Music first
7. Words first
8. Pictures first
9. Demonstrations and comparisons
10. Bisociation (unusual combinations)
11. Illustrating slogans with images and/or sounds

There will undoubtedly be other approaches to executing a selling proposition on television in the future, but these are the major techniques currently in use. Let's look at each and discuss their pros and cons.

USING A STAND-UP PRESENTER

Probably the simplest use of an actor in a TV commercial is as a stand-up presenter. Often referred to as a *talking head*, this word-oriented approach deals with eye-to-camera close-ups meant to suggest sincerity. I've always believed that this approach is a holdover from radio. It is the electronic form of basic human communication: one person talking to another. This approach works best when the product needs a human being to demonstrate it, when it is an abstract service with nothing for the viewer to see, or when you want the "personal" effect of a forthright salesperson talking to a potential buyer.

Casting is the key to the stand-up presenter approach. The best way to initiate your search is to write out a complete description of the person you are looking for. The description should respond to such questions as the following:

- Should the presenter be a man or a woman?
- Should this person be friendly or authoritative?
- Would the commercial be stronger with an actor who would become identified with the product or with a known personality whose reputation would enhance its appeal?

PROS The stand-up presenter technique can be very inexpensive, using a simple backdrop or wall instead of a set. The camera may stay very close to the presenter, which practically eliminates editing costs. Also, the technique can be riveting if the presenter is able to hold the viewer's attention in a one-on-one eye-to-eye presentation.

CONS This technique tends to look "cheap" rather than inexpensive. It is so simple that it can become simple-minded. It is quite a trick to hold viewers' attention with nothing going on except a person looking you right in the eye. There are three keys to this approach: good casting, good direction, and, most important, hardworking copy. People truly want to learn about products or services that might benefit them.

THE PERSONALITY TESTIMONIAL

The personality testimonial method consists of finding either an authority or a star personality who will associate himself or herself with your product in some positive fashion that will help establish its worth or enhance its popularity with the TV audience. This method has been used with all sorts of personalities from Lee Iacocca, former CEO of Chrysler Corporation, to movie stars and astronauts. Bear in mind that on-camera personalities, including movie stars, musicians, and sports figures, achieve enormous popularity by appearing in this type of commercial. The trick is to be sure that the popularity spreads over to the product or service advertised.

Again, there are advantages and disadvantages to using the personality testimonial. In my experience, using the personality/authority approach is like the old nursery rhyme: When she was good, she was very, very good; but when she was bad, she was horrid.

PROS

If the personality selected to promote the product or service has a believable reason to be in front of the camera, the technique can work very well. The person must have the electricity to light up the TV screen while making simple, direct statements. If this quality is present, the resultant commercial can have a profound impact on acceptance and eventual sales.

CONS

The personality testimonial approach lives or dies on the believability and relevance of the personality chosen. There are many well-known people who just can't project their personality in a TV commercial. There are two additional difficulties to be aware of in using this approach: expense and verification of claims.

Personalities can be very expensive, demanding yearly fees of $500,000 and more. There have been many successful campaigns using the testimonial approach, but if you choose the wrong person for a large fee, you can make a very expensive mistake. Conversely, if you have found the right person and you wish to make a long-term commitment, be sure to initiate legal documents about future payments.

Although all commercials are governed by rules concerning product claims, these rulings are even more stringent when it comes to a personality claiming product usage. If a personality says, "I've used Brand X for years, and the whole family loves it," this statement must be backed up with documented proof. There are no shortcuts here. Both government and broadcast advertising groups demand verification. Government agencies involved are the Federal Trade Commission (FTC) and the Federal Communications Commission (FCC). The broadcast groups include the National Association of Broadcasters (NAB) and the TV networks.

SHOWING "REAL PEOPLE" REACTIONS AND OPINIONS

Actors in TV commercials memorize a script, but "real people" (or non-actors) give spontaneous reactions to a product or service. Commercials that feature satisfied buyers can be highly believable. Viewers can identify with real people who share their problems and concerns.

A good example of this technique is seen in a commercial for Bays English Muffins. A supermarket manager agreed to let us videotape some of his customers right after they had selected Bays Muffins. They were then interviewed by a true genius at such interviews, Ray Van Steen from Chicago; their comments on how they used the product became the strength of this commercial approach.

There are two ways to produce real people commercials. First, you can use a hidden camera and microphone to get natural reactions that the paraphernalia of production might inhibit. An off-camera interviewer usually asks questions, which are later cut out of the film or tape, leaving only the "real person" comments. Afterward, the interviewee signs a release, and if the comments are used in a commercial, that person receives the equivalent of Screen Actors Guild payments.

Second, you can use real people as interviewees with the camera and the microphone out in the open. This open camera technique elicits an entirely different type of response. But I have found that it can be handled in a manner that allows the person interviewed to act naturally. It takes a particular talent to accomplish this. Two of the best directors I have worked with in this area are Ray Van Steen in Chicago and Albert Maysles in New York. Both have the innate ability to put people at ease. As a result, they get answers that are quite natural and unforced.

It is also possible to actually cast professional actors, and then film them as if they were "real people" giving their opinions. (Of course, everything they say has been previously scripted and approved by the client.)

PROS

Given a good interviewer, the comments elicited from actual product or service users can be very convincing. Also, the technique can be very inexpensive, particularly if videotape is used rather than film. The reason is simple: with videotape, you can check the recorded comments immediately. If they don't come up to the standard you have set, the tape can be erased and used again for the next interview. Also, videotape cameras are absolutely silent, which cuts down on distraction. In addition, minimal additional lighting is needed.

CONS

Because of a basic distrust on the part of many viewers when it comes to "real opinions," this technique can become suspect. If this lack of belief exists, then the commercial is wasted. Also, the technique has been used and misused so often that there is a wear-out factor involved for most viewers.

Creating a Slice of Life

The slice-of-life technique involves writing and producing a brief dramatic episode that reflects a problem facing the viewer, and ending with the advertised product or service as a solution to the problem. This technique has been very successful in the past for Procter & Gamble, Colgate-Palmolive, and General Foods. In classic examples, this technique used "Katy Winters" in problematic personal situations, which she resolved by suggesting the use of Secret deodorant. In another classic series, "Madge the Manicurist" dipped her customers' fingers into Palmolive dishwashing liquid to prove how soothing it was to hands. And "Mrs. Olsen" entered many household situations to suggest that Folger's coffee could smooth frayed nerves.

A new genre of slice-of-life is being used by Taster's Choice instant coffee. The series features a very attractive unmarried English couple who live in the same apartment building. Their casual meetings revolve around a cup of Taster's Choice.

A Kellogg's cereal called "Nut & Honey Crunch" has utilized humorous slice-of-life episodes to promote the brand name. Each commercial features a misunderstanding between two people based on a literal translation of the two words, "nothing, honey," instead of "Nut & Honey," the name of the cold cereal flavored with nuts and honey. (See Exhibit 3.1.)

PROS   As originally used, the dramatic episodes became quite memorable, and the technique could be repeated in a variety of situations. There followed an instant recognition of the protagonist and the product, which seemed to solve all tough situations around the house. The production cost was average, depending on the contract agreements with the featured actor.

CONS   The technique soon became thoroughly predictable and eventually quite boring. As the techniques of production have become more varied and sophisticated, slice-of-life has fallen into disrepute. As a matter of fact, a creative director in a New York advertising agency once remarked, "Any way you slice it, it ain't life." The future of the slice-of-life technique depends on the ability of commercial writers to keep the approach fresh and different.

Animation

Up to this point, I have been talking about having *people* on camera, whether they be celebrities, personalities, actors, or ordinary people. Now we come to the use of artwork and animation as a mode of commercial expression.

Exhibit 3.1

1. WOMAN: (SPEAKS FORIEGN LANGUAGE)

2. INTER: Mmm, that looks yummy.

3. MAN: It's Nut & Honey.

4. INTER: (SPEAKS FORIEGN LANGUAGE)

5. WOMAN: (LAUGHS, SPEAKS FORIEGN LANGUAGE)

6. INTER: Oh baby...

7. I love it when you lie to me.

8. ...

9. SONG: KELLOGG'S NUT & HONEY CRUNCH.

Slice-of-Life Commercial

A masterful job of emphasizing the product name (Nut & Honey Crunch) occurs in conversational misunderstandings of the words "nothing, honey." This has become a long-running campaign, fueled by good writing and casting and a less-than-subtle use of humor surrounding the product name.
Courtesy Leo Burnett USA.

Animation covers a wider spectrum of image possibilities than many people realize. Animation includes not only cartooning, à la Walt Disney, but also many other types of graphic expression. (See Chapter 11 for more information.) Using animation to express ideas is particularly effective if the idea will benefit from any one or a combination of exaggeration, graphic demonstration, humor, or a new look.

Exaggeration

There is a certain reality to live-action photography. On the other hand, animation allows the use of hyperbole and exaggeration, which bypass legal requirements for factual presentation. An example of this type of exaggeration would be "Charlie the Tuna," a talking fish who finds out that people don't want tuna with good taste, but tuna that tastes good.

Graphic Demonstration

If the selling proposition has to do with traveling through the inside of an engine, animation is the answer. Computer graphics can take viewers into "virtual reality."

Humor

This can be accomplished by a combination of humorous writing and unusual voicing in the sound track, plus the imagination of the animator.

A "New Look"

Volkswagen has accomplished this by combining live-action photography with computer animation to take you through the inner workings of the VW motor.

Because of the complete freedom animation offers, a great deal of time should be spent discussing the idea before final planning begins. Usually, these discussions start with a commitment to animation as a technique. Next, the writer develops a general plot or story line. The art director then draws either a key frame or a sequence of drawings. Finally, the animator enters the discussion as soon as the visual approach is agreed on.

PROS

One of the true strengths of television is its power to give a fresh look and feeling to a product or service. The cost of animation depends on the type of animation. Cel animation (the artist's drawings photographed frame by frame) can be relatively inexpensive.

CONS

Although you can draw anything your imagination will allow, costs can become prohibitive if the computer becomes the ruling production tool. Many commercials that use Computer Graphic Imaging (CGI) are very imaginative—and very costly. Originating in the production of the movie "Terminator II," the continuing spin-off of visual effects has become highly experimental—and computer equipment and expertise are expensive.

Music First

In some TV commercial campaigns, the music becomes a distinctive background for a wide variety of advertising approaches. The consistent use of a musical theme from commercial to commercial is a constant reminder of the product or service being advertised. Just hearing the music, even from another room, will bring an image of the product or service to mind.

A good example of "music first" is United Airlines' use of George Gershwin's "Rhapsody in Blue." For several years, this melody has driven commercial after commercial for the airline, to the point that merely hearing the music makes viewers think of United. Through sight and sound, the melody and the airline are combined in a unique way.

When music dominates the sound track, the viewer is left to substitute individual words and thoughts. This is a memorable way to produce a commercial with story-telling visuals. As a New York composer justifies the use of such descriptive music instead of a voiceover announcer, "You don't hum the announcer."

PROS Adding music to the commercial, with or without the voice of an announcer, can be quite simple and inexpensive if library music (existing music) is used. If this route is chosen, several hours should be spent listening to the prerecorded melodies and rhythmic patterns that are available in special compact disc (CD) music libraries. These CDs are purchased by TV and radio stations as well as recording studios. They are available for commercial use for as little as $100. On the other hand, if the budget will allow original music to be written, scored, and recorded, the result will be individual and exclusive. The melody will be owned by the client, and no one else can make use of it.

CONS If library music is selected, be aware that any other advertiser, for any other product or service, can also purchase the same music for its commercials. The drawback to original music revolves around money. If a unionized recording session is held, recording fees, as well as residuals, will have to be paid to both the American Federation of Musicians (AF of M) and to the Screen Actors Guild (SAG) for the singers.

However, chosen for the right reasons, and within budgetary limitations, music can establish a mood, help identify a product or service immediately, and give additional selling top spin to the commercial.

 ## Words First

Words can actually become the visual, replacing live action or animated images on the screen. In some commercials, the technique superimposes the voiceover announcer's script over shots of the product, as is the case in a commercial for the Subaru automobile. As you see performance

---

A PICTURE IS WORTH 150 WORDS

As "Rhapsody in Blue" opens, a young working mother is shown dropping off her 4-year-old daughter at nursery school in the morning, then boarding a United Airlines plane for New York. The plane lands at LaGuardia, and she takes a taxi into midtown Manhattan. Meanwhile, between these scenes, the viewer sees the daughter with her little friends in nursery school. As the mother joins in conversation at a meeting in New York, the daughter whispers a secret to another 4-year-old.

The mother eats lunch in the boardroom, and the daughter has a sandwich at school. When the little girl takes an afternoon nap, the mother relaxes, homeward bound on a United Airlines plane. The nonverbal commercial ends as the mother arrives at the nursery school, her daughter runs to her, and they embrace.

Although not a word is heard over the Gershwin music in the sound track, it has taken me more than 150 words to describe the silent action of this contemporary heart-tugger of a commercial.

Director: Michael Grasso, New York. *Editor*: Bob Carr/Optimus Chicago. *Music*: Warner Chappell, Inc.; arranged by Manny Mendelson/Comtrack Chicago. Courtesy United Airlines.

---

shots of the car, the actual words in the sound track are superimposed on the screen in a very artistic way. The imprinted words crawl up the screen, but in different sizes to show their relative importance.

A more arresting use of the "words first" technique was utilized by Nikon Cameras. Although pictures are what a camera is all about, not a single picture appeared in this Nikon commercial. Instead, words imprinted on a black screen described memorable photos from American history. The sound track was completely silent, except for the sound of the film transport of the Nikon camera between the shots being described.

Only the words appeared on the screen, describing the pictures not shown: "A little boy salutes as his father's casket rolls by," "A president picks up his dog by its ears." "Five men raise the American flag on a mountaintop." So strong were the original pictures being described that these verbal descriptions immediately brought them back to mind. And the final imprinted words made sense: "Chances are these pictures were taken with a Nikon camera."

PROS   Produced for a sound selling reason, this technique can be effective and inexpensive. Many variations can be employed: the words can crawl up the screen over the visual of the product or service, or they can be artistically framed around the commercial's visuals.

Exhibit 3A

LEO BURNETT COMPANY, INC.   UNITED AIRLINES
AS FILMED AND RECORDED   (2/93)   "Her Day/ United Airlines Logo" :60   UAPE9136

1. (MUSIC: THROUGHOUT)

2. (MUSIC)

3. (MUSIC)

4. (MUSIC)

5. (MUSIC)

6. (MUSIC)

7. (MUSIC)

8. (MUSIC)

9. (MUSIC)

10. (MUSIC)

11. HACKMAN (VO): For a half century and more...

12. business travelers have depended on United Airlines...

13. to get them to their most important meetings.

14. United, rededicated to giving you the service you deserve.

15. Come fly the friendly skies.

CONS   There is an inherent danger of visual dullness lurking here. The technique is so inherently simple that its application includes the possibility of becoming boring. Monetarily, the technique can be inexpensive or not, depending on the art forms used.

PICTURES FIRST

Many commercial ideas start in the mind of a talented art director. Visualization comes naturally to these folks, and some of the most effective commercial campaigns begin with the picture. J Walter Thompson in New York originated just such a campaign for Eastman Kodak, with a series of commercials showing "True Colors." Each of these commercials centered around people-oriented snapshots, with Kodak film capturing the true colors of the scene. Art direction initiated the commercials—the pictures were chosen first, and the copy was written to accompany them.

Approaches like this one show the emerging force and importance of the art director in creative planning for the production of TV commercials. Finally, after years of almost complete writer domination, the visual origins of the TV commercial are coming to the fore, and the art director becomes either an equal partner or the leader of the creative team. Many of the more complicated visual effects made possible through digitized computerization of images originate in the minds of art directors rather than writers. In either case, the combined efforts of writers and artists are fusing, and many of the most effective commercial campaigns of the 1990s are the team efforts of two people: the writer and the art director.

PROS   If the picture is strong enough, it can become the complete reason for the commercial. From a budget standpoint, such commercials are usually quite inexpensive.

CONS   If the picture is only so-so in appeal, the emotional response will be dulled, and the commercial will be a waste of time and money. This approach only works when the visual is arresting and tells a complete story.

DEMONSTRATIONS AND COMPARISONS

These two approaches, although related, offer different selling opportunities. In a demonstration commercial, viewers actually see the product in use. The advertiser hopes the viewer will find the demonstration interesting and instructional. In a comparison commercial, the product is demonstrated alongside a named or unnamed competitor.

Demonstration Commercials

An example of a good demonstration commercial is for the Black & Decker Hot Glue System. We see a 105-pound woman fastening ladder rungs to a ladder frame. The rungs are made of various materials, from wood to ceramics. After she finishes gluing the rungs, she climbs the ladder to a platform. On the platform is a man who weighs 200 pounds: he climbs down the just-glued rungs without mishap. This is a very straightforward demonstration, which graphically shows the ability of a TV commercial to sell the benefits of the product. (See Exhibit 3.2.)

PROS   Demonstration commercials satisfy the viewer's wish to see how a product actually works. Properly edited, such a commercial can become an informational tool as well as a selling vehicle. They need not be expensive.

CONS   If the product doesn't lend itself to graphic demonstration, such a commercial will seem forced and out of place. There must be a legitimate reason to explain the inner workings of the product and a graphic way to either photograph it or illustrate it with graphic animation.

Comparison Commercials

In essence, comparison commercials go one step beyond demonstration commercials. An integral part of such a commercial involves demonstrating your product in a direct comparison with its competition, which is shown and named. This can be effective if a direct comparison fortifies the results of the demonstration.

Government regulation has encouraged comparative product demonstrations. The competition may not only be shown, but also identified by name. The key to the approach, from the government's standpoint, is that all head-to-head comparisons must be backed up with verifiable and repeatable proof.

PROS   If the sponsor's product has a clearly discernible edge on competition that can come alive in a commercial, by all means use this demonstration/comparison approach. Be sure, however, that you can prove and document the comparative test. Unless many on-camera actors are used, which is unusual, this can be a fairly inexpensive type of commercial to produce.

Exhibit 3.2

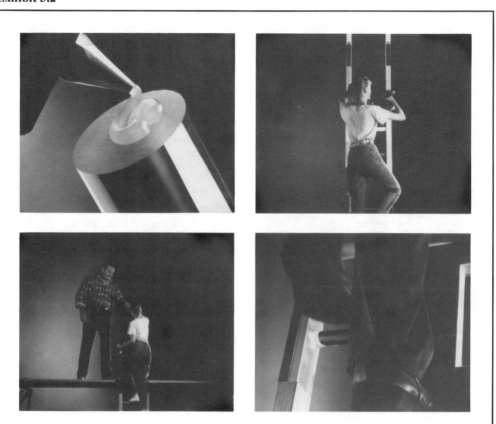

"Ladder" Product Demonstration

McKim Baker Lovick/BBDO in Toronto produced a straightforward demonstration for Black & Decker's Hot Glue Gun. A 105-pound woman is shown gluing a rung on a ladder and then climbing to the top of the ladder on the newly glued rung. To make the demonstration even more convincing, a 200-pound man then climbs down the ladder, putting his full weight on the rung glued into place by the Black & Decker Glue Gun. This is a most direct—and most convincing—use of demonstration as a commercial production technique.
Courtesy McKim Baker Lovick/BBDO Toronto.

CONS   The big drawback to this creative approach is that you give the competition free time in your commercial. This can be a big risk, because research shows that confusion is often caused by such comparison commercials: Is the commercial for Coca-Cola or Pepsi? Two makes of tires were mentioned in the commercial—which one is supposed to be better? Many advertising agencies vote against this approach, thinking it is better to talk about a product's good points than to give the viewer even a glance at the competition.

BISOCIATION: UNUSUAL COMBINATIONS OF SIGHT AND SOUND

The world *bisociation* was coined by Arthur Koestler. He wanted to show that you could come up with something new by taking unrelated factors and associating them. This becomes a good definition of the word *creativity* in advertising: combining seemingly unrelated elements of sight and sound to create a new selling tool.

One of the best examples of bisociation is the Marlboro Man. There is no logical connection between a man in a cowboy outfit who is smoking a cigarette while riding a horse. But that unusual scene has become the setting for presenting a filtered cigarette that is now the leading cigarette in the world. Before cigarette advertising was banned from American television (with other countries following suit), re-creations of cowboy scenes from the Old West were combined with music from an old movie, *The Magnificent Seven*. This bisociation became the cornerstone of one of the longest-running commercial campaigns in U.S. TV advertising history. It continues in the media that still accept cigarette advertising, primarily magazines and billboards.

PROS

If an unusual combination of a sight and a sound brings freshness and newness to a product or service, this bisociation can spell lasting recognition (as in the Green Giant saying "Ho Ho Ho"—or Tony the Tiger saying "They're Grrrreat!!").

CONS

Repetition is a key to this approach. The combination must be seen and heard over a long enough time span to take hold in the minds of the viewers. On the other hand, if there is no logic—or seeming logic—to the sight-and-sound combination, it can become a very expensive waste of TV commercial time and expense.

ILLUSTRATING A SLOGAN WITH IMAGES AND SOUNDS

The double-barreled ability of TV advertising to combine what you see with what you hear has created memorable slogans. No other advertising medium offers this combination. Television, with its appeal to the eye and the ear, provides this opportunity to separate an advertiser's slogan from its competition and make it memorable at the same time. In a few seconds, usually at the close of the commercial, the slogan can remind the viewer of the entire sales message.

One of the shortest and most effective sight-and-sound slogans is for Nabisco products. At the very end of each Nabisco commercial, the Nabisco logo appears in the corner of the closing scene as a voice sings, "Nabisco" in three notes, followed by a single musical note. In solfeggio, the three musical notes would be sol-re-mi, with the accent on the middle note, as when the word is spoken. And—wonder of wonders—the entire closing logo treatment takes only 1–1/2 seconds.

Many worldwide advertisers have gone to graphic interpretations of their logos, some with a slogan, with a sound effect to drive the visual. Sprint, the telephone company, claims its digitized and laser-assisted phone system is so quiet, "you could hear a pin drop." What you see is a pin dropping in slow motion. As it hits a surface, around-the-world phone lines are activated on the TV screen.

Add the sounds that connote the property of the product, and the effect becomes doubly memorable. Coca-Cola has done this with several closing slogan treatments by adding a gurgling sound in the background, as if a Coke is being consumed during the singing of the slogan. They have done this with various slogans over the years; "Coke Adds Life," "This Is It," and so on.

To further make the commercial lead the viewer to a purchase, the two major competing soft drinks, Coca-Cola and Pepsi Cola, have used music-driven campaigns featuring celebrities. There have been so many used that there is a confusion factor involved. Was it Coke or Pepsi who used Elton John? How about Ray Charles, or Michael Jackson? In each competing commercial, the goal was to leave the viewer with a final musical slogan impression that would trigger a purchase.

PROS The goal of such closing treatments is to leave a memory-hook in the viewer's mind as the commercial ends. Research has proven that the two most memorable parts of a commercial are the beginning and the end. Slogan treatments to start and end the commercial can make 30 seconds of airtime just that much more effective.

CONS The danger is taking time away from the selling portion of the commercial in order to make room for the closing slogan or musical treatment. If the closing memory-hook is more than three seconds long (ten percent of the entire commercial's length), then it defeats its purpose. Brevity is essential.

A variety of techniques can be employed to make commercials more effective. The choice should be made early on for maximum effectiveness. That choice can be dictated by the idea itself. If you are advertising a food product, appetizing close-ups of the product may be the selling key. If, on the other hand, the product must be explained by showing it in action, demonstration may be the right technique. Let the idea itself be the guide to the choice of technique.

Agency Review of the Idea

After the mode of production has been chosen and the idea has been translated into a script and a storyboard, an important quality control

A BLEND OF WORDS AND PICTURES

There are ways of expressing the selling idea so that both what is seen and what is said have equal selling impact. The Clemenger advertising agency in Melbourne, Australia, combined words and pictures for maximum impact in a Mercedes Benz commercial. (See this ad's execution in Chapter 9.)

The commercial opens with a tight close-up of the left rear fender of what appears to be a brand-new Mercedes Benz sedan. As the copy starts, the camera slowly travels toward the front of the car. The copy states the problem as the camera finally gets to the left front of the windshield, which is smashed. As the voice tells us of the horrible broadside crash that almost totally destroyed the right side of the car, the camera continues around the front of the car to show the devastation caused by the high-speed crash. But, says the voice, the passenger compartment held together, even though everything else was totaled. And then we see a family of four standing by the right rear of the car. They are obviously unhurt—a tribute to the safety of the car.

There is no music in the sound track, no tricks, no fancy titles or quick cuts. Just a very serious voice telling a very serious story over a thoroughly wrecked automobile, which was obviously constructed to completely protect the family of four who were in the Mercedes when it all happened. What could be more effective as a safety commercial?

---

point has been reached in the production process. This is the agency review of your commercial idea. It is the first time anyone other than the creative people have been exposed to the idea. Unless the idea can stand up to the critical scrutiny of other agency people, it may not be as strong as you thought. Unless you can describe the thrust of your commercial in one or two sentences, you probably have an overly complicated commercial in mind. The idea should stand on its own and not depend on production techniques to make it a good idea. Ask yourself these questions about the idea:

1. What is the intent of this commercial?
2. Does the commercial fit into the creative strategy?
3. Is the commercial strong enough to be a prototype for a TV campaign?
4. How can the production technique be presented for the agency review?

WHAT IS THE INTENT OF THIS COMMERCIAL?

Why are you asking the client to invest in producing and telecasting it? Is it in line with the client's marketing objectives? How does it further those objectives? Does it help build public awareness, move merchandise, and fit into the client's total marketing scheme? Unless your commercial can meet these criteria, you may be spinning your creative wheels and preparing to waste your client's money.

Most agency reviews include people from account management, who may play devil's advocate in passing judgment on your idea, They, in effect, represent the client. Unless the client can be convinced that your commercial will fit into a larger merchandising and marketing plan, the commercial will not be produced.

Does the Commercial Fit into the Creative Strategy?

There should exist, in writing, a creative strategy. Most agencies, working closely with their clients, write a strategy statement for their advertising in all media. Its preparation is usually the dual responsibility of the account management team and the creative director. The creative strategy states the purpose and aim of all the advertising that will be placed in all media. It is the written goal to be sought in every ad and every commercial produced for that particular product or service. No matter how good or how original the idea, unless it fits the overall plan for the product, service, or brand, it will not work.

Is the Commercial Strong Enough to Be a Prototype for a TV Campaign?

The best ideas are those that are strong enough conceptually to become campaigns, rather than one-shot commercials that live and die in 13 weeks. (Thirteen weeks is the quarterly cycle into which commercials are placed.) Repeatability can be based on any of a number of techniques, including music, casting, or graphic presentation of a copy claim. As you present your commercial for review, suggest that it can be "pooled up" (extended into a series) in one of these ways:

- Present a copy claim in the same unique and memorable way in every commercial. Palmolive dishwashing liquid claimed it was "soft on hands." To illustrate this claim, they produced short vignettes with "Madge the Manicurist," who showed how soft Palmolive was by dipping her customers' fingers in this dishwashing liquid.
- Use an unusual technique (music, casting, or editing style) to identify the idea throughout the series. Charmin toilet paper touted its softness by casting a bungling grocer who couldn't help "squeezing the Charmin."
- Stick to your "points of difference" through an entire pool of commercials.

Here is an example of what I mean by points of difference. Maytag washers and dryers have claimed to be so reliable that no one ever has to call for a repairman. They cast the Maytag repairman as the "loneliest man in town." The campaign started with Jesse White as the Lonely Repairman and continues with Gordon Jump in the role. There's even "La Reparateur Qui S'Ennuie," who is the Maytag Lonely Repairman for French-language Canadian commercials. These Maytag commercials have been running for more than 25 years. Research and sales results have proven that the idea was well worth "pooling up."

Another example is "Ronald McDonald," a clown who has starred in McDonald's commercials aimed at preschool kids. The series has run for more than ten years.

How Can the Production Technique Be Presented for the Agency Review?

Realizing that you are trying to describe something that hasn't happened yet—the production of a new commercial idea—inexpensive ways must be found to explain the idea and get it accepted within the agency, so that ultimately it will be presented to the client. Remember, at this point in commercial planning, you are spending the agency's money. This money represents what is left from commissions and/or fees derived from working for clients. I refer to these as the *hard dollars*. Each buck represents approximately $90 in billings (depending on how your agency has worked out remuneration with advertisers). Most of that money goes for overhead, including your own salary. These dollars should not be wasted, any more than you would waste the advertiser's money that will pay for producing and airing a comercial.

To help explain the execution of the commercial for the agency review, there is a choice of several inexpensive methods:

- Rather than record special music at this point, find prerecorded music that will fit your idea. If the idea hinges on a specific rhythm to guide the edit, choose a rhythmic cut or drum solo from one of your own tapes or CDs to show your intent.
- Use the same technique when it comes to explaining your visuals: If there are appropriate existing visuals, use them.
- Put together a "Ripomatic": scenes from other commercials cut to the rhythm and flow of your idea. With today's digitized editing equipment, this can be done quickly. WARNING: This is not "for air." It may represent very expensive scenes from other commercials that would not be available to you on the budget assigned to your commercial. Point out these discrepancies before showing your Ripomatic. This method can also help illustrate the editing style of the proposed commercial.

There's one key rule to remember at this early stage. Don't overspend on the initial presentation, because suggestions made during that agency review may appreciably alter the look and sound of the eventual production. Also, your idea may even be rejected outright.

Here are a couple of additional thoughts about this inexpensive first look at your commercial idea. If you feel that a storyboard is absolutely necessary, consider having an art director draw one master frame, instead of a multi-frame storyboard. With a master frame, you can often lead your review board through your commercial in a logical sequence. Then, if the idea is accepted for client presentation, you can either work from a complete storyboard or put the storyboard on videotape. This last method is a good one, like the Ripomatic, because your commercial idea will then be presented in "real time," which gives your client a much better feeling for the end result.

Finally, don't be resentful if the agency review board sends you back to your typewriter or drawing board for changes and alterations. This is the purpose of the review—to bring fresh thinking and other viewpoints to bear on your commercial idea. Even if your idea is rejected, take a deep breath and go back to work. That is easier to say than to do, but this is not an easy business. It will require all the self-discipline you can muster, demanding at the same time that you show no stress or strain in preparing the material. It's a neat trick, but it's worth learning, and the agency review is often where you learn it quickly. I'll never forget my friend Rudy Perz, an executive creative director at Leo Burnett. He presented three completely boarded ideas, and they were summarily rejected by the review board. Rudy picked up his storyboards, walked to the door, and turned with this exit line: "Lions three, Christians nothing." That remark became a classic at Burnett, and Rudy came back to win many a creative battle in the same war room.

Presenting Ideas to the Advertiser

So, step one was getting the idea, step two was the agency review of the idea, and now comes the crucial test: presenting the idea to the advertiser.

If the agency review has been thorough and your idea has been honed and sharpened by this in-agency confrontation, you will find yourself well prepared to present your idea to the advertiser for approval.

Ideally, you have gone through a tough screening in the agency review, with your peers asking all the probing questions about your idea that the advertiser might ask in this final step of idea acceptance. You now have two major areas of concern facing you.

REALISTIC PRESENTATION OF THE IDEA

First, be wary of turning your presentation into a "dog-and-pony show," a razzle-dazzle description of the upcoming commercial that might be misleading. It is entirely possible to unintentionally misrepresent how the commercial will look and sound. Enthusiasm is all well and good, but don't overdo it. I have often seen a performance by a creative director that would do honor to a Barrymore, followed eventually by a commercial that left the advertiser saying, "Is THAT what he was describing to me when I bought his idea?"

In other words, don't try to "snow" the client. Either they will be turned off by your overselling, or they will be turned on and expect a commercial that will never meet expectations.

ACCURATE COST ESTIMATES

Second, and equally important, in your eagerness to get advertiser agreement, do NOT misrepresent the cost to produce the commercial. When the advertiser says, "Sure, it's a good idea, but I'm not sure I can afford to produce it," DON'T answer with, "Don't worry about a thing. We can easily produce the idea for what you want to pay." *Remember, production costs are typed into a commercial by the writer and drawn into the commercial by the art director.* The more the writer and art director know about production costs, the more they will be able to control cost as they prepare the original idea for production.

Unless you have actually priced out your commercial before you present the idea to the client, don't "ballpark" a price. It is much wiser to say, "I don't know what the commercial will cost, but I can give you a range estimate in a couple of days." You can get such a rough production estimate when you describe your idea to a knowledgeable production company.

You may have done your money homework and be able to say, "Our experience with similar commercials indicates that this idea is not inexpensive, but we think it will last a long while and be well worth the cost."

The wisest course is to be ready for this inevitable question when it arises. There are two ways you can prepare yourself without taking the time to actually bid out your storyboard or production notes. First, as you are working on the idea, make a phone call or two to a production company you think will be included in the eventual bidding. Don't talk to a "rep" or salesperson, but to the production people who actually put costs together. An accurate description of your idea should elicit a cost estimate within 10 percent of the final figure.

Second, if your commercial structure is similar to one used in other commercials (e.g., using a stand-up presenter in a bare-wall setting or showing food preparation in close-up on a tabletop), a call or two to production companies that do this sort of work will again give you a range estimate of the cost of the commercial.

The main thing to remember at this stage is never to quote final production costs. Before actual production, nothing is final. Any addition to or subtraction from your idea will affect the eventual production cost. However, the more familiar you are with production costs, the better you will be prepared to say things like, "Well, we could change the idea that way, but it will increase the final production cost."

Smart agency people will know beforehand the range of production expenditure the advertiser has in mind. Backed by hard-dollar knowledge, they will present ideas to the advertiser that will be good sales tools and affordable as well. It is the irresponsible member of the creative department who does not take the financial responsibilities of production into account. The more you learn about production, the better equipped you will be to prepare a contemporary commercial and to present it realistically to your client.

Do you remember the various visual aids I suggested you use in presenting your idea for agency review? They are twice as important for the client presentation, because the client's primary business is marketing the product, not producing commercials. You will do yourself and your idea a big favor by providing as many visual aids as possible when you present your idea to the client.

This is a delicate matter. It should be approached with as much information and control as you can muster. Chances are the agency has spent weeks or even months preparing for this meeting, and every effort should be made to make it successful.

Preparing for the Presentation

Let's consider the atmosphere of the conference room where the presentation is to be made. In most instances, there is an expectant air. The stage has been set. Usually, there is a cork-board wall on one side of the conference room, with a rail on which are resting the storyboards to be presented. They face the wall and will be turned around one at a time as they are presented to the client. Also, there is a TV monitor and cassette player in the room, in case the storyboard is on tape or a Ripomatic is to be presented.

The number of people at the meeting varies considerably. Attendance is usually in direct ratio to the importance of the commercial being presented: the more important the commercial, the more people at the meeting. If there is a chance the commercial will be developed into a long-running campaign, or if the commercial is to introduce a new product or service, key people from the agency will be in attendance. And people from research will also attend to add their expertise to the discussion.

THE CLIENT'S VIEWPOINT

One of the best ways to prepare for a presentation is to put yourself in the client's shoes and judge whether the commercial will meet the client's needs. Spend at least 30 minutes preparing a list of questions that you think may arise. This list should include the following:

1. Does this commercial fit the client's marketing strategy? (Such a written statement should exist.)
2. Does it fit the client's budget?
3. Does it separate the product or service from its competition? (List competitors and their advertising strategies.)
4. Does it suggest the positive aspects of the product? (List them.)
5. Does it suggest some quality of the product that has not been featured in previous advertising?
6. Is the commercial likely to surprise the client? (Pleasantly or unpleasantly?)
7. One more time—does it fit the client's budget? Leave lots of white space between the questions so that you can make notes during the presentation. Make sure you show the list to an account executive at the agency. In this way, you'll win support for your idea, and the agency will go into the presentation with a unified approach.

REMEMBERING THE COMMON GOAL

This is not an "us-against-them" meeting, although I have seen meetings go in that direction. The thing for both sides of the table to remember is this: The agency is trying to find a way to improve the marketing thrust for the product, and so is the advertiser. It is such an important meeting that sometimes wise advertisers ask for a day to think over an idea, rather than reacting to it immediately. The best meetings end with the advertiser saying, "Looks and sounds fine to me. Let's produce it!"

In Summary

The entire production of a commercial quite often depends on how the idea is presented to the advertiser. These factors are essential to a successful presentation:

1. Don't exaggerate the commercial.
2. Be sure your presentation stays factual, even at the risk of losing a dramatic impression that might be misleading.
3. Be sure you have a rough idea of what the commercial will cost to produce. If you don't know, don't guess at a figure. Say, "I'll get back to you with a rough estimate tomorrow." Then, do some checking before making a money statement.

The presentation is key to the future success of your TV commercial production. Be sure you are prepared for it.

4 PRICING THE COMMERCIAL

I n general, an advertising agency does not direct, film, edit, or finish its own commercials. Rather, the agency creative people—writers, art directors, and producers—supervise the production of the commercial, which is directed, filmed, and edited by independent commercial production companies.

Problems with In-House Production

Several large agencies have tried to produce some of their commercials completely in-house, but this has not been a roaring success. These agencies include Young & Rubicam, New York, and Leo Burnett, Chicago. The effort was to produce the simpler commercials in-house, using agency creative people as directors and producers, and hiring camera people and production crews from free-lance sources. This has not been successful, and Young & Rubicam has closed its in-house production unit.

The two main concerns with in-house production units are cost recovery and the need for top-flight talent. Whereas all costs incurred by using outside production sources can be billed to the client as part of the production cost, this is not the case with in-house units. The overhead expenses of such units become a general cost of doing business for the agency. Because each commercial is deemed to be different and special, in-house personnel may offer too subjective and narrow a creative view. The best people in the field usually prefer the independence of working outside the advertising agency. In order to obtain top creative direction, lighting, and editing in the production process, the preferable method is to hire outside experts and then supervise their work, from pre-production through to the finished commercial, ready to be aired.

Finding Production Companies for Bidding

There are more than 2,000 commercial production companies in the United States. Your choice ranges all the way from the local TV station to huge New York and Hollywood film and tape production companies, complete with back lots. Those back lots also include the Orlando area of Florida.

How do you go about finding the right production companies to give you price-quotes on your commercial? The first clue is in that hyphenated word, *price-quote*. Before you call any production company, determine what price your client can afford to spend on the production of the commercial.

CONSIDER THE CLIENT'S BUDGET

Is your client operating on a tight budget? And what exactly *is* a "tight budget"? To a national advertiser, doing a national commercial, a tight budget for a 30-second commercial might be a gross of $200,000. (*Gross* means that all production elements are included: music, editing, finishing, agency commission, air prints, and the principal filming.) To a local or regional advertiser, $5,000 might be a tight budget.

So start with two hard facts: First, the client has only so much money to spend for production, out of the total media budget. Second, even if the client is a local or regional advertiser, the commercial will share airtime with expensive national commercials. This means the commercial needs to be inexpensive without looking cheap.

The challenge of making a good commercial on a tight budget becomes more difficult all the time. To understand how costs have changed over the years, consider this: In the early 1980s, the average cost to produce a 30-second national commercial was $150,000. The average gross cost to produce a single 30-second national commercial in the 1990s is more than $275,000. We are talking serious money here. In 1992, I supervised the production of a 30-second commercial that cost the client $1 million. And there have been many commercials that have cost more than that.

COST-SAVING IDEAS FOR COMMERCIAL PRODUCTION

Rapidly mounting costs make it imperative to determine budget limitations *before* deciding on production companies to bid on your commercials. If you have $100,000 to spend, consider producing in cities other than New York or Hollywood. It is possible to get top-flight production for less money in Chicago, Minneapolis, Indianapolis, Boston, Atlanta, Miami, or Portland. Also, if your production is for a local or regional client, consider shooting in 16mm film instead of 35mm. Filming in 16mm involves less expensive equipment, less expensive film stock, and often less expensive union crew requirements. Filming in 35mm is the ultimate in professional commercial production. If the dollars for production are even more scarce, plan a simple videotape production to pull costs down.

Your might also consider choosing a city as close as possible to your home office to save additional back-and-forth travel and living expenses. Cities other than New York and Hollywood are less expensive for two big reasons: First, the union requirements in other cities (including crew size) are reduced. Second, directors and camera people in these cities are willing to accept lower fees for their work. This doesn't necessarily mean they are less talented, just not as well known. In general, if the company features a "name" director, its overall production costs will be higher.

Specialization of Production Companies

Another factor that will affect your choice of production houses is the type of production planned. Very few companies produce both in animation and in live action, or in film and on videotape. And there are now companies on both coasts that specialize in the latest adaptations of computerized and digitized special effects. These companies offer the use of cutting-edge computer software in achieving visual effects, all of which comes at a price.

To sort out the production companies that are best equipped to produce the commercial you have in mind, there must be an understanding of the differing abilities of each, as well as their comparative production costs. Let's start our discussion then with companies that produce in animation.

ANIMATION COMPANIES: FROM DISNEY TO DIGITIZING

The word *animation* has taken on several new meanings in the 1990s. Animation originally referred to frame-by-frame drawings drawn by artists on clear "cels" (a word derived from *celluloid*), and filmed at 24 frames per second. Today, animation encompasses all sorts of live-action and artwork combinations that were not even considered until digitized finishing procedures became the norm. To get an accurate price-quote for your animated production, it is necessary to contact production companies that specialize in the specific type of animation you have in mind.

It is still possible to find artists who draw in the traditional frame-by-frame animation mode. And because no two artists draw alike, it is wise to review examples of their work before deciding which animators you should invite to bid. The choice depends on your design and execution needs and the client's production budget. The better known the animator's style, the more money he or she commands.

While most animation companies are either in New York or the Los Angeles area, it is also possible to find animators at a lower cost in Minneapolis, Chicago, Pittsburgh, Boston, Atlanta, Indianapolis, and even Waterloo, Iowa. Union rules and wage requirements vary by city, which helps dictate price differentials. If your animation is very simple, without great movement or background changes from one frame to the next, you may do well with a smaller company in a smaller city. This is particularly true if your basic art elements are already established and you don't need the expertise of a top designer and director of animation.

In cel animation, using the best artists and the most professional work, a 30-second fully animated commercial will cost between $80,000 and $150,000, depending on the animation specifications. When you get into the realm of computerized and digitized origination, the sky's the limit—particularly if your visual is breaking new ground. Remember, these computers are priced by the hour, and hourly rates can run from a few hundred dollars to well over a thousand. The main difference between cel animation and Computer Generated Imagery (CGI) is that the human hand draws cel animation, while the computer manipulates images.

LIVE-ACTION COMPANIES

If your commercial idea calls for live-action filming, you have a much wider selection of production companies than are available to you in animation. The range extends from big-name directors who command fees of more than $15,000 a day, down to the local TV station that tapes your commercial between station breaks, with total costs of less than $1,000 for a simple commercial.

So, what should you do? Will you go for the top of the line or settle for the smallest production facility and the cheapest production mode? Or will you recall the charming sales rep who took you out for that great lunch and take your commercial to that company? My suggestion is: *none of the above*.

Your decision should be made after considering the following questions:

1. Is the client local, regional, or national?
2. Has the agency determined how much money is available in the total media budget for producing the commercial? (As a rule of thumb, large budgets spend no more than 8–10 percent for commercial production. The smaller the budget, the larger the percentage for producing commercials.)
3. What type of director does the commercial call for? An exciting dialog director? An expert camera director who knows how to shoot downhill ski footage? Or a tabletop wizard who will make food close-ups mouth-watering?

Be aware that director's reels are available to help you find just the right companies to bid on your commercial. Most agencies with clients who advertise on television are staffed with producers who have built a knowledgeable answer to the above questions. As the production companies add and subtract directors from their ranks, advertising agencies must make it their business to keep up with these important personnel changes. They should know which directors have started their own companies, which camera people are free-lancers, and which editors are best known for specific editing styles.

Once you have established your specific production needs, you are ready to make the final decision on which companies to ask for bids. However, first you need to know a bit more about the various types of production companies. The more information you can obtain, the wiser will be your choice of companies to bid. Following are some facts that separate production companies.

Big Companies with Their Own Stages

This category seems to slim down, year after year. Those that are left are usually found either in New York, on the West Coast, or in the Orlando region of Florida. They quite often have direct relationships with major motion picture companies and access to large stages and fully equipped back lots with standing exterior sets. If you commercial needs the full range of live-action production facilities, this type of company should be chosen to bid on your commercial. For example, most song-and-dance commercials of the Michael Jackson type need huge stages to handle the scope of the photography. The same can be said of some automobile commercials, which show cars in huge settings that require controlled lighting.

Production Boutiques

A growing list of smaller companies rent stages or locations and hire free-lance crews for specific jobs. They may also rent equipment on a job-by-job basis. These smaller companies, or boutiques, are usually owned and operated by excellent directors. They offer a highly customized service, and the price may well reflect this. If your commercial relies primarily on specific casting and close attention from a top director or camera person, you would do well to include such boutiques in your bidding, if your budget allows this luxury. Their forte is personalizing your production, so the end product will bear the stamp of their individuality and taste. Such boutiques can be found not only in New York and Los Angeles, but also in many smaller cities across the country.

Videotape Production Companies

Although some live-action film companies also produce on videotape, the specific equipment requirements of tape have spawned production companies that specialize in that production mode. To keep up with state-of-the-art equipment can be costly. Each improvement in video-tape equipment costs thousands of dollars, making it financially difficult for a tape production company to stay on the leading edge. However, videotape production is usually less costly than film production, and tape companies can be found in many smaller cities, serving mostly local and regional advertisers.

Local TV Stations

Continuing down the production-cost scale, many TV stations will produce tape commercials for local or regional clients. The stations will be glad to show you the work they have done for other local clients. This lower production cost also brings along some big problems. If you decide to work with a local TV station on their stage, your commercial will be shot either on 16mm film or videotape. The reason for this is that these are the production tools used for news-gathering by the station's staff. Being accustomed to instant news coverage, the same crew will usually not take the time you would like to devote to producing a commercial. The result is lower production quality.

If videotaped in the station's studio, be aware that the crew working on your commercial may also be working to keep the station on the air. If they are, the crew ignores your videotape during station breaks to concentrate on the on-air commercials, and you are out of business for several minutes. Not only that, but you may have lost the interest and attention of the crew, and your commercial will suffer. If the crew producing your commercial also produces live news, weather, and sports on the same work shift, guess what gets top priority. Right. Your commercial production takes a back seat to staying on the air.

Reviewing Production Company Cassettes

Assuming that you now have determined how much you have to spend and where you wish to shoot your commercial, how do you choose the companies to bid on production? One way is to look at director's sample reels from several production houses that fit your budget and creative needs. These tapes are either on 3/4-inch videotape, 1/2-inch videotape, or laser discs. Some companies keep samples on CD-ROM, ready to play back in your personal computer. Reels are the production companies' calling cards, and they represent their best work. Larger agencies with TV production departments have a library of company tapes. The agency's producers and creatives can stay up to date with present production by keeping such files. These cassettes are a great help in determining which companies to bid. Also, many agencies hold weekly screenings of new reels. The audience usually includes writers, art directors, and producers who are about to go into production. A secondary, but important, added attraction at such screenings is a chance to see the commercials being done by the competition.

STRATEGIES FOR SMALLER AGENCIES

If you work in a smaller agency outside the major advertising cities—New York, Chicago, Los Angeles, San Francisco, Minneapolis, Miami, and Orlando—it helps to know a producer at a larger agency who can bring you up to date on the kind's of work various production companies are doing. Because of the greater number of commercials produced by large agencies, their people have access to information that can be very helpful to people like you. So if you can, talk over your requirements with a producer at a larger agency and get some opinions. I have always found that this type of information is given freely.

Beyond that, your chances of looking at sample reels in a smaller agency are really quite good. I have heard production companies state that often the smaller agencies are better to work with than some of the bigger ones, because they have fewer "experts." Therefore, the smaller agencies allow the production company director, camera person, and editor to do their best work without interference.

THE CRUCIAL QUESTION: THE BUDGET

Before you call for a sample tape, ask yourself two questions. First, can my client afford a star director, like the one whose work I'm asking to see? Second, can my agency afford to send me to a distant city for a week or more? It seems like money has lots to do with your choices, doesn't it? Consider these cold facts: If you produce your commercial on the West Coast, the per diem cost for meals, hotel rooms, and rental cars will run at least $250 per day. In New York City, your costs will run about $300 per day.

To put it another way, to stay in the Los Angeles area for a week for pre-production, production, and editing will come to $1,750. A week in New York will run $2,000. That's per person, and usually two agency people must attend those duties. The agency will have to add a minimum of $3,500 to the West Coast bid, and $4,000 to the New York bid. In most cases, these costs are billable *net* to the client, but not for more than two people. Beyond that, those dollars come from the agency's potential income and profit.

JUDGING SAMPLE REELS

Once you have a solid idea about which production houses can give you the kind of commercial you want and keep within your budget, phone, fax, or write for their sample tapes. But when you get down to judging those tapes, be aware that a sample tape is the showpiece of a production company. And be aware also that you must separate the creative *ideas* on that tape from their *production*. That's not easy to do, but it is important; in 99 out of 100 instances, the ideas come from advertising agencies, not from the production company. The agency brings an idea, fully conceptualized, to the production company, and the *production* of the idea is the only contribution of the director, camera person, and editor. Although the two parts blend together into a commercial, it is important to differentiate between them if you want to have a clear idea of what you can expect from the production of your commercial idea.

When you view a consistently superior sample tape, you realize that the nation's best creative agencies are working with that production company. Top production companies attract top creative work, and the higher production price tag usually reflects this combined excellence.

When you have run the tapes and want to make a judgment concerning that company, have a clipboard handy, with a checklist including the following points:

1. Direction (who directed, and your opinion)
2. Casting (good, bad, indifferent)
3. Camera work (who shot the commercial, and your opinion)
4. Lighting (good, bad, indifferent)
5. Editing (who edited, and your opinion)
6. Cost of producing the commercials on this reel

These six items are the basic responsibility of the production and editorial companies you will employ. As you watch the sample tapes, make notes on the commercials you think are as good as you want yours to be. Those notes will come in handy in your production discussions with the companies you ask to bid on your commercial.

When you see a commercial you particularly like, based on your six criteria, find out who the director was, who did the casting, who was responsible for the lighting and camera work (usually the dual function of the director of photography or the camera person, and the editorial company that was used).

One further note about sample tapes. When you are through with them, return them promptly, unless there is an agreement that you will keep the tape on file. The tapes are a production company's calling cards, and they need those tapes sent back so they can call on the next agency.

Production Company Personnel

Remember, when you choose a production company, you are not choosing equipment or mechanical things. You are choosing people. The best way to find the best people for your purposes is to see the work they have done for somebody else. It's all there on those sample tapes. Only experience, information, exchange, and conversations with individuals will reveal these idiosyncrasies.

DIRECTORS

You'll note that most directors are better at some types of commercials than at others. Some love the challenge of a tough location shoot, with the vagaries of weather forcing them to make instant decisions. Other directors find their reward in the quiet, controlled atmosphere of a sound stage, working intimately with on-camera actors. And some directors' best work is done with tedious lighting of close-up food shots. The likes, dislikes, and individual abilities of the production people shine through in their work. There are even some "people" directors who don't like to stick around for the product close-ups, even though that is really what the commercial is all about.

If you have a humorous commercial to produce, it only makes sense to choose a director with a keen eye for casting and a sense of humor. But even humor comes in flavors and shades. If you want broad, burlesque humor, you will find the right directors in large cities, where they have the opportunity to direct on stage as well as on film. If you want subtle humor, look for that quality in the sample tape. It is truly an individual directorial ability.

CAMERA PEOPLE

The same goes for camera people. Some are better at stage shooting than location shooting. There are indoor camera people who love to take the time and trouble to light the smallest object. Look closely at the size of the product you are advertising in your commercial, and note whether you require that kind of attention. The top-flight lighting experts achieve stunning results through their close control of lighting on a product, no matter how small.

On the other hand, you would never ask these camera people to shoot from a helicopter, where the sun (the "key light in the sky") is constantly changing its position in their lenses. Flying camera people are a special breed, and there aren't too many good ones around. Some actually look forward to risking life and limb to capture a scene that has never been shot before. For example, one man jumped out of an airplane with a camera in his helmet to shoot other daredevil parachute jumpers who were taking still pictures with a certain brand of camera. Another camera person filmed parachute jumpers on skateboards as they plummeted to earth in a soft-drink commercial.

The secret to selecting three production companies well qualified to bid competitively on your commercial is a combination of three elements.

1. Finding companies whose bids fit your budget
2. Finding production people with the particular abilities to complement your idea
3. Inspiring these people to give their best effort to make your commercial special

That's the trick, to combine those three elements—the budget, the people, and the desire for excellence.

The Bidding Procedure

Let's assume that the client has approved your commercial for production, and you are now preparing to send your idea out for competitive bidding. In most agencies, it is policy to get competitive bids on all commercials to be produced. This is particularly important for large pools of commercials, which are usually produced in the leading production centers of Chicago, New York, or Hollywood. In smaller production centers where there are fewer companies, the competitive bidding may be limited to two companies or will not happen at all, if only one company exists to produce the commercial. Competitive bids can be sought from companies in more than one city, but this tends to be both cumbersome and inconclusive. In fact, differences in union jurisdictions and crew sizes often make multi-city bidding less than competitive. (A bid from New York will invariably be higher than a bid from Minneapolis, for example.)

THE BIDDING PACKAGE

Whether you seek bids from three companies, two companies, or only one company, the bidding procedure should be similar. It should start with the agency furnishing the production company with basic materials, which I will call the "bidding package." This bidding package should contain at least four basic elements:

1. A specification sheet, including a checklist for bidding
2. The script (or scripts, if more than one commercial is involved)
3. Storyboards or Ripomatic (storyboards on videotape)
4. Writer's production notes
5. Additional materials (e.g. prerecorded music tracks)

Let's examine each of the basic elements in the bidding package.

Specification Sheet and Checklist for Bidding

This sheet, prepared by the advertising agency, lays out in detail all areas of financial reporting and responsibility and assigns each to the agency or production company. It may look like a dull, tedious document, but both cost and quality control depend on the amount of attention given to the specification sheet. It covers two areas of financial responsibility.

1. Who pays the talent: the agency or the production company? These payments can easily amount to several thousand dollars if a pool of commercials is to be produced over several shooting days.

2. Who does the editorial work on the commercial? Does the agency want the production company to handle post-production, or will it have the editing and finishing work done by a separate editorial company? This post-production cost has become a major item with the advent of digitized finishing.

Don't be overwhelmed by the massiveness of the specification sheet (a sample is included in Appendix One). There will probably be many items listed that don't pertain to your commercial, but every item that does should be checked off and the responsibility assigned.

The specification sheet should be a printed form on which you fill in the facts about your commercial. These facts include the following:

1. The name of the advertiser and product
2. The name, address, and telephone number of the agency, and the same of the assigned agency producer
3. The title, code number, and length of each commercial
4. A check mark, indicating whether the production company should base its bid on the complete job (from pre-production to final broadcast materials) or merely through production and viewing of the dailies
5. Film or tape preference: film (35mm or 16mm) or videotape (1-inch, Beta, etc.)
6. A statement that the bid should include negative-to-tape transfers or finished for-air materials
7. A statement that pricing should be based on a firm bid or on a "cost-plus-fixed-fee" bid (these two bidding methods will be discussed later in this chapter.)

The specification sheet becomes a factual basis for bidding and should also include a space for additional information, such as the following:

1. Is pickup footage to be used (i.e., scenes from previous commercials or stock footage from a film library)? Jot down the sources of this footage so that the bidding studio knows where to find it and so it can determine who will pay for it—agency or production company.
2. Are "special payments" to be made? If so, by whom? Such payments would include ongoing contracts with talent paid more than union scale.
3. If music is involved, who will pay for it?
4. Are there existing props or sets? Who will pay for the storage, pickup, and return of this material?

The second page of the specification sheet should include the "checklist for bidding." This is a further spelling out of responsibility, this time including the client as well. Here are 16 pre-production elements for which financial responsibility must be established:

1. Set design (or location search)
2. Character sketches (if animated)
3. Casting (where it is to be done; videotape the session?)
4. Preparation of special releases (legal)
5. Signing of performer releases (who handles them?)
6. Paid-up status of union talent (who checks this?)
7. Product props (special bowls, mugs, etc.)
8. Actual advertiser's package (camera-ready copies)
9. Actual advertiser's product (in bulk?)
10. Color-correction of package and/or labels
11. Home economist (and grocery suppliers)
12. Wardrobe (talent's own or rented/purchased?)
13. Technical advisor
14. Stylist
15. Stock footage search and purchase
16. Pickup footage from previous commercials

These responsibilities and their assignments continue into the production and post-production of your commercial. Here are three more for your production checklist:

1. Talent session fees (who pays?)
2. Talent reports, union forms, W4s (who files?)
3. First edit (who does and who pays?)

Talent conditions.   Speaking of talent, before any bid can be considered complete, the exact number of union performers must be determined and payment assigned to either the agency or the production company. By law, talent must be paid promptly. Talent includes members of the three major performing unions: Screen Actor's Guild (SAG), Screen Extra's Guild (SEG), and American Federation of Television and Radio Artists (AFTRA). SAG and SEG members must be employed in all of the population centers over which they have jurisdiction for film commercials. As of this writing, AFTRA has a parallel jurisdiction over radio and videotape commercials. And if you have a music track which involved a recording session by musicians, you must pay the American Federation of Musicians (AF of M).

Responsibility for the sound track.   Now, let's discuss responsibility for the sound track as it is detailed in the checklist:

1. Who owns the music? Is it in the public domain? Is it library music, involving a payment to a recorded library company? Does the client own it? If it is original music, who pays for its recording? Is it an existing copyrighted melody for which rights must be negotiated (by whom and who pays?)? Is it new music that the client will purchase outright? Who will produce it and pay for the session?
2. In recording the voices and/or music for the sound track, who is responsible for the following?
   a. Recording the sound track
   b. Paying the voiceover talent session fee
   c. Making out the talent report for subsequent payments (as required by union agreements)
   d. Filling out the music reports, whether original, public domain, or a version of copyrighted material
   e. Storing and identifying the sound track elements for possible reuse and remix
   f. Mixing of sound track elements
   g. Transferring sound track elements

After the agency fills out the specification sheets and gives them to each of the production companies bidding on the commercial, all of the bids will be based on the same information. There will be less margin for error in pricing and less misunderstanding about what the production consists of. As a result, the bids should be truly competitive.

Scripts

There is a classic form for a commercial script. The left half of the page is the VIDEO or picture side. It describes each scene that will appear in the commercial in its chronological order. The right half of the page is the AUDIO or sound side. It describes the elements of the sound track, i.e., the words and/or music that occur in conjunction with the video picture.

The main functions of the script are (1) to get client agreement on the copy, and (2) to serve as a timing device. The first consideration must be to fit the copy into the slightly less than 30 seconds of track time that is normal for a 30-second commercial. I say "slightly less," because, even though commercials are transferred to videotape for broadcast, there is a very slight lag between the start of a sound track and the picture. For sake of convenience, however, we will always refer to the length of a 30-second commercial as 30 seconds.

All copy should be read aloud and timed before submitting the script for approval. There is nothing more frustrating than trying to cram 32 seconds of great copy into a 30-second sound track! No script should ever be presented for client approval or for production until it has been properly timed. When you are timing copy, be sure to allow for the physical movement called for in the video description. The action as well as the words must fit into the overall timing of 30 seconds.

Storyboard

Storyboards are visualizations that coincide with the video descriptions in the script. Traditionally, the storyboard was a series of either artist's drawings or actual photographs. Under each of the storyboard frames are tabs, or typewritten parts of the audio and video descriptions that match the storyboard picture. Each scene, each written description of each sound, and each bit of important action thus become directly connected by storyboard frames in sequence.

The traditional concept storyboard can be nothing but stick figures, or a highly detailed series of drawings. It is also possible to do a one-frame master scene as a storyboard. This type of board is useful if all the action takes place in one area and if all the movement can be visualized in one drawing.

Animatics.   A second and much more complete depiction of the hoped-for commercial is called an *animatic storyboard*. The key frames of the commercial are either drawn or photographed and then put on videotape in their proper sequence, in sync with a voiceover and any other sound effects or music.

This is the preferred way to present the commercial idea to the client and for use in bidding, because it is actually 30 seconds in length and thus shows the relative length of each storyboard frame in seconds. This is not possible with the traditional storyboard.

Ripomatics.   A third mode is called a *Ripomatic* (or *Stealomatic*) storyboard, because existing scenes from other commercials are edited together to explain the concept. This running footage sequence is then put on videotape, along with a sound track including a voiceover and any other sound effects or music. The one major problem with a Stealomatic is that the choice of expensive footage from other commercials may over-promise the end result of your commercial. This can be a serious flaw. Aside from that possible problem, both the animatic and Stealomatic storyboards are preferable, in my opinion, to the concept storyboard approach.

Before the production day, many directors will draw a "shooting board": their own suggestion of how each scene will be structured. This can be most helpful in the pre-production meetings that precede actual photography.

Writer's Production Notes

These notes can be some of the most important planning documents of all. I refer to these notes as the writer's because most originators are writers. But if the art director originated the idea, then the notes should be written by the art director. The point is that whoever had the idea should describe it in writing with production notes.

Here are the various aspects of the idea that should be fully described in the writer's production notes. Although television is basically a visual medium, production costs can often be best determined from a written description.

Casting. When you describe your protagonist in writing, you can describe him or her more in depth than an artist can draw the person's image. You can describe age, education, likes, dislikes, and all the psychological as well as physical clues that will help in casting the right actor.

For example, in looking for an ingenuous 16-year-old girl for a Heinz ketchup commercial, the art director had drawn the usual sexy young Hollywood type. But, based on the writer's production notes, we cast a slightly overweight but honestly attractive girl who could actually blush! The written description, not the drawing, led us to the right girl, out on her first date.

Set design. The storyboard is mainly to get the general feel for the final commercial and usually should not be taken literally. Rather than drawing an elaborate set that is often too wide for the camera's eye, describe the action in words. Follow the same procedure for commercials that will be filmed on location. Talented directors and camera people, working with competent production companies, will add their input to the written descriptions.

This happened several years ago, and I hope it will never happen again. A storyboard was drawn for a commercial with a beautiful ending scene: a snow-covered mountain peak on the right side of the frame, a sunset in midframe, and a smaller mountain with a lake in the foreground, in the left part of the frame. The client loved the drawing, and the agency promised to find it for the commercial. A three-person team from the agency, plus the director and a pilot, spent five flying days and $15,000 looking for that drawn storyboard frame. They never found the exact scene. Had the writer's production notes been the guide instead of that fanciful storyboard frame, $15,000 and five days would have been saved. Here's what the writer had written: "At the end of the commercial, a mountain lake reflects the sunset, with silhouetted mountain peaks in the background." Colorado is loaded with scenes like that.

Lighting.   Because mood is a by-product of lighting, a description of the mood desired will suggest the lighting in a more complete way than a drawing can.

We once worked with a storyboard that showed a highly reflective black floor for two interpretive dancers. The art director felt the mood of the commercial would be strengthened by the mirror images of the dancers on such a floor. Well, I must tell you that a reflective floor surface for dancers that will show their reflections but not their footprints is very expensive to construct and to light. However, a quick look at the writer's production notes saved many thousands of dollars in lighting, construction, and shooting time. Here's how the writer described the dance scene: "Because our product is only five inches high (a canned food product), we will not want to be further than waist high from the dancers at any time." That sentence meant that we would never see the floor. The lighting would be specific to the dancers, not to a reflective floor. The commercial made monetary sense to the advertiser and advertising sense as well.

Even though a storyboard, an animatic, or a stealomatic is needed for client presentation, the actual bidding and pre-production planning need well-written and well-thought-out production notes, plus specification sheets. Words, in each instance, become much more exact and definitive than art frames and help make competitive bidding truly competitive.

Additional materials.   The name of the game is information. Any additional information you can furnish the production companies will sharpen their ability to bid intelligently and economically on your commercials. Additional materials should include any test sound tracks you have recorded, no matter how amateurish. By listening to the type of music you have chosen or the way you have directed an announcer in a test voiceover track, a production company can get a clearer idea of the intent of the commercial.

If you have shot experimental film or tape, even 8mm, this can also be helpful. One of the classic commercials of all time began with an 8mm home movie shot by the late Gene Kolkey of Leo Burnett. He filmed his very young son and showed it to camera-director Howard Zieff, who then shot a commercial for Campbell Soup called "Flower Pot." Kolkey's home movie became the additional material that communicated the idea to Zieff.

The entire process of bidding a commercial is like rubbing your head and patting your stomach at the same time. On the one hand you are trying to create a new piece of advertising, and on the other hand you are trying to be economical. Bidding on commercials is business art. To overplay either side of the equation does violence to production and to the eventual effectiveness of the advertising.

FIRM BID VERSUS COST PLUS FIXED FEE

To help control possible production waste as well as to spell out what is hoped for in production, commercials are bid in two basic ways. Let me explain the strengths and weaknesses of both bidding systems.

Firm Bid

This was the original method of pricing commercials for production, and it continues as the dominant mode today. In general, a firm bid has the following ramifications.

1. We, the production company, will produce a given commercial for X dollars.
2. If the commercial costs more than X dollars to produce, we will not charge that extra cost to the agency and client. We will take it from our own projected profit.
3. If the commercial costs less than X dollars to produce, we, the production company, will make a larger profit on the production.

This mode puts a great deal of the burden on the production company, because it must accurately assess the working methods of the agency so that it can come as close as possible to its assigned profit. (Profit for the production company usually is between 20 and 35 percent.)

The possible weakness of the system is that too high a bid costs the advertiser too much, and too low a bid takes profit from the production company. As bidding procedures became more sophisticated and as large companies such as Procter & Gamble became more cost-conscious, an alternative method of pricing was introduced, cost plus fixed fee.

Cost Plus Fixed Fee (C+FF)

This method consists of projecting all the direct costs of production, exclusive of any profits, cushions, or pads that are sometimes used in computing firm bid estimates, and adding them together. A fixed fee (or markup) is then applied to the direct cost total. This fixed fee remains constant unless one of three changes occurs:

1. The number or complexity of the shooting days changes because the concept of the commercial is altered
2. The agency or client decides to change the number of commercials to be made
3. The agency agrees to a fee change requested by the production company

Thus, direct costs are out-of-pocket costs that the production house incurs to provide labor, equipment, materials, and services to satisfy the production needs of the commercial. They usually grow out of the specification sheet and the bidding checklist.

The fixed fee should include all overhead costs and the production house's margin of profit, which is usually between 20 and 35 percent. Usually, there are several items that are not marked up, i.e., not listed among the direct costs to which the fixed fee is applied. These items may include talent session payments, travel and living expenses, weather day and/or cancellation charges, and the director's fee. These are quite often billed out on a net basis.

The fixed fee in many instances becomes the negotiable part of the production cost. Depending on the complexity of the production, the fee will quite often be adjusted up or down before production approval, which is consummated in writing.

There are several advantages to the C+FF bidding method. Because the bid is based on direct costs supported by bills, it is possible for the agency to audit the various cost elements after production is completed and before final payment is made. Though this is a tedious, labor-intensive way to go, it will help determine whether the direct costs are accurate and will help keep a clean separation between direct and overhead costs.

Also, C+FF will guarantee the production company its margin of profit, because any additional expenses agreed on after the production contract is signed are billed out directly and do not have to be absorbed by the production company. These additional expenses would include rental of props, costumes, etc., later requested and not agreed upon when the C+FF bid was approved. These additional expenses will be billed directly to the agency by the production company.

In paying the direct costs involved in the union talent session payments (to which the fixed fee is not applied), it is customary for the production company to charge the employer's share of taxes plus a handling fee. This fee is usually about 10 percent of the total talent charges, which include fringe benefits (such as Pension and Welfare) as well as the session fee. These direct costs are then billed to the advertising agency.

Whether the bid is based on C+FF, firm bid, or any other mode, it is customary for the production company to be responsible for the following related aspects of production:

1. Reshooting due to loss of or damage to the film negative or videotape. This may involve an adjustment to the fixed fee.
2. Reshooting and overtime penalties for the crew and talent due to equipment loss or malfunction.

3. Studio or location liabilities, either to persons or to property.
4. Filling out all appropriate talent reports and prompt payment of talent (if so indicated in the specification sheet). The talent report is vital, not only to the payment of session fees, but also for purposes of future payment of residuals.
5. With the C+FF bidding method, the studio must also fill out a "Final Cost Detail Sheet." When this sheet is approved by the agency, final payment is made to the production company.

Here is how the payments are usually made by the agency to the production company under the C+FF bidding system:

1. Fifty percent of the total bid price is paid on acceptance of the production company bid.
2. Twenty-five percent of the total bid price is paid on delivery of the first cut (if done by the production company). If the editorial finishing is done by the production company, the final 25 percent is paid on delivery of the final approved edit. If all editorial is done away from the production company by separate editorial and finishing companies, the remaining 50 percent of the total bid price is paid to the production company on approval of all dailies.
3. The final payment to the production company is made only after the production company has turned over all contract elements (negatives and all other elements listed on the specification sheets) and has completed two important additional items:
   a. All talent reports and talent contracts, including W4s (if the specification sheet says the production company has to pay).
   b. A filled-out production cost sheet that shows the actual production costs.

Payments under the firm bid system can be made in the same way as under the C+FF system, or in any way agreed upon by the agency and production company. For example, if the production company is only responsible for the pre-production and production of your commercial, the agency might make a one-third payment on acceptance of the production bid, one-third on the delivery of all negative and production elements, and one-third on completion of talent reports, talent contracts, and the filled-out production cost sheet.

One final word on the bidding procedure: Over the years as an agency producer, I have worked with many fine production companies staffed by business-oriented artists. These production experts not only studied the boards, the scripts, the specification sheets, and the production notes, but they also knew enough about the aspirations of the agencies and clients involved to help them attain the level of excellence so eagerly sought. In order to make your own commercial goals completely understood and to help make the production company's bid accurate, be sure to prepare an informative bidding package.

Judging Competitive Bids

At this point, you have selected three companies to bid on your commercial and have sent each of them the identical bidding package. You have also indicated whether you want a firm bid or one based on cost plus fixed fee (C+FF). The three bids have come back for your inspection and final selection. How do you determine which bid represents the best value for the advertiser's dollar and the best commercial from the agency's quality-control standpoint?

Whether you bid firm bid or C+FF, in nine out of ten cases your bid come back with the Association of Independent Commercial Producers Cost Summary Forms (see Appendix Three). This six-page document has been prepared by the production company, which is a member of the Association of Independent Commercial Producers (AICP), representing nearly all of the commercial production companies in the United States. This form has helped standardize the way competitive bids are submitted to advertising agencies by production companies, enabling the agencies to make direct comparisons among competing bids. Let me give you an example.

Suppose two of the three bids are almost identical in total production cost. Is it possible to choose between them on a logical and practical basis? Yes it is, if both bids are on the AICP form. You can compare important cost factors by checking the *internal* costs of one bid against the *internal* costs of the other.

Here's how it works: Let's say Bid A has $8,000 listed as the cost of "Director/Creative Fees" (line 10) and $2,000 for "Location and Travel Expenses" (line 3). The total of those two items is $10,000. Bid B has listed $5,000 as the cost of "Director/Creative Fees" and $5,000 for "Studio and Set Construction Costs" (line 5). Again, the two items total $10,000.

Company A apparently believes that your commercial should be shot in a real house (a location) instead of on a set. It also thinks its director is worth a higher fee than does Company B. Company B has a different interpretation of your bidding package. It apparently believes that your commercial should be shot on a specially constructed set on a stage. And its director commands a lower fee than does Director A. Now you must make an evaluation over and above the comparative costs:

1. In the opinion of the creative department, is Director A that much better than Director B ($8,000 vs. $5,000)?

2. Is there an advantage in shooting your commercial in a real house on location rather than building a set ($2,000 vs. $5,000)?

These are questions you should weigh carefully, because how you answer them will affect the final look and sound of your commercial. Also, the prices quoted above are from the top sheet of the AICP form. The detailed description of the costs can be found in the following five pages of the form. For instance, "Studio & Set Construction Costs" on the top sheet are the total of F, G, and H, to be found on page 3 of the AICP form.

Although the differing items in the two bids come to the same total, they arrive in different ways. Your decision can also affect the overall production budget. For example, if you decide to go with Bid B, but instead of opting for a $5,000 set, you tell the production company you want to shoot in a location house, the saving could amount to $3,000.

Or you could go the other way. You could accept Bid A with the more expensive director, and tell the company to build a set instead of shooting on location. This decision would raise your overall budget by $3,000. That's a swing of $6,000 on two estimates that originally totaled the same.

Sometimes the bids are not equal at all. When this happens, the AICP form will give you clues to big dollar differences. At the top of the first page is the "Studio Cost Summary." Among the headings is "Number of Pre-Production Days" and "Pre-lite." If this is where the cost discrepancy lies, it may be that the low bid is the result of not allowing sufficient pre-production time. Also, it might be wise to spend time before principle photography pre-lighting the product (if this is called for). To accept that lower bid might be penny wise and pound foolish.

It is also possible that another item, "Number of Studio Days," will vary on the forms you receive from your bidding studios. If one studio bids only one day of studio shooting, and the other two studios bid two days, the cost differential can run into six figures in the gross cost. You may find, with questioning, that the studio that says it can shoot in one day has planned a more efficient shooting schedule than the other two companies. It might be worth your while to go with the much lower bid, after you thoroughly discussed how they plan to save all that shooting time.

The AICP form is a boon to the production companies as well. Until this standardized form was adopted, it was very difficult for them to handle the myriad bills that came in from free-lancers and independent contractors hired to help produce the commercial. Now, each of these people (who work in assigned departments) is given a standard billing number on the AICP form. If a person is hired as a carpenter on set construction, his costs are listed under number 169, "Carpenters," and every carpenter charge will be assigned to that department number. "Inside props" are number 172, and so on. Thus, the AICP form will help in cost accounting and will eventually aid in item-by-item computerized billing.

In Summary

In choosing a production company, then, bear these facts in mind:

1. If you are debating between three companies of equal ability, the lowest bid should be seriously considered.
2. If you prefer one company over the others, and its bid is not the lowest of the three, be prepared to explain why you think it is better than the lowest bid, or find ways to bring their bid down by discussing the various interior costs listed on the AICP form. Whatever you do, do not select a company you won't want to work with.
3. Be sure you choose a company that can meet all your schedule requirements, from pre-production right through to the end of the production assignment.

Mies Van der Rohe, the great architect, said something about his craft that also is true for commercial production: "God is in the details." Careful study of the AICP form may not make you godlike, but it will certainly make you better able to control the many details that cost money in production. And remember, we're talking lots of money. The average national 30-second commercial cost more than a quarter of a million dollars to produce in gross cost to the client.

It should be understood that one of the most important parts of commercial production occurs long before a camera rolls or an actor utters a line. The way a production company is chosen and the conversations that lead to a final production bid are absolutely key to the eventual success of the commercial to be produced. The importance of these initial steps will become even more evident as you prepare to actually produce the commercial.

5

Casting the Commercial

The intent of 30-second commercials that feature actors or spokespeople is to give a microcosmic look at life—a compressed view of people, their likes and dislikes, their wants and needs. In that half-minute, commercials try to do many things: tell a story, establish characters, portray elements of personal conflict, and achieve a final resolution. In addition, the commercial must do all this while focusing on a particular product or service. The product, not the actor or spokesperson, must be the hero.

Commercials that strive to achieve this seemingly impossible task rely mainly on the people in front of the camera. It is they who deliver the message and persuade viewers to try out the product or service. This means that casting is one of the most critical decisions a TV commercial producer makes.

Sources for Casting

In casting there are three sources you can draw on: actors, personalities, and "real people." First there are actors. These are the men and women whose profession it is to create characters of every description. They are trained to perform roles and to make those roles appear real. They are cast mainly in commercials that either have tightly scripted dramatic action or rely on spontaneous reaction.

Second, there are personalities: people from all walks of life who stand head and shoulders above the crowd and are immediately recognizable. This includes star performers from every professional sport, as well as recording artists like Michael Jackson and Elton John. The implication in the use of personalities is simply this: if they think the product is great, so should you.

If you choose to cast a personality for your product or service, be sure your product won't be upstaged by the personality's physical or psychological presence. The casting of a personality is intended only to add acceptance and credibility to a product or service.

Finally, there are the rest of us—the nonactors, noncelebrities—the real people of the noncommercial world. Referred to as "real people" (as opposed to actors or known personalities), this group is important in certain types of commercials, particularly those that call for believable endorsement by ordinary consumers. The implication here is that a neighbor is telling you candidly about a product or service that has worked well for him or her and will work for you as well. These commercials are usually not completely scripted, and they may consist only of a list of questions to be answered by the on-camera nonactor. Real-people commercials rely on actual reactions and verbal endorsement. Such commercials usually require a signed statement from the real people that opinions expressed are truly their own.

The Importance of a Casting Director

All three categories of people are located by casting directors who work in the major production centers. Talented and efficient casting directors are available either through the production company or on a free-lance basis. Some of the huge advertising agencies have their own casting directors.

YOU'VE GOT THE CUTEST LITTLE BABY FACE

Every mother on earth thinks her child should be in a commercial. The problem is, which child is the right one for a particular commercial?

To my mind, the best person to answer that question is a Chicago-based director, Bob Ebel, head of Ebel Productions. He has shelves full of awards for his work with the younger set and reels of commercials promoting Fisher-Price, Tyco Toys, Carnation, Chex Multi-Grain, Michael Reese HMO, Clorox, Oscar Mayer, and Kraft, to name a few.

What's his secret? First, his studio is a children's dream. A child's easel with a picture painted by tiny hands greets visitors as they walk in the door. Miniature tables and chairs for the tiny hopefuls are covered with crayons, coloring books, and stuffed animals. Says Ebel, "When the kids come in they think they are coming into a playroom to talk to me. The camera is completely hidden. That is why our kids are so relaxed. After the kids trust me, I weave them into the product story."

To prepare for that trusting moment, massive pre-production occurs. Kathy Hurley, Ebel's executive producer, may see as many as 400–500 kids, and callbacks may involve as many as 100 kids in one day.

Three kids are chosen for each role. Why three? "Because," says Ebel, "any child may be having a bad day: an earache, a recent fight with a sister, or just a bad mood at the moment."

Precious moments with small children are a fragile commodity. In a commercial for Michael Reese HMO, Ebel kept the audition camera rolling as he asked children under the age of two to jump into an oversized easy chair. What they did was so good that the footage was edited to James Brown's classic "I Feel Good," and the ensuing commerical won every award in sight. The audition footage became the finished commercial!

Ebel credits his Midwestern upbringing and value system for a great deal of his success. He adds, "Treat kids with respect, just like adults. Turn work into fun. Understand that they have good days and bad days, just like adults."

Exhibit 5A

Bob Ebel adjusts the formalwear of one of his young actors.

A production company's casting director is part of the production package, but a free-lance casting director charges by the day—and his or her services are usually well worth the money. These people keep current with the talent pool available for commercial auditions. They know all the agents as well as all the talent that is performing in theater, on TV, or in other noncompeting commercials. They know who is coming back to acting after a period of absence, and who will soon be available. This kind of information is the key to successful casting. A list of casting directors can be obtained from an office of the Screen Actors Guild (SAG) or any major production company.

A good casting directior has the rare ability to sense what is meant when you describe how you want the part to be played. This intuitive ability enables him or her to bring the right actors to your casting session. One of the best ways to determine which casting director has this unique quality is to find out who was responsible for casting a commercial which is particularly successful due to the cast.

Exhibit 5B

Treating kids with respect allows Ebel to capture precious moments like this.

Hiring Professional Actors

Professional actors are a distinctive breed. (The term *actor* is generic, referring to both men and women.) Many of them hold jobs outside the acting profession, always with the hope they will be cast in a play or in commercials that will allow them to pursue an acting career full-time.

Therefore, professional actors keep in touch with casting directors. They learn to respond to the specific requirement of each commercial role. For that reason, it is wise to furnish the casting director with a written list of cast requirements. Consider the following points, and compile the key information to guide the casting director.

Exhibit 5C

The audition footage for a Chicago hospital's HMO was so good that it became the finished commercial.

What is the personality of the role? Is the person humorous, serious, naive, well-informed?

Is this a test commercial that may be used for only a few weeks? Test commercials can tie actors up for long periods and keep them from auditioning for competing commercials, even though the test may eventually fail.

Is the commercial to be local, regional, or national? Some actors do not want to appear in regional commercials, thinking they might be excluded from casting sessions for national commercials. Other actors will gladly work in regional or local commercials, if you will guarantee that the commercial will not go national. This gives them the freedom to accept roles in commercials for competing products or services in other parts of the country. Bear in mind that actors will NOT be cast in commercials that show them in on-camera roles for directly competing products. It is up to the casting director to be sure this requirement is met before sending an actor to a casting session.

Does the role require physical skills, such as the ability to play golf, tennis, baseball, etc.? If so, the actor should be prepared to prove this ability. I have been tripped up in such situations. Once, an actor was required to dive from a three-meter diving board, which he said he could easily do. When we arrived at the location, the actor froze; he wouldn't even approach the diving board. I ended up being the diver. So, if the role requires a special physical talent, hold your casting session at a location where you can judge that talent. For instance, if the role requires the ability to ride a horse, hold your casting session at a stable. If swimming is a requirement, hold your casting session at a swimming pool.

If you are coming to the casting session from out of town, be sure to make all this information available to the casting director before you arrive. If time allows, ask the casting director to send you the actors' sample tapes for you to judge before you travel in for the actual casting session. In this manner, it can be determined whether the advertising agency and the casting director are on the same wavelength. Although the casting director's time and the videotaping will cost you money, you will save an early trip to the production center, and the casting sessions will go more smoothly, saving everyone's time.

What Happens During a Casting Session?

A casting session is a most unusual, rather emotional experience for the first-timer. In the waiting room sit eager actors. Any of them could make many thousands of dollars as a result of this casting session, because they are paid "residuals" each time a commercial is aired.

If it is a major national commercial produced in a large city, the actors will be members of the Screen Actors Guild (SAG). These actors pay yearly dues to their union and maintain a high degree of professionalism. There is no charge for asking an actor to appear in a casting session, but if they are asked to return for a second callback, the actors might be paid for up to two hours of the actor's current daily rate. And don't ask them to improvise in an audition. Actors can be directed in a casting session but not asked to improvise your copy. The reason that it is unfair to ask an auditioning actor to improvise your copy is that the actor has not as yet been hired, and improvising goes beyond the bounds of an unpaid audition. The actor is auditioning to act out the agency's copy—not to write it.

THE CASTING SESSION BEGINS

One at a time, or in groups if the interaction of actors is key to the audition, actors come in and read for the commercial roles. In many instances, the casting session looks like a mock trial. The talent sits on one side of a long table, opposite several somber-faced people from the agency and production house. These folks include agency creatives, the director, and perhaps the client and the agency account executive.

Introductions are made, the director discusses the part briefly with the talent, and the actor does a reading. (It is wise to have copies of the script, called *sides*, available in the outer waiting room so the actors have time to prepare before coming into the audition.) After the initial reading, if the director thinks there is a possibility that he or she is the right actor, he may ask for more than one interpretation of the lines, just to see how the actor reacts to direction.

It's a subtle game: "What do they want from me?" "What can I offer in the part?" "Does she look right for the part?" "Is he taking this audition seriously enough?" The actors are looking for some clue that will help them. Should he or she try a different body attitude (a lift of an eyebrow, a double take) or a different reading rhythm to catch the attention of everybody across the table? The agency folks and the director, who are looking for the right actor to help guarantee that their $500,000 commercial will be a sales hit, apply their own criteria to the selection.

Even if the commercial is supposed to be funny, casting is a serious business. Everybody brings his or her individual set of hopes, wishes, dreams, and biases. It is truly a wonder that people ever agree on the cast for a commercial. Some gentlemen prefer blondes. Some ladies prefer bald-headed gentlemen. And everybody has his or her own idea of what a hero and a villain look like.

As to the logistics of the casting session, the casting director brings in the talent, but the commercial director should direct the audition. The director's rapport with the actors is crucial to their performance, and, after all, you are paying the director to direct. Directing starts with the casting session. Too often I have seen agency creative people or clients make a choice in casting that ends up in disaster because the director was not involved in the casting, or the director's selections were overruled. Hire a director you trust, then give the person free rein to direct. Casting is an integral part of direction.

HINTS FOR GOOD CASTING

Listen to the Dialog

If your commercial involves dialog, give the actors time to learn the lines and to understand their meaning. Then, as the auditioning actors read, listen carefully. Are the words written to be spoken? Too many commercial writers stay with the written words instead of the spoken word. No viewer will ever see the copy; it will only be heard as conversation. So in the audition, listen to the written words as they are being spoken.

Perhaps the copy isn't yet polished, and a change of tense or sentence construction will sharpen the meaning. If it is decided to make copy changes during the casting session to improve verbal flow, be sure there is client approval for the change and also that any change will meet all the legal and network copy requirements.

Cast in Combinations

If the commercial uses two or more actors in one scene, audition the cast in complete units. If the commerial calls for the interaction of a family of four, direct the auditions in groups of four. Videotape the four-actor unit. Remember, if the director likes two of the four in one group and someone else in another, they can always mix and match the best actors at the callback. If a line is to be delivered in a two-shot with one other actor, the audition tape can capture the relationship of these two people for casting comparisons. (See Exhibit 5.1)

Videotape the Casting Session

One of the very best ways to look at talent is on a videotape monitor. It is, in essence, a TV screen. By taping the actor and playing back the performance, the actor can be seen the way the viewer will in the finished commercial. For instance, if a line is to be delivered with an actor's face in tight close-up, the tape camera can move into a tight close-up in the audition.

There are several other advantages to casting on videotape. First, the director can learn how the actors react to direction with a camera present and with readings being done to that camera. Second, by casting the actors in the same groupings as in the actual commercial, the director has a good opportunity to see how the actors relate to each other. The success of a 30-second commercial with several actors involved depends heavily on immediately identifiable relationships. Casting on videotape helps to find workable combinations.

Also, when casting on videotape, the actors' auditions can be reviewed after they have left. When faced with live actors in a casting situation, all sorts of unrelated influences may appear. Someone may not like one actor's perfume or another actor's tennis shoes or any number of inconsequential things that have nothing to do with whether the actor is right for the part.

Exhibit 5.1

1. (MUSIC: UNDER THROUGHOUT) GIRL: I've got a shell and two star-fishes.

2. (AVO): It's called Me Day. BOY: My Mom says he looks like my Daddy's boss.

3. (AVO): It's the day when everyone in Mrs. Meyer's first grade brings something from home...

4. JUDY: My Daddy caught it for me.

5. (AVO): ...and shares it with the rest of the class.

6. On this Tuesday morning, Jack Moore brought something different.

7. JACK: This is my Dad. His name is Jack, like me...(WHISPERS) sit down. KIDS: (LAUGH)

8. JACK: Last Saturday, we built a dog house. Maybe someday I'll get a dog.

9. Every Saturday morning...

10. we let Mom sleep, and we go to McDonald's together. That's where we tell each other things...

11. we'd never tell anybody else.

12. (AVO): At McDonald's, we never planned...

13. on being part of Jack Moore's Me Day...but we're glad we were.

14. JACK: This is my Dad.

15. He's my best friend.

"Me Day"

One of the reasons television advertising for McDonald's has been so successful for so long is the great degree of realism achieved in casting their commercials. Leo Burnett USA, working with Joe Pytka, one of the top directors in the country, has taken the viewer into a traditional school room. The "realism" was achieved by constructing a set, rather than going into an actual school. This three-way combination of believable casting, a believable school room set, and sensitive directing has made this commercial one of the most memorable in a sea of commercials.
Courtesy: McDonald's Corporation and Leo Burnett, U.S.A.

The Danger of Casting from Photographs

Unless you have no other choice, **do not cast from composite photographs**. These retouched photographs may have been taken several months or even years earlier—at least several haircuts or hairstyles ago. It is imperative to know how the actor currently looks and acts, and recording the audition on videotape will show this.

Another problem can arise from casting from still photographs. I faced such a situation when asked to produce breakfast cereal commercials involving models whose still pictures appeared on cereal boxes. The models didn't actually have to do any of the physical stunts portrayed in the still photographs, because they had been cast only as still photographic models. But when it was decided that these same models should also appear in TV commercials performing these stunts, a real problem arose.

The girl in a cowboy hat couldn't ride a horse. The college boy with a towel around his neck who was now required to dive from a 3-meter diving board couldn't swim. The girl with ice skates thrown over her shoulder didn't know how to skate. And the 10-year-old girl shown skipping rope in the still photograph had never skipped rope.

The models were cast for their looks in still photographs, not their physical abilities. In order to convert these nonathletes into performers, we had to hire doubles for all of their athletic activities, cutting back to the models in close-ups. The use of stunt doubles made these commercials quite expensive.

Incidentally, if you find yourself in a similar situation, it is wise to work with a casting director who understands the problems of doubling. Stunt doubles are usually found in Hollywood, where doubling has been used in feature films for years. Doubles have to be cast not only for their ability to do stunts, but also for their physical similarity to the people for whom they are to double. And if the stunt is difficult, you will have to pay double the on-camera SAG rates for their appearance. Be sure to check with the local SAG office on this.

Here is a final reminder that when it comes to casting actors for commercials, it is imperative that the director be part of the decision group. The director will be expected to get the best possible performance out of the talent, so his or her opinions are vital.

Using "Real People"

In casting a commercial, there are instances when "real people" (nonactors) are better suited than professionals to satisfy the creative approach. This is particularly true if the commercial is testimonial in nature. If the selling thrust has to do with the sincere opinion expressed by an actual user of the product or service, the real-people approach becomes a basic part of the commercial's success.

At this point, amateurishness is a virtue. The mere fact that the real person doesn't have the smoothness and acting ability of a professional can give credence to what he or she has to say. So casting takes on an entirely different tone. Instead of working only through a casting director and bringing in actors with agents, you will be looking elsewhere.

For instance, in putting together real-people commercials for Bays English Muffins, we went directly to a supermarket where Bays were on display. We waited until we saw someone put a package of Bays in their grocery basket, and then we asked them if we could interview them. We wanted to know how they planned to prepare those Bays English Muffins.

We used videotape rather than film for two basic reasons: First, we could keep the equipment unobtrusive. Videotape needs very little auxiliary lighting, and the tape camera is absolutely silent when in action. Second, we had budget considerations. After each interview was over, we could privately view it, and if we decided not to use it, we could rewind the tape and be ready for the next interview, using the same tape stock for the next person. If we had used film, we would have had to develop and either print or transfer each interview to tape before accepting or rejecting it. This would have meant many thousands of feet of film, rather than a relatively small quantity of videotape.

Some people say the results on tape are different than on film, and they are right. Tape has a tendency to look "live" and immediate. And that was a plus rather than a minus for these particular commercials.

We guaranteed the success of these interviews by using an expert interviewer named Ray Van Steen. This mode of production calls for very low-key direction. Very often, the director doesn't seem to be directing at all, but merely asking questions of the real person on camera. His or her relaxed attitude elicits a response from the person that protects the realism of the commercial. Van Steen stood just out of range of the camera. The customer's eye contact was with him, rather than with the camera. In the edit, we cut out Van Steen's questions, using only the answers his questions elicited. (See Exhibit 5.2.)

We told each person that we were doing some research on the purchase of Bays English Muffins, and that there was a possibility of using their remarks in a commercial, if they so agreed in writing. Not a single person refused to discuss the product with us in front of the camera. And we paid each one a small sum of money on signing the release form.

We divided the questions asked by Van Steen into three categories:

1. What people said about the freshness of the product
2. Some of the ways they had prepared the muffins
3. In general, why they bought the product

Exhibit 5.2

JOHN MARSHALL MARKETING CORPORATION

PRODUCT: BAYS ENGLISH MUFFINS
AS FILMED TV COMM'L NO: BEMT-87-3
TITLE: "REAL PEOPLE" - USES

DATE: 11/12/87
LENGTH: 30 SECONDS

1. ANNCR: (VO) Here are some of the ways

2. people are using Bays English Muffins.

3. WOMAN 1: You know, make a little pizza out of it.

4. WOMAN 2: I love 'em with jelly.

5. WOMAN 3: I always put peanut butter on mine.

6. WOMAN 4: Put a little crab salad on it... toast it.

7. WOMAN 5: Soft cream cheese with strawberries.

8. WOMAN 6: Like grilled cheese and ham sandwiches.

9. You can put them in the toaster oven or even put them in the microwave.

10. (MUSIC UNDER) ANNCR: (VO) In your grocers' dairy case.

11. Bays.

12. WOMAN 6: Make about thirty of them and they're all gone in five minutes. (LAUGHS)

Bays "Real-People" Commercial

Interviewed by Ray Van Steen off-camera and shot on videotape by Northwest Teleproductions, Chicago, these real people tell why they bought Bays English Muffins and how they intend to prepare them.
Courtesy John Marshall Marketing Corp.

The portions of the interviews pertaining to the categories were edited into separate commercials, each of which began with a voiceover announcer asking the key question, answered by the comments of these "real people."

In New York City, one of the premier companies doing real-people commercials is Maysles Films. Albert Maysles has made a career out of "reality" filming—from documentaries on a wide variety of subjects to commercials using the real-people approach to casting. Some of his most impressive commercials have been done for the Wal-Mart chain of stores, featuring the employees and their viewpoint concerning Wal-Mart customers. (See Exhibit 5.3.)

Exhibit 5.3

Maysles's "Real-People" Work

The ability to direct and photograph nonactors is an art, and one of the best at it is
Albert Maysles of New York City. Here's a "real-person" shot from one of the
Maysles commercials for Wal-Mart.
Henry Corra, director; Albert Maysles, director/cameraman. Courtesy Maysles Films, Inc.

In general, Maysles Films shoots on film rather than on videotape.
They believe the added quality of film is to the advantage of the
commercials involved. The costs are higher than the videotape method
I described above, but if the dollars are available, the results are of
higher quality.

In each instance, the people interviewed were comfortable in
front of the camera, because they were being interviewed in familiar
surroundings. This is a great plus when it comes to putting amateurs at
ease.

Not all production companies are at ease themselves in this type
of production. The best way to determine which companies to bid on
real-people commercials is to watch the real-people commercials that

are on the air. Then find out who did them by contacting the agencies that handle those specific accounts.

Casting and Directing Celebrities

In an effort to call attention to a product or service and at the same time to imply endorsement, well-known personalities are often hired to appear in commercials. These internationally recognized men and women command a great deal of money and a special type of production attention. The trick is to find the right combination of personality and price that will add recognition and top spin to the marketing of the product or service.

The main effort is to find a personality (1) that has some logical connection to the product and (2) whom the client can afford. However, there have been cases in which both of these requirements have been ignored in an effort to take advantage of a star's recognition. Such was the case with Michael Jackson's appearance in Pepsi commercials. He would not agree to hold the product in his hands, and his fee was a matter of conjecture, somewhere in seven figures. However, both considerations seemed sufficiently unimportant to the advertiser, because Michael Jackson is instantly recognized by the teenage audience Pepsi was trying to attract.

On the other end of the equation, the use of Lee Iacocca as a spokesman for the Chrysler Corporation made eminently good sense. First, who better to discuss the Chrysler product than the top man in the corporation? He reportedly was paid one dollar to appear in his company's commercials. Iacocca was the right choice at that time (and the fee was right as well).

Writing copy for such a personality also presents its own set of possibilities. Because of the personality's stature, should the copy be written by the star? Should the star have editorial control of the final copy? And who should direct the star? All of these decisions have a direct bearing on the success or failure of the star approach to commercial production.

In most instances, a mature director is chosen, one who can command the attention and respect of the personality whose performance largely hinges on direction. Although most personalities made their reputations in front of live audiences, turning that positive recognition into a believable commercial depends on the talent of the TV director. In the case of Lee Iacocca, the direction was handled by two or three directors, including Albert Maysles, who made his reputation as a director of documentaries. Maysles's ability to capture a natural performance by Iacocca on film had a great deal to do with the success of these particular Chrysler commercials. The same attributes held true for Neil Tardio, who directed many of the 61 Iacocca commercials over a 14-year period.

In Summary

Reality is an interesting consideration in casting commercials. Disparate things are "real." The big-city slums are real, and so is the White House. Street people are real, and so are millionaires. Your first consideration in casting is to determine the type of reality you want, not the degree. Then decide whether this type of reality can best be portrayed by an actor, a well-known personality, or a real person. Through casting, you can sharpen your chosen "reality" by selecting on-camera people who best give top spin to your selling idea.

And remember, there are specific directors who can elicit the type of performance you are looking for. The best way to find them is to learn who directed other commercials that demonstrate the type of performance you are striving for.

6 USING LOCATIONS OR SETS

A major decision arises very early in the production of a TV commercial: where the production will take place. The decision has serious implications for costs, scheduling, and the quality of the final product.

Let's assume the commercial will be produced in live action rather than using animation. It will involve on-camera actors who will act out the script in the rooms of a house. A decision has to be made at this point: Should the commercial be produced on location or on a set?

Let's say the commercial calls for a kitchen. The kitchen can be built as a set on a rented stage, or a location search can be made to find an actual house that has a suitable kitchen. When it is found, the house can be rented for the necessary day or days of production, and the commercial will be done "on location."

Let's look at the advantages and disadvantages of each mode of production.

Shooting on a Set

Let's say it has been decided to build a kitchen set. First, consider the budget. The sharpest increases in costs for many years has been in those involved in set construction. This is due to increases in the cost of materials and construction labor. So the budget must be carefully considered before deciding whether to build a set.

THE CASE OF FOOD COMMERCIALS

Even so, there are often good reasons to shoot on sets. For example, certain types of commercials are naturals for sets rather than locations. (See Exhibit 6.1.) Let's say the commercial is for a food product, and the preparation of food, including actual cooking shots, is part of the commercial premise. The home economist who is hired to do the food preparation will probably need more than one oven to prepare the food and keep it hot for the actual shooting. Very few homes are so equipped. Also, bear in mind that when a commercial shows a real kitchen, chances are that the food was not cooked in the "hero" oven

Exhibit 6.1

LEO BURNETT COMPANY, INC.   HALLMARK CARDS, INC.
AS FILMED AND RECORDED   (3/92) "Dance Card/Revised" 2:00   (Page 1 of 2)   HMHF1229

1. (MUSIC: UNDER THROUGHOUT)

2. SHEEHAN: Hey, Tony...
who you taking to the dance?
TONY: Patti Harney.

3. JERRY: Oh man, Patti Harney?
She said "yes" and everything?
TONY: Well...no. I haven't really
asked her yet.

4. But I'm gonna.
SHEEHAN: In...person?
TONY: No way! I'll probably
just call her on the phone.

5. FERGIE: Yeah, a phone call.
I think that's what I'm gonna
do.

6. TONY: So who are you going
with, Jerry?

7. JERRY: Oh well...see there's
this kid on my street...his name
is Bill Shallcross...well, see he
plays hockey...

8. with the brother of Rachelle
Tasker, and she has gym class
with Mande Moore...

9. and Mande Moore has a locker
next to Cheryl Berman...

10. and Cheryl Berman who's
like really good friends...

11. with Nancy Eaglin. So she's
gonna ask her.

12. TONY: Who?
JERRY: Cheryl's gonna ask Nancy
...for me.
TONY: Oh...right.

13. FERGIE: Get a friend to
ask for you...I think that's
what I'm gonna do.

14. JERRY: What about you,
Sheehan?
SHEEHAN: Well, I was thinking...

15. what if you, uh...slipped a
card into a girl's notebook?

Hallmark "Dance Card"

Produced by Leo Burnett with sensitive casting and direction by Joe Pytka, this tells a
complete story of boy-meets-girl in the study hall. When one boy tells his buddies he
invited a girl by putting a Hallmark card in her notebook, he becomes the object of
their derision. ("You put it in writing? Your reputation is ruined.") But she walks
over, tells him the card was nice, and accepts his invitation. The realistic lighting is

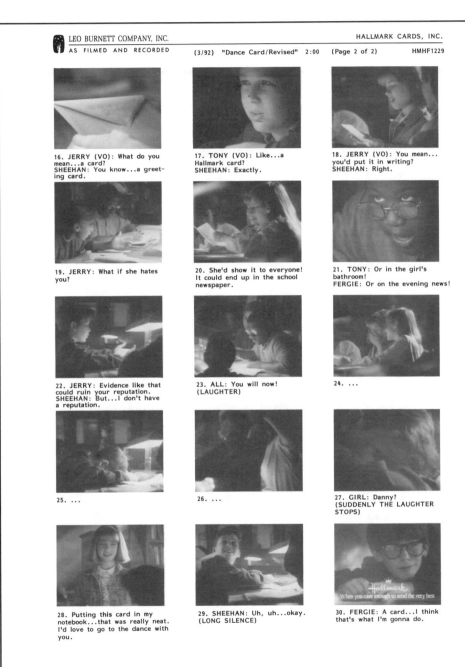

LEO BURNETT COMPANY, INC.
AS FILMED AND RECORDED

(3/92) "Dance Card/Revised" 2:00 (Page 2 of 2)

HALLMARK CARDS, INC.

HMHF1229

16. JERRY (VO): What do you mean...a card?
SHEEHAN: You know...a greeting card.

17. TONY (VO): Like...a Hallmark card?
SHEEHAN: Exactly.

18. JERRY (VO): You mean... you'd put it in writing?
SHEEHAN: Right.

19. JERRY: What if she hates you?

20. She'd show it to everyone! It could end up in the school newspaper.

21. TONY: Or in the girl's bathroom!
FERGIE: Or on the evening news!

22. JERRY: Evidence like that could ruin your reputation.
SHEEHAN: But...I don't have a reputation.

23. ALL: You will now! (LAUGHTER)

24. ...

25. ...

26. ...

27. GIRL: Danny? (SUDDENLY THE LAUGHTER STOPS)

28. Putting this card in my notebook...that was really neat. I'd love to go to the dance with you.

29. SHEEHAN: Uh, uh...okay. (LONG SILENCE)

30. FERGIE: A card...I think that's what I'm gonna do.

just as subtle as the direction. It was achieved by producing on carefully lit sets rather than on location. This commercial was shot over a two-day period. "Dance Card" won Best of Show in the International Mobius Advertising Awards.
Film Editor: Marty Bernstein, Cutaways. Music: Steve Ford Music/Chicago. Courtesy Leo Burnett USA.

(Hero refers to the oven or the food that is seen in the commercial.) The food was probably cooked in an area off the set and brought to the set at the last minute for photography. Food preparation for commercials takes more space than most "location" houses have available.

The convenience of off-the-set cooking areas is very important to food commercials. Stand-in food is prepared as the lighting for the commercial progresses, and when the lighting is completed, everything will go forward with almost military precision. At the very last moment, the home economist brings in the hero plate or pan, the stand-in plate is removed, and the photography actually starts while the prepared food is at its hottest and best-looking. This type of close timing can best be accomplished on a stage set, rather than in a location house.

Also, very often extensive lighting is needed for close-up food photography, and a set allows the additional room in which to move lights at high and low angles in front of and behind kitchen ranges and other appliances. Remember that sets usually don't have ceilings, which gives the lighting people unlimited space for high-angle lights.

OTHER REASONS TO USE A STAGE SET

Camera Angles

Food commercials are not the only type to benefit from shooting on a stage set. If the commercial calls for unusual camera angles in a home setting, a set is much easier to work with than a real home. For instance, if a shot requires shooting from the top of a stairway down into a first-floor room, the camera can be mounted at that high angle, ten feet above the floor, and it may not even be necessary to see (or construct) the stairway. The angle implies that the stairs are there.

There would be times in a location house when the camera person would wish the walls were movable—and they always are on a set. The crew would simply move a "wild wall" in or out. A *wild wall* is a set element that resembles a wall of a room, but it can be moved very easily, thus allowing freedom in altering the shape and dimensions of the set.

Camera Motion

When you use a set instead of a house location, you can use the whole range of heavy-duty photographic equipment. This includes camera dollies—wheeled platforms that can "boom up" a camera ten feet or more. (*Boom up* means to place the camera on the end of a long movable arm and then raise the camera far above floor level.) Such equipment can't be used efficiently in a home, and, as a result, camera positions are limited to small moves or the in-and-out moves of a zoom lens on a stationary camera.

The ability to move the camera during the scene can often give added vitality to the commercial. And if the move is straight in toward the scene, don't think that zooming a lens will give you the same motion as dollying the camera. When the lens is zoomed in to a scene, the lens actually brings the scene to the camera. On the other hand, when the camera is dollied (moved) physically into the scene, the lens components don't change, and the camera actually goes to the scene. There is a noticeable difference between zooming in and dollying in. Usually you can benefit from the freedom of a dolly on a set, but not in a location house.

Lighting

When a location house is used, extreme care has to be taken in placing the lights. Great damage can be done to house walls, and the additional power needed to light a location house can blow fuses and otherwise wreak havoc.

Sound

Another good reason for using a set instead of a location has to do with shooting "sync" sound. *Sync sound* is the on-camera dialog of actors, which requires the recording of sound during the actual filming. The sound is thus "synchronized" with the on-camera action.

If the on-camera sound of dialog must be completely controlled, the soundproofed quality of a sound stage cannot be matched in the ordinary location home. Incidentally, it's called a *sound stage* because it has no sound. A sound stage is soundproofed.

Also, the wild wall capability of a set on a stage allows the crew to get the microphone boom into position in ways that would be difficult if not impossible in a home location. The fact that walls can be moved, angled, removed, and replaced gives the nod to a set over a location in many cases.

Unique Sets

If the backgrounds are artistically unique to the commercial (as in many automobile commercials), an art-directed set is the answer.

To summarize, set construction makes good sense when the commercial dictates extremely careful light, including lights high overhead, which is impossible to achieve in a location house. If the commercial features close-up food preparation, where several stove and ovens must be available for immediate photography of hot food, a stage with such facilities is the answer.

Shooting on Location

Now, before giving up on the use of locations at all, let's talk about some of the advantages locations have over sets. First, there is an authenticity to a home location that is hard to get on a set, or is quite expensive to duplicate. For instance, suppose ceiling detail is important to the commercial. All homes come fully equipped with ceilings, at no extra charge. Normally, sets do not. This authenticity extends to other things found in a real house. In a house location, the camera can look from one room to another without the expense of constructing a second room. In a real house, the camera can show stairways, hallways, windows with exterior detail, and all the other components of a house.

POINTS TO CONSIDER IN SELECTING A LOCATION HOUSE

In the major filming centers, there are location experts who have books filled with still photographs of houses available for photography, including their exact location and their daily rental cost. When you decide to go the location route, there are several points to check out carefully.

Lighting

If natural light is important to the commercial, be sure someone finds out what the sun does to or for that exterior location. Where does the sun come up and where does it go down? How long is the sun effective? That is, are there mountains, tall buildings, or other obstructions that block the sun and shorten the full-sun shooting day?

Sound

If sync sound is being shot on location, the following items should be carefully researched:

1. Nearby superhighways or business streets with stop signs
2. Construction of any kind that would be heard in your sound track
3. Nearby playgrounds, swimming pools, etc.
4. Airports and the take-off and landing patterns that extend for several miles around them (Nothing is more frustrating than to have the sound person stop a sound take because he or she can still hear a plane overhead in the earphones.)

Here's another deceptive noise: the ocean surf. It is a very pervasive sound that cannot be edited out of your sound takes. Even if you want the sound of surf in your track, it should be added after the edit is completed, as part of the final sound mix.

Equipment

Are the house's ceilings high enough to accommodate the lighting, sound, and camera equipment? The rooms must be sufficiently large to hold all the camera equipment and personnel. On a sound shoot, the crew can number more than 15!) Space must be allowed for the cast and the action planned for them.

It's a good idea to take the director and/or the head electrician along before a location is chosen. They will check out other essentials. Is there sufficient electrical power within the house for the lighting and camera equipment, or should a generator truck be brought along for auxiliary power? If a generator truck is needed, can you park it on the street? Are there local ordinances against such equipment?

Rental Cost

The production house producer or the assistant should make the arrangements for the location, including the advance payment of the location fee. Many homeowners make a practice of renting out their homes for photography, and they are well aware of the possible damage that can be done to their property. They will adjust their rental prices accordingly and also ask the production company to sign damage waivers. Prices vary according to regions of the country, size of the house, number of rooms to be used for filming, etc. In all instances, the property must be returned to its original condition immediately following production.

Be aware that many outdoor locations are available for rental as well. It is possible, for instance, to rent the Rose Bowl in the off-season and to rent hotel dining rooms on the one day of the week they are normally closed. All sorts of deals can be made, including shooting in supermarkets from midnight to 8:00 a.m., if the market is usually closed at that time.

If set construction costs are prohibitive, there are many more options available to you in the real world of houses, stadiums, tennis courts, stores, etc. It is also possible to work out arrangements to shoot on government land. Be sure to get permission from the proper authorities before attempting this, however. More and more commercials are produced in the "natural world," from Hawaiian beaches to Colorado ski slopes. These commercials range from soft drinks to automobiles, from cold remedies to sports equipment.

In Summary

If you believe sets are better for your commercial, it may be money-wise to choose a production company affiliated with a major motion picture company. These can be found in the Los Angeles area, as well as in Orlando, Florida. Many of these companies have "standing sets," complete rooms on huge sound stages that are left standing. You may be able to use one of these sets at a minimal rental cost, with only painting and redressing to be done. Also, these companies have large storage areas, where set components can be brought out and reassembled for less cost than new set construction.

In general, if the commercial calls for the use of one or more rooms of a house and there is no sync-sound shooting involved, shooting on a location is a wise way to go, if you can find a proper set for your purposes. You will undoubtedly save more than the cost of construction, and if you have chosen a location house carefully, you will be rewarded with an authentic look at a lower price than constructing a set.

It is also possible to approach a home builder who has not sold a new home, rent it, and "prop it" with the exact furniture you wish for your commercial. Furniture can sometimes be rented for this purpose.

Carefully consider what you hope to achieve visually with your commercial. Then consider the on-camera sound problems that you may meet with on location. From these considerations, make your decision as to whether sets or locations are better for your commercial.

7 USING MUSIC

Music can be to the commercial what a rug is to a floor, what furniture is to a room, what wallpaper is to a wall, what curtains are to a window. Music can complement the commercial and give it a viewpoint. Music can make the commercial cohesive, highlight it, and define it.

Music plays a part far beyond mere melody and harmony. Properly applied and balanced, it becomes an integral part of the visual image, even though it is an aural experience. Music can give color, emotional content, and meaning. It can add life, style, and selling impact.

Sources of Music

Music for commercials can be very costly, or very inexpensive, depending on how you approach its use. But first things first: Where do you find music to do all those marvelous things for your commercial?

HIT TUNES

Rights can be purchased for the use of an existing melody and also, if desired, for the lyrics. If the tune is or was a hit, prepare to spend a lot of money. It is possible to pay more than $100,000 for music and lyric rights to a popular song. What's more, that's only the beginning.

It is quite often possible to use the original recording, both instrumental and vocal, but this again adds a great deal to the cost. More often than not, the lyric has to be altered to fit the product's marketing approach.

To change (or parody) the lyrics to include the product name or to fit the selling message in other ways, singers, arrangers, and an orchestra, plus recording time, will have to be added to the budget. In any case, the hit tune will have to be re-recorded to fit the commercial timing exactly and to allow room for the voiceover announcer and other elements in the commercial track.

Fortunately, competent help is available, not only in Chicago, New York, and Hollywood, but in many other cities as well. This help is available through music production houses, fully equipped with composers, arrangers, and musical directors. They know which singers are right for the commercial and who can compose, arrange, and perform the music effectively to the exact commercial length and requirements. In most cases, music production houses are quite complete. They will even negotiate for existing music rights, if that is one of the requirements.

If you plan to use a popular tune in a single commercial or for a campaign composed of several commercials, it is best to attempt to establish costs before presenting the idea to the client. These costs would include the following elements:

1. Music rights (This includes length of time, plus down-the-line renewals if the campaign is successful and continues to run on television.)
2. Music rights for radio (Find out whether radio rights can be included as "broadcast rights.")
3. Lyric rights (Were the lyrics written by the music composer, or someone else?)
4. Costs of re-recording to fit the commercial format, including hiring singers, arrangers, copyists, musicians, and recording/mixing time
5. Additional royalties due to the composer and musicians if the original arrangement is used

Make every effort to estimate these costs before going to the client for approval; there is nothing worse than agreeing on the use of a popular tune, only to find that the exact costs will be out of reach.

Realize from the start that this is an expensive way to originate a commercial music track. The pricing on such a production varies, with several factors affecting the cost:

1. Is the song's popularity on its way down? This could bring the cost down.
2. Would the commercial enhance the popularity of the song? This has happened, and it might also bring the cost down.
3. How sharp are the negotiators? Often the cost of rights depends on this.

There are no hard-and-fast rules about how much well-known music will cost for a commercial. Also, some advertisers believe that if a piece of music is recognizable, it will weaken the commercial instead of strengthen it. These are subjective areas, but they must be addressed, or the costs of using hit-tune music can be wasted.

Also, bear in mind that rights for the use of published music is usually for one year, with an option to renew for additional periods. If the creative plan is to have the music become the basis for a long-running campaign, keep future use in mind. The more agreement there is in the first contract regarding future use, the more the music is protected for both use and cost.

Sometimes the well-known melody, rather than the lyrics, is the key to the creative plan. Such was the case with Leo Burnett's commercial campaign for United Airlines. In looking for a musical theme that could become identified with United, Burnett came up with a rather unusual solution: Use the main theme from George Gershwin's "Rhapsody in Blue." At first blush, it's hard to imagine the connection between Gershwin and United Airlines, but the sweeping, majestic music now seems a natural complement to United's lofty service. It takes a certain leap of faith to undertake that type of synergism, but this particular combination has worked well for at least five years—a long time in the business of creative TV advertising.

Of course, rights had to be paid for the use of Gershwin's original score, which was re-recorded for each commercial in order to support the visuals. In a commercial involving the Art Institute of Chicago, paintings were shown that portrayed various musical instruments being played; the same instruments were also featured in the musical arrangement. The arrangement was unique to this particular commercial, but the Gershwin theme was an instant reminder that this was a commercial for United Airlines. And that is what the consistent use of a recognizable musical theme is all about.

New Music

The second way to procure music for a commercial is to have new music composed, arranged, scored, and recorded specifically for the product or service. This is also the second most expensive way to use music commercially. For one thing, unions govern the recording of music (American Federation of Musicians) as well as the recording of singers (Screen Actors Guild and the American Federation of Radio and Television Artists, known as AFTRA). This means that union rates will have to be paid for recording, and residuals will have to be paid for continued use of the music. But the entire recording will be done by professionals, and that is the best way to guarantee an absolutely top-notch production job. Music composition and creative rights for original music tracks can run $30,000–$60,000, and the recording costs can add another $15,000–$20,000 to the total.

Foote Cone & Belding, San Francisco, used new music in a commercial for Taco Bell, meaning that the music was completely proprietary. It incorporated the Mexican slogan, "Head for the Border," along with the ringing of the Taco Bell, as integral parts of original music tracks composed for the client. This sloganized use of original composition maximizes the purchase price of custom music tracks. And the use of musical tracks that include slogans put a double hook into the audience's memory.

These are big sounds with big budgets, which brings up two of my favorite commercial words: *perceived value*. If a commercial is being prepared for a national advertiser, and it is hoped that the commercial will be the first of a long-running commercial campaign, the perceived value of such an expensive track would be great and probably well worth what was paid for it. On the other hand, if the client's products don't have national distribution and the commercial is a one-time-only idea, then such an original music score and recording would be a waste of your client's money—and the composer's work.

Not all original music is as grand as United Airlines' use of "Rhapsody in Blue," or even the Taco Bell tracks. Some of it is much simpler in melody as well as arrangement and doesn't bear the big price tags I've been talking about. But if a qualified, professional musician is asked to compose special music, chances are that two things will happen: The commercial will be enhanced, and the cost of the commercial will go up. Again, it all depends on how the client perceives such value.

PUBLIC DOMAIN MUSIC

On we go down the "price of music" scale for commercials. If the budget is too slim for either parody lyrics of a well-known piece of music or specially composed music, there are ways to procure appropriate music for much less money.

One way would be to find public-domain music. Music in the "public domain" is no longer covered by copyright and is therefore available for anyone's use without payment to the original composer. For example, the "Blue Danube Waltz" has been used numerous times without composer payments. This is because the melody is in the public domain.

Although public-domain music may be used without paying the composer, there is a "publisher's fee" charged for the use of a particular arrangement in a commercial. There is a definite drawback to public-domain music: not only can you use the music at a low cost, but so may anyone else. Exclusive rights are not usually given, though some publishers will assign regional exclusivity. This, of course, raises the cost of using the tune.

RIGHT-TO-WORK STATES

By definition, a "right-to-work" state is one in which workers agree to a specific payment, without union affiliation. If the client is regional, and the region is made up entirely of right-to-work states (Texas, Arizona, etc.), then it is possible to find a composer who will agree to write and direct music for a "buy-out" fee, including a one-time payment to the musicians. This method is not recommended, because the client may decide to add states that are covered by union jurisdictions, and the right-to-work commercial cannot be used without union payments. This has happened more than once. Each state makes its own determinations in such matters, and a vote of its citizens could change the state's status and thus negate any right-to-work buy-out payments previously made to musicians, singers, etc.

LIBRARY MUSIC

Most recording studios and radio and TV stations subscribe to music libraries. These specially recorded CDs have been prepared specifically for broadcast use as background music. Many of these recorded music libraries list their music under headings such as love, hate, hope, fear, and so on. So if you're looking for specific mood music, this is a source open to you (and to everyone else, because these libraries are for common use). If you wish to use such music in the commercial, the recording studio or station will probably charge you a small fee (in the $100 range) to make a recording of it. You can then use it without further payment. But then, so can everybody else who pays the fee.

I have found a way to use library music that comes close to making it exclusive. Take a two-minute piece of library music and edit it down to 30 seconds. Then take a different piece of library music, being careful that it is in the same musical key and musical tempo. Finally, edit the two pieces together to make an entirely new 30-second track. The chances of anyone else achieving the same music edit are truly remote. If you do this, check for similar keys and tempo; otherwise, the musical result will be a mishmash.

MUSIC AND STILLS

There's another simple, inexpensive way to use music that I think is worth mentioning. First, take a well-known piece of music in the public domain, perhaps an old march, and add a bunch of pertinent still photos to the recipe. Then, using an animation stand, edit the stills to the rhythm of the march. The stills might be various shots of the product, ending on a tight close-up of the label. If the still photos are from a photo library, their use may include a fee, however small. The resultant commercial can stand alone and be quite striking. It's worth a try, and the cash outlay is minimal.

ELECTRONIC MUSIC: DIGITAL AUDIO TAPE

Some of the newest and most innovative music is not music at all, at least not in the traditional sense of the word. It is born in a computer and printed out on Digital Audio Tape (DAT). DAT achieves its own auditory effect as it is further manipulated. This digital recording technique takes sound waves, transfers them into computer information, and then adds layer after layer of this information without loss of quality and without distortion of any kind.

A DAT machine resembles a cassette tape recorder. It can record sounds digitally as well as play them back. To watch a musician working in this mode is a most amazing experience. But with every miracle comes a warning: perfection in sound is not "human." The computer is so exact that even Bach sounds too perfect. So it may be necessary to throw in a few slightly off-key effects to return the humanity to the track. Too often, these synthetic sounds become hard, mechanical, and unemotional. This doesn't have to happen, particularly if the melody stays more important than the treatment, or computerized effect.

It's possible to work with only one person in this mode, but don't expect to save a lot of money by using these computer bells and whistles. Those esoteric pieces of equipment are expensive to buy and to maintain. You pay for the operator's expertise and equipment, and the final cost will be pretty close to a full orchestra track.

Up to this point, we have been talking about the *tools* of music production, not the *essence* of music, which is the composer and the musician. I have mentioned many of the specific tools to illustrate the possibilities of providing atmosphere and emphasis to your sound tracks. But the sound track is made or missed by the special abilities of the composer and musicians.

Music as Atmosphere

Another way to use commercial music is to use it for complementary atmosphere with the announcer's copy and the visuals. To make your product more exciting, use exciting music, even if it's only in the background. If your car is the newest convertible, a bit of happy, "racy" music will help position and sell the car. Remember, you have only 30 seconds of airtime, and the right choice of atmospheric music can help make the sales message memorable.

If your commercial is based on emotional response instead of copy points and hard facts, music can guide you into a separate world of persuasion. Eastman Kodak and its advertising agencies have been doing this for years. One of their more recent emotional successes involved a very simple lyric: "True Colors Shining Through." This theme was used in a variety of "memory picture" commercials. One featured babies and another featured a volunteer fire department made up of small-town buddies. (See Exhibit 7.1.) The music itself was the soul of simplicity, as were the visuals.

MUSICAL BOOKENDS

You might consider using music as commercial "bookends." Some agency people call it creating a "doughnut." This method uses a words-and-music selling phrase to open the commercial and a repeat of the opening phrase to close the commercial. The voiceover announcer's

Exhibit 7.1

KODACOLOR GOLD FILM
"FIRST MOMENTS" :30

CLIENT: EASTMAN KODAK

COMM'L NO.: EKVR 9203

(MUSIC UNDER: "TRUE COLORS")
ANNCR: (VO) The baby in this picture

is going to have a very special year

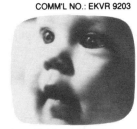

A year of first steps, first words, first birthday.

And none of these things will ever happen again.

Now, if you were this baby's parents,

which film would you choose?

No other film in the world

gives you truer color than Kodacolor Gold film.
SINGER: I SEE YOUR TRUE COLORS...

Aren't your pictures worth Gold?

Kodak's "First Moments"

Quite often, utter simplicity wins the day, as with this single-scene commercial for Eastman Kodak, featuring a very young lady. Produced by J Walter Thompson, New York, the result is truly mesmerizing—and an effective tool to help sell Kodak Film. *Courtesy Eastman Kodak Company.*

voice fills the hole in the middle. Don't be bashful about taking the words of the selling phrase to a commercial composer. They can put almost any phrase into a musical setting. The great advantage to producing "bookends" for the commercial is that there is no doubt about what is being advertised—beginning to end.

Remember that practically without exception, the two most important parts of a commercial are the beginning and the end. The beginning is important because if you don't capture attention immediately, you've lost a prospect, multiplied by the number of homes watching. And the end of the commercial is just as important, even if only as a memory-jogger. The last five seconds can help the viewer retain your message. The use of music bookends can help accomplish both of these important aims.

Prescoring and Postscoring Music

The next decision to be made regarding the use of music in the commercial is whether it should be prescored or postscored. In prescoring, the music is originated and recorded before the filming. In postscoring, it is not until the film or tape is fully edited that a music track is written and recorded to fit the finished picture.

PRESCORING

In prescoring, it is assumed that the picture can be shot to the prerecorded music track. This method is used to great advantage when the visual is a series of silent scenes that can be edited rhythmically to the prerecorded music track.

A whole category of picture-oriented commercials begins without a storyboard, but rather with a basic music track to which any number of different storyboards for any number of different commercials can be drawn. The lyrics to the prerecorded music track may change from one commercial to the next, but the melody remains the same.

There are several good reasons for originating a commercial series in this manner:

1. A large part of the commercial (the finished sound track) can be approved before any of the visuals is shot.
2. It is a great way to present an idea to the client, because the finished track not only tells the client how the commercial will sound, but also gives an idea about how the commercial will look.
3. If the idea needs major adjustments, prescoring offers an opportunity to do so at a fairly early stage.
4. In pricing the commercial before production, the prerecorded track will help competing production companies to make intelligent bids,

because all the storyboard scenes are pretimed and positioned by the prerecorded sound track.
5. The prescored track also becomes the template for discussions in the pre-production meeting.
6. On the production day, the prescored music-and-lyric track becomes a guide to the length of the various scenes, merely by timing the phrases of music and lyrics.

With a prerecorded track, the music and lyrics become the focal point and driving force of the commercial. Also, in producing your prerecorded melody, stay contemporary with the style of music chosen. To take the prerecorded mode a step further, many such melodies can be prerecorded for different commercials in the campaign in a variety of tempos and musical styles.

POSTSCORING THE MUSIC TRACK

To this point, I've discussed music that is prescored and prerecorded. Music can also be postrecorded. This means that the music recording is the last thing done to the commercial, instead of the first. The music is thus written and scored to the edited picture. The theory behind this procedure is that in some types of commercials, the track will be stronger if it takes its cue from the picture, rather than the other way around. Also, the picture becomes more emphatic if the edit gets its energy from such musical emphasis.

Here's how postscoring is done. First, if tempo is important to the actual filming, a "scratch track" is done so the timing of the edit can be understood early on. A *scratch track* is a simple piano-and-rhythm sound tape recorded before production begins and used as a guide to the actual filming. The final track is then "postscored" after the film has been edited to the basic scratch track rhythm. The more information the director has about the rhythm and basic attitude of the commercial, the better the scenes will be shot. Incidentally, the editor will probably do the first picture edit with the scratch track as the guide.

When the edit is agreed upon, the composer comes to the editor and "reads" the rough cut and takes his or her "counts." This means that the composer will build the musical timing chart by counting the time-rhythm of the picture edit and then compose the postrecorded music to fit that count.

To determine the exact rhythmic speed of the music in relation to the picture edit, the composer will decide on the speed of a "click track." The click track is an actual rhythm pattern of clicks that sound like a metronome or rim-shots on a snare drum. In the recording session, each musician will wear earphones in order to hear the rhythmic beat of the click track. In the postrecorded music mode, it's a good idea

Exhibit 7A

NOT to lock the picture completely in place, because it's conceivable that something in the final music will suggest the need for the alteration of a few frames of the picture in one direction or the other. The editor can easily make this change after the postrecorded music has been completed.

In Summary

Music can replace words in a commercial, thus making it more thoroughly understood far beyond the English-speaking world. There is a wide choice of how to originate a music track, and the choices are varied enough to be affordable to a wide range of budgets.

There are good reasons to prerecord your music track, and the same can be said for postrecording the track. It is the wise person who takes the time to decide which is the better course.

MUSIC CHORDS AND COMPUTER BOARDS

The new world of music is peopled by computer scientists who also double as musicians. Their combined knowledge of the digital world and musical composition finds full expression in commercial music tracks. Such a man is Fred Weinberg of Connecticut.

His mother was an opera singer, his father a professional piano player, and Weinberg's first paying job was as a recording engineer. He also played the flute and the accordion. He won the right to attend the High School of Music and Art in New York while working at night as an audio engineer. So the unusual combination of playing music and understanding sound mixing prepared Weinberg to set up his own sound laboratory. His basement is filled with exotic equipment: MIDI (Musical Instrument Digital Interface), DAT (Digital Audio Tape), and data cartridges with RAM (Random Access Memory) and ROM (Read Only Memory).

He can digitally record the voice of a cat and then multiply it into a chorus of cats singing in harmony by playing the "samples" on an electronic keyboard. The same effect can be achieved with any sound. For instance, a single male voice can become a 50-voice male chorus.

Fred Weinberg is one of today's leading-edge sound engineers who find a home for their talents in sound tracks for tomorrow's commercials.

Music in many cases transcends words, setting a mood and atmosphere. Music allows the viewer to exercise the mind as well as the eyes and ears. It is music's ability to speak to every individual in his or her own language that makes the correct sound combinations so important to the success of the commercial.

8 CHOOSING FILM OR VIDEOTAPE

Film has a long history of artistic development, whereas videotape began as an expediency. For more than a century, film has been used artistically in many negative sizes and with many camera types, from huge bellows cameras to the miniaturized automatic cameras that fit easily in a shirt pocket.

Shooting with 35mm Film

There is a "look" to 35mm film ("mm" stands for "millimeter") that is hard to describe. One of my film mentors, the talented graphic designer and filmmaker Mort Goldsholl, believes the film look relates to the eye-to-camera speed combination of 24 frames per second passing through the camera, which softens the moving image to the human eye. As you know, motion picture film is actually a series of still pictures that emulate motion. When these sequential "stills" pass through a projector at 24 "stills" per second, the result is a motion picture.

Often, when looking at running footage one frame at a time, a slight "smear" will be noted in the picture. However, when played at the normal speed of 24 frames per second, this "smear" disappears, and the picture is softened.

This contrasts with the image on videotape, which is formed by racing dots (or pixels) that originate in the upper-left corner of the monitor and race horizontally and down until they finish at the lower-right corner. This gives videotape a different "feel" visually—a clarity and hardness—even though it fits the electronic TV projection system perfectly.

Another advantage of film is emerging: Film is continuing to adapt as the imaging revolution caused by the computer continues. Film negative packs a high density of picture information (up to 2,000 lines per frame) that can be translated into any future carrier medium, including the high-definition TV (HDTV) systems being developed. The present TV transmission system of 525 lines of picture information barely touches the possibilities of film, with its 1,400-line capability. As these high-definition systems evolve, film will be ready to complement them.

The most important feature of film, presently and in the future, is the capability of photographic emulsions to record, store, and accurately reproduce the greatest amount of pictorial information with extremely high sensitivity to light, of any present or envisioned imaging method.

Although most commercials produced for local advertisers are still produced on videotape for budget reasons, the quality of film continues to be the bellwether of the industry.

Also, because of 35mm film's long history, there is a fraternity of talented people in every aspect of filmmaking. Filmmaking is a craft, and the entire membership of film crews earn their respective positions, from camera people, directors, and lighting people to the editors who help edit and finish film commercials on computers. Because it is a craft, film is peopled with experienced, highly qualified personnel—at a price.

ADVANTAGES OF 35MM FILM

There are whole categories of commercials for which 35mm filming is preferred. This would include any commercial that features close-ups of food products. The ability of the 35mm negative to absorb subtleties in lighting makes for mouth-watering shots. Nuances of light and shadow are best captured on 35mm film, as are shades of color and hue.

In the hands of a talented cinematographer, 35mm film can "paint" a live-action scene, and when this filming is kept in the first generation by digitizing it into a computer, the results can be truly spectacular.

Again, because of the bigger negative size (compared to 16mm), the variations of depth of field become acute. For instance, if the commercial features a carefully lit automobile on a turntable, the three-dimensional feeling of 35mm film gives an all-around sheen that is amazing.

DISADVANTAGES OF 35MM FILM

The disadvantages of using 35mm film have mostly to do with cost and production time. Because 35mm filming is highly unionized, the crews are quite large—more than 20 people in a West Coast production. Also, because the equipment is quite bulky, it usually takes longer to set up and light a scene for 35mm photography than it does for 16mm filming. Conclusion? If it's affordable, 35mm filming is the best way to produce commercials. If not, there is always 16mm film and videotape.

Shooting with 16mm Film

The use of 35mm film has been the standard for filmmaking for more than 75 years, but during World War II a smaller format, 16mm, emerged and became important for lower-cost photography. The U.S.

military developed 16mm film in 1941–1945, and its use was not controlled by the Hollywood moviemaking unions.

Having been developed away from Hollywood moviemaking, 16mm film found a home in TV stations and less-expensive commercial production. While 35mm filming was ruled by the Hollywood unions, 16mm film was part and parcel of TV station operations, with their own union, NABET (National Association of Broadcast Electrical Technicians). Crews for 16mm were smaller, and, as a result, production costs were lower.

ADVANTAGES OF 16MM FILMING

One of the major advantages of using 16mm filming is the greater speed with which smaller crews work. Where film is your choice and portability is important, 16mm camera equipment can come to your rescue. Very often, action photography, like films of downhill skiing, can best be covered with a 16mm camera mounted in the skier's helmet, or even on the skis themselves.

DISADVANTAGES OF 16MM FILMING

A major advantage of 16mm filming is that, because the negative is much smaller, great care must be taken to shoot with exactly correct exposures. This can become of greatest importance as you choose the camera person to work with. Be sure that person is familiar with 16mm cameras.

FILM INNOVATIONS BY KODAK

There is a certain love affair between Eastman Kodak and me. There's a good reason for this: Kodak saved my commercials for Helene Curtis in London way back in 1954. It happened this way.

I had flown to London to direct a location commercial for Helene Curtis Spray Net, showing how beautiful hair could look when "you know what" was used.

The problem was that London weather was, as they put it, "seven-eighths cloudy," which means just short of a complete downpour.

The English cameraman came to the rescue. He showed me three, 400-foot rolls of a new, experimental black-and-white 35mm film sent to him by Kodak, something called Tri-X. (In those days, all commercials were short with black-and-white film, not color.)

We quickly changed negative stocks and tried Tri-X, which had a very fast ASA rating. Voila! Although our shots were without shadows, the entire production looked much brighter than the rainy weather indicated, and the production was saved.

There is a continuing improvement of film stocks and emulsions, and it was a thrill to be part of one of the early innovations of 35mm motion picture film.

When to Produce on Videotape

There has been a long-running argument in the broadcast commercial industry about whether it makes more sense to produce on film or on videotape. This argument can usually be settled on the basis of budget alone. Obviously, for local and regional advertisers working with limited budgets, this decision is critical. Whereas the average national advertiser rarely spends more than 8 percent of the entire broadcast budget on commercial production, local and regional advertisers are forced to spend as much as 20 percent and more.

If, for example, a local advertiser has a budget of $100,000 to cover media buying as well as production costs, the budget available for commercial production is only $20,000, leaving $80,000 to buy the time on television. The commercial must then compete on the air with national commercials, which generally cost as much as $250,000 to produce—an amount that is more than twice the entire local budget! One answer to producing a commercial as effective as those of the national advertisers, but at less cost, is to choose videotape production over film.

As discussed in other chapters, the subject of producing TV commercials covers an extremely wide base of creative approaches and available budgets. This ranges from a local merchant to a multinational advertiser with nearly unlimited funds to spend on the production of commercials. Let's look for a moment at the local and regional advertiser, whose dollars must be carefully counted as commercials are being produced.

Certain types of commercials are ideal for videotape production, if budgets are limited. Remember, although the average national film commercial costs approximately $250,000 to produce, it is still possible for the local and regional advertiser to produce simple, direct commercials on videotape for less than 10 percent of that amount.

CHOOSING A VIDEOTAPE PRODUCTION COMPANY

Most TV videotape production houses have their own complete crews: producers, directors, camera operators, lighting personnel, tape editors, etc. They understand the possibilities and limits of tape production and can be of much more help to you than the local TV station crew, for which production houses charge more money. But given simple, direct commercials, TV station crews can do competent, time-efficient production on tape.

In simple, direct commercials, I would include interview and testimonial commercials, which can be shot at existing locations without building sets or renting stages. (See Exhibit 8.1.) Tape lends itself to such commercials, because unacceptable takes can be viewed and

Exhibit 8.1

On-Location Testimonial Commercial

Ray Van Steen is a Chicago-based voiceover announcer and speech coach who
specializes in eliciting candid remarks from nonactors for use in testimonial
advertising. Here we see him asking questions from his off-camera position as he
interviews homeowners whose homes have been devastated by an earthquake. This
Allstate Insurance commercial had to be on the air quickly, so videotape was used for
overnight editing and next-day on-air projection.
Courtesy Allstate Insurance Company.

rejected, and retakes can be made immediately. For further budget
savings, unacceptable takes can be erased and the tape reused for the
next take.

Whenever a commercial evokes a feeling of immedicay or "news,"
videotape can be of help. The overall brightness of videotape adds to
this feeling. What might be considered by some people a "raw" look
adds to this "right now" aspect and helps make such commercials more
believable and thus more effective.

Another plus for videotape has to do with lighting. Videotape can
accept lower light levels than can most film, and it thus requires fewer
lights for each setup. This can save a great deal of production time.

INEXPENSIVE VIDEOTAPE COMMERCIALS

Videotape production can be very inexpensive, if multiple cameras are used to shoot in "real time." This means that the various shots in the commercial are actually being edited in the control room, as the director instructs the video engineer to switch from one camera to another in a continuous sequence, which will become the final commercial. Many TV station crews are accustomed to this mode because of their nightly coverage of local newscasts. This use of videotape is the least expensive way to produce commercials, but it is only effective if the commercial is very simple and direct.

VIDEOTAPE INNOVATIONS BY AMPEX

The Ampex Corporation in California developed videotape for TV program delays on the West Coast in 1956. I was producing commercials for the Bing Crosby Pebble Beach Tournament, and this was to be one of the first uses of videotape to show the West Coast TV audiences the tournament on local time—a delay of three hours from the New York telecast.

I asked CBS if they would allow me to make a one-minute commercial with Bing, using their videotape machines. They said yes, but they would have to charge me $500. I asked Bing if he would agree to do a standup minute for my client, using videotape. Bing agreed to do it for nothing, saying "I'd like to see what I look like on this new thing, videotape." All went well (Bing looked and sounded like Bing), and the whole one-minute commercial cost my client a total of $500!

This experience is particularly novel, considering the cost of star talent today—$100,000 and more for one commercial, not done as a favor—and the cost of a national commercial—not $500, but more than $200,000!

DISADVANTAGES OF VIDEOTAPE

There is no such thing as a "name" video camera operator. Most video camera operators are basically engineers, rather than artists, as is often the case with film production. As a result, the framing of scenes, as well as the lighting, is often inferior to film production.

Additionally, videotape cannot accept as much video information as film. This results in a lack of richness of color and detail. If close-ups of food or other products is key to the "look" of the commercial, film has the advantage.

Reasons to Produce on Videotape

To a large extent, videotaping local and regional commercials is a money-saving alternative to either 35mm or 16mm filming. Most local TV stations have videotape crews who may be available for hire (particularly if the advertiser is a client of the TV station). Deals can be worked out if the commercials will appear on that station. But don't think that the high-quality look and direction of a top-flight film crew will be the result. You get what you pay for, and one of the trade-offs of local videotape production is a definite "hurry-up-and-let's-get-it-done" approach to the entire production process.

If the commercial is local or regional, and it has been decided that videotape is the way to go because of the budget available for production, there are several cautions that should be heeded.

ASK FOR PRE-PRODUCTION DISCUSSIONS

Too often, the videotape crew involved in TV station operations doesn't usually take the time to pre-produce. Remember, the major duty of a station videotape crew is to jump in a van and cover a fire for the 6 o'clock news. They pride themselves on "instant production," as well they might. After all, their primary responsibility is to supply the station with instant pictures and sound bites, and this takes a racehorse mentality. But this is not what you need in commercial production. Make sure that the crew is clear on the objectives of the production and knows exactly what you want to achieve. Once the decision is made to produce a commercial, a pre-production meeting should be set up,

Most videotape production companies will insist on pre-production meetings. It is only TV stations, whose crews are charged with keeping the station on the air, that must be reminded of the need to hold pre-production discussions. (Who should attend the pre-production meeting is covered in detail in Chapter 9, "Producing the Commercial.")

BE SURE NEW VIDEOTAPE IS USED

This may sound needless to emphasize, but it's not. Quite often, the videotape is used more than once, and unless you ask you might be given second-hand tape for commercial production. The erase-and-reuse capability of videotape is both a privilege and a problem. The privilege is that a great deal of tape stock can be saved with judicious reuse. The problem is that there is a loss in quality as tape is used over and over again.

As mentioned earlier in this chapter, there are types of commercials that can be well served by the reuse of tape. For instance, if the production is a long string of interviews or personal on-camera opinions, the unacceptable ones can be culled out by rolling the tape back and erasing them as new material is put on the tape. The loss of quality in one reuse is minimal. Don't go too far, however, in the reuse of tape.

DON'T SETTLE FOR LESS THAN THE BEST

Because it is possible to see a take immediately after completing it by simply rewinding the videotape, everyone has an instant opinion about whether it's a good take or not. Too often, the tendency is to settle for less than the best, to say, "That looks OK to me," when another take of that scene might be ten times better.

This happens often when a station crew is involved. Again, their first responsibility is to keep the station on the air. The quicker they get back to their area of responsibility, the better it is for them. To such a crew, more than one take per scene can seem like a complete waste of time.

The reverse is actually true. Haste truly makes waste in such a situation. To settle for less than the best makes the commercial unnecessarily dull and a poor sales tool.

When Possible, Use a Tape Production Company

If it's affordable, produce with a professional tape production company, preferably one that specializes in TV commercial production. All major and most secondary cities have fully staffed videotape production companies, and they are well aware of the budget restrictions of many commercials they are asked to produce.

They also have staffs who are young and eager, having been trained either in college schools of communications or local TV stations. Their orientation is to videotape production rather than film production, which prepares them for simpler, faster commercial production.

Again, economics helps spell the difference between production on videotape or on film. In most cases, video production is charged by the hour, while film production is charged by the work day. This difference has its genesis in the origins of each mode: videotape was first used in TV-station operation, which has an hourly base. On the other hand, film comes from major motion picture production, where stages and locations are rented and used by the work day (often including overtime). So careful planning of a videotape production can again save dollars by calculating the crew's time on an hourly basis. All of this makes good sense if the commercial lends itself to videotape instead of film production.

Film for Animation

When the commercial is done in "traditional" animation, 35mm film is the tool of choice. By traditional, I mean cel animation, in which each of the 24 frames of film that represent one second of real time is inked and painted by hand on a "cel" (short for "celluloid"). This is only one type of animation, however.

It is also possible to feed visual information directly into a computer and manipulate that picture or "animatie" it. There are as many variations of this computerized approach to animation as there are artists to conceive the visuals. (More about these possibilities will be covered in Chapter 11, "Producing with Animation.")

Special Effects with Film and Tape

As we will discuss in later chapters, many leading-edge commercials make use of computers to control camera moves and motion-control motors to achieve the picture by shooting one frame of film at a time. This picture manipulation continues in the use of the computer to edit film and to add layers of information without loss of that wonderful picture quality which is the trademark of 35mm motion picture film.

As a matter of fact, the combination of computers and film has brought truth to the statement that when it comes to visual effects, if an art director can think of it and explain how it should look, that visual effect can be accomplished. This new marriage of film, tape, and computers has opened a Pandora's box of visual and auditory possibilities. The compatibility of film, tape, and computers had brought about an unusual array of TV commercials, some of which will be discussed in Chapter 14, "Computers and Special Effects."

Be aware that some of these perfect visual effects are also perfectly cold and inhuman, missing the emotional effect that was hoped for. In too many cases, the possibilities of the computer have become more important than the reason for the commercial in the first place: to sell a product or service.

The neophyte's temptation is to use as many of these tricks as possible. Fight that urge. Some computer technicians will be more interested in experimenting with their electronic wonders than in promoting a product or service in the finished commercial. Nothing is more disturbing than trickery without a reason. The best production doesn't call attention to itself; it generates an overall selling force. Use only the tricks that will add top spin to that selling force.

In Summary

Remember these basic reasons for using film:

1. If lighting is important
2. If depth of field is important
3. If superior camera work is important
4. If budgetary considerations are secondary to overall quality

By comparison, the basic reasons for using videotape are the following:

1. If the budget is low
2. If you are looking for a "live" look
3. If the commercial is simple and direct
4. If time is of the essence

9   Producing the Commercial

Let's assume that you have chosen the company to produce your commercial, the client has approved the cost of production, the bid sheets are signed, and you owe the production company the first payment on the bid. The next step is what I will call a "pre-pre-production meeting."

This is the first time the agency creative group sits down with the principals of the production company, after the bid has been approved, to discuss the details of the commercial shoot. This meeting will be held either at the agency or at the production company, whichever location is more convenient to all concerned. At this first meeting, the complete production schedule is agreed upon. This schedule will start immediately, and exact dates will be set for the pre-production meeting and the actual shooting day or days.

This early checkpoint is crucial for making early decisions on how the commercial is to be shot, including whether it will be shot on a stage or on location. After this early meeting, stage rentals are agreed upon or location pictures are taken for client and agency approval. The agency and/or the production company starts casting, and preliminary set sketches are initiated, if sets are to be built. All necessary camera and lighting equipment is reserved, and crews are hired for the necessary days of production.

The Pre-Production Meeting

As soon as the details of production are in hand, the actual pre-production meeting is set up. This is the final checkpoint for everything that has to do with actually producing the commercial. It will be held either at the agency or at the production company. In this meeting, all the final decisions are made. What should happen in this meeting, and who should be involved?

First, the meeting should be held several work days before the actual shooting. There are logical reasons for this time spread. You may, as a result of the pre-production meeting, wish to make changes involving casting, set design, locations, or other production details—all of which takes time. If such changes are agreed upon, you need several working days ahead of production to achieve the changes.

105

Assume that the pre-production meeting is set for Monday morning, and actual production will occur the following week. Mondays are usually better for meetings than for actual shooting, because it's always helpful to have a work day available just before shooting to give everything a last-minute check. This isn't possible if you decide to shoot on a Monday, unless you are willing to pay overtime for production people on the preceding Sunday.

WHO SHOULD ATTEND THE PRE-PRODUCTION MEETING?

From the Agency

The agency producer, writer, and/or art director should be present, as well as any other people from the creative department whose input would be helpful. Don't crowd the room; include only the people who can make a valid contribution.

The agency person in charge of the production should run the pre-production meeting. It is imperative that an agency chain of command be established before this meeting. Pre-production meetings are not democratic. They must be strongly chaired by the agency production leader.

This leader must not let the pre-production meeting wander. He or she should keep the discussion on track. Advertising is full of bright, volatile people who bore easily. The subject must be kept clearly in focus. The pre-production meeting is being held for one reason: to thoroughly prepare for the controlled production of an effecitve commercial—within budget.

From the Client

While some agencies and clients don't feel the need for client attendance, my experience tells me that it is often wise to have a client representative at the pre-production meeting. This is particularly useful if the product is technical or if questions might arise about how it should be handled, displayed, or operated. It is important to have the client there to advise on such matters, even at this early stage, because his or her decision may add to or subtract from the number of crew members assigned to the shoot. When the client is in attendance, a member of the agency's account management team is usually there as well.

From the Production Company

A key person at the meeting will be the director, who will run the actual shooting day, directing the talent, setting up the shots, and, in effect, orchestrating the entire production. The director's role in pre-production is to ascertain the agency's wishes and to examine all the elements that will comprise the production day. Also in attendance should be the producer and/or production assistant (P.A.), who is responsible for carrying out the myriad details that make up the production: from making sure the talent is ready at the right time and place to making sure lunch is served the moment the director releases the crew. The P.A. reports to the director and is a very important member of the studio's staff.

The casting director should be present, because one of the purposes of the pre-production meeting is to make final cast selections. Most casting selections are viewed on videotape in the pre-production meeting. If there are problems in this area, the casting director must be prepared to solve them by producing additional actors for auditions. Large agencies have their own casting directors, as do large production companies. Smaller companies and agencies use free-lance casting directors who charge by the day and are available in the major production centers.

The set designer and/or property master should attend if sets are to be built. The pre-production meeting is the last look at the plans for final construction.

The home economist should be in the meeting if food is involved in the photography. The type of equipment needed to prepare food will be discussed, as will the general appearance of the food, plates, place settings, and so forth. Home economists for motion picture photography are truly specialists. They must understand the needs of the motion picture camera person. They must continually work one step ahead of the camera person, providing a "stand-in" plate of food so he or she can set up the lighting long before the "hero" plate is put in position for the actual shooting. It is a good idea to let the production company choose the home economist. Production people know who works quickly and efficiently and cooks appetizing-looking food as well. Time is money on the set, and a slow home economist can keep the whole crew waiting and cost the production as much as several thousand dollars in nonproductive shooting time.

A stylist should attend the meeting if wardrobe or costuming is required. Cast members can bring their personal wardrobe for the shoot if so desired, and they will be paid a small amount to do so. If in the final casting session you don't think their clothes are right for the commercials, a stylist should be brought in to work with the actors in finding the right clothing. Also, if for creative reasons the commercial calls for specific "costuming," such as a full suit of armor or a hula skirt, a stylist can quickly obtain the needed costumes from well-stocked rental facilities—at least if you are shooting in New York, Chicago, or Hollywood.

Finally, there is the camera person. In some instances, the director is also the camera person. If this is not the case, the camera person need only attend a portion of this meeting if the commercial relies heavily on lighting or special camera effects.

Most of the specialists discussed here need attend only that part of the pre-production meeting that pertains specifically to their part of the production. The well-run meeting will schedule these specialists in for only 15 to 20 minutes and hold to that schedule. Bear in mind that in major production centers you pay for the time these experts spend in your meeting. The costs are not exorbitant, so if you need them in the meeting, have them there. But don't keep them longer than you need them.

The Agenda

Now that we know who is coming, we'll proceed to the structure of the pre-production meeting itself. The agency should prepare packets for all those attending the meeting, including the following items:

1. Writer's production notes
2. Storyboards and scripts
3. Tape of the music track (if prerecorded)
4. Videotape of final casting suggestions
5. Stills of locations (if a location shoot) and alternative locations (Stills should show the position of the sun, indicate north, and include time of day they were taken.)
6. Set designs (if on a set)
7. Production specification sheets, which assign responsibility for all details to either agency or production company
8. Copies of the AICP form, in case there is a discussion of agreed-upon costs, or if additional costs become a consideration during the meeting

In tandem with the director or assistant director (A.D.), the agency should also prepare an agenda for the meeting. The elements of the agenda are as follows:

1. Statement of the commercial's intent, written by the creative director or producer
2. Discussion of the storyboard, frame by frame
3. Play and discuss the prerecorded track (if one exists)
4. Director's shot list (Often, this list is illustrated with stick figure drawings. The director will describe the various scenes and camera angles he or she has in mind. This list gives everybody a preview of what the director plans to shoot. This is a very good time to discuss additional shots or angles. The shooting day is really too late for this discussion.)

5. Review of the casting videotapes (Usually, in addition to the agency's and director's first choice for each part, the videotape contains a second choice for each role. Final selections will be made or, if necessary, recasting will be begun immediately.)

6. Review of the production schedule (The production company should provide a daily time shooting schedule, including maps and arrival times at locations, crew calls, and cast calls. A post-production schedule should also be available if the production company is to stay with the job to the end.

7. Meeting with the home economist if food photography is involved (This includes final planning and a look at dishes, silverware, and other food-related props, either with pictures or the actual materials to be photographed.)

8. Session with the stylist (If styling or costuming is involved, a look at the wardrobe is in order. The stylist either gets approval or makes changes as requested.)

9. Plans for product handling (If the product to be advertised requires special handling or operating procedures, these matters should be discussed at this time. Also, agreement should be reached on who will furnish the product and when and where it should be delivered.)

10. Special considerations (For example, if an animation house has prepared animated titles for your commercial, you should have layouts of the titles in the meeting or, better yet, the animator should be present to discuss positioning and timing of the titles. This clarification will allow the director and/or camera person to plan the framing of the shot to accommodate the titles. Or if special optical digitized effects were planned to separate your scenes, this information should be shared at this meeting.)

Remember, the overriding reason for a thorough pre-production meeting is to avoid surprises on the shooting day. Misunderstandings at this late date can corrupt the commercial as well as cost additional and unproductive dollars. How the "look" of the commercial is planned can make a difference of thousands of dollars, as we will discuss in a later chapter on digital effects and combinations. I will touch on the cost difference between cel and computer animation, plus all the digital wonders now possible for the finished look and feel of the commercial. Consider those alternatives carefully, because they can either save or cost time and money, often more than the advertiser can afford. The pre-production meeting is none too soon to address these alternatives.

The Shooting Day

Now the time has arrived to put all that planning to work. No more discussions of whether this is a better way to shoot than that way. The moment of truth has arrived for your commercial. This is the shooting day.

If the planning was complete, if the pre-production meetings were conclusive and understood by all, then the day should go smoothly. As Louis Pasteur put it, "Luck favors the well-prepared." Here's hoping that beautiful state of affairs exists on the set or location, because that shooting day will cost the client up to $10,000 an hour. (Most location shoots with a full crew will run close to $100,000 in major production centers.) To put it another way, a half-hour of indecision and un-necessary discussion during a location day will waste about $5,000. And it also might result in going to unexpected overtime, with additional costs. So it pays to be prepared. (See Exhibit 9.1.)

DO'S AND DONT'S ON THE SHOOTING DAY

Let's assume that the pre-production went well and all has started well on the shooting day. What else can the agency or client representative do to help the shooting day go smoothly?

First, don't be late getting to the stage or location. No matter how well things have been planned, nothing is perfect, and decisions may have to be made right at the beginning of the day. Arrive on time to help make these decisions.

The first thing a director will do is set up the first shot. The agency person in charge should be there, too. There is nothing more counterproductive than for someone from the agency to show up after the first shot is ready and say to the director, "Hey, hold on. That's not how I visualized that shot at all!"

When such a situation occurs, the momentum of the production is affected. The shooting day, which should start with controlled energy, grinds to a stop just as it is getting started. The director is halted in his or her tracks while the agency or client representative makes eleventh-hour suggestions and the camera crew loses its early-morning eagerness. The attitude of everybody concerned changes perceptibly, and the cutting edge of the production is dulled.

This may sound odd to some readers, but I've always felt that a successful commercial production is like a love affair. In both cases, there is a willingess to cooperate and eagerness to have things work out right. When the attitude on the set is one of cooperation and understanding, the happy results will show up on the screen. When the opposite occurs, the sense of loss will be reflected in a weakened selling tool.

Don't be put off by the amount of time it takes to light the first setup on stage. Lighting is a critical ingredient in good photography. Competent camera people and directors will not shoot until the lighting effect they have decided on is ready. It is the wise agency or client representative who respects this fact and doesn't become impatient at this point.

Exhibit 9.1

Mercedes Benz Car Crash

This is the final frame of a commercial that shows a family standing unscathed beside their badly damaged Mercedes Benz. The commercial was accomplished in one shot, starting from the right rear of a seemingly undamaged car, then trucking around the car to show the terrible damage, and finally showing the unharmed family that survived the crash. The voiceover announcer copy is stark and direct, adding to the realism of the commercial.

Courtesy Clemenger, Melbourne, Australia.

The Crew

Good things happen on the shooting day because of the combined efforts of a group of professional people who know their jobs. Let me introduce some of these people by talking about a typical IATSE crew on either coast. (IATSE is an acronym for International Alliance of Theatrical Stage Employees.) In other cases, your film crew might be members of NABET (National Association of Broadcast Electrical Technicians). IATSE sprang from the legitimate theater, as its name implies, while NABET originated in the TV industry. Both are recognized for their competent membership.

Chances are, if you are producing in either New York or Hollywood, your IATSE (or "I.A.") crew will include 15 or more people. This rather large number is due mainly to union requirements that have had the effect of departmentalizing the film production industry. For example, there are some union jobs to be handled only by electricians and others to be handled by prop people, who work with nonelectrical items such as furniture, paintings, and other props. If you plan to produce in a major film or TV center, be prepared to abide by the area's union rules.

A film crew has a well-defined pecking order, or chain of command. This is to your advantage, because a shooting day is expensive, and time must be used efficiently. The best way to maximize the time is to know the roles of each crew member and then allow them to play their roles. A good film crew is like a well-oiled machine; it can get a great deal done in a very short time. Here is what a crew of 15 does on a Hollywood shoot.

THE DIRECTOR

From the crew and agency standpoint, the person that makes it happen during the shooting day is the director. He or she is in charge. The director gets the biggest salary and has to accept the most responsibility. The buck truly stops with the director. Ideally, the director is involved in the talent selection, because he or she is responsible for directing the cast. The director knows through experience which actors—and actor-types—will respond best to his or her style of direction. It may be costly for the agency and client to agree on the cast without also getting the approval of the director.

In addition to directing the cast, the director also directs the crew. All decisions are cleared through the director, who has the final say on the set. The director alone decides what time lunch is and how long it will be. Most important, the director must be able to respond to concerns such as the following: "The agency doesn't think that last take was as good as it could be." "Don't you think the lighting is a bit dreary?" How skillfully the director copes with problems in every area of responsibility, from simple to complex, helps determine whether your director is superior or merely competent.

It is useful to acquaint yourself with the prevailing directorial styles. Some directors are swashbucklers. You can literally feel their presence when they walk onto a set. Others are almost self-effacing, but they have the ability to say yes or no without hesitation and with quiet authority. And there are directors who seem almost casual in their approach to the production day, but their power is evident in the way the crew and cast respond to their relaxed authority.

Someone once asked me if all directors are egotists. I guess my answer will always be, "No, they're just tremendously self-confident." They express this self-confidence in various ways, but it all adds up to the ability to lead.

THE CAMERA PERSON

Second in command is the DP (director of photography), also known as the camera person. The working crew reports to him or her in the placing of lights, with the counsel of the director. Lighting is vital to achieve the visual mood of the commercial, so shooting doesn't start until the lighting is to the camera person's satisfaction. The "look" of the commercial is up to the camera person, and no excuses will be accepted in the screening room if he or she hasn't achieved it. In major motion picture production the camera person reports to the DP, who sets up the shot. In producing commercials, the role is assumed by the camera person.

Knowing the whole art of lighting is the duty of a top-flight camera person. Prior to the shooting day, he or she must know and inform the chief electricians about what type of lighting equipment is needed to achieve the desired look for the commercial. Camera people often rise through the apprentice ranks as assistant camera people. The factor that separates one camera person from another is how he or she has learned to apply this studio and location lighting knowledge.

The camera person must be completely familiar with the equipment. If the commercial has to do with varying the speed of falling flakes of breakfast cereal, the camera person must know precisely which variable-speed motors to order for which cameras, and how to support this "overcranked" camera mode with all the other related lighting appurtenances. A good camera person can come up with suggestions beyond those made in pre-production. For example, if the agency's intent is to show falling flakes of breakfast cereal with every flake in sharp focus, a knowledge of strobe-light photography will be most useful. In this mode, each frame of running film footage is separately lit by a high-speed strobe-light flash. This is a most precise and difficult camera procedure, eating up lots of film negative, but it is possible to accomplish it with a knowledgeable camera person and proper equipment.

In more and more instances, the roles of director and camera person are becoming fused in one person—the director/camera person. Unless on-camera dialog is the major technique of your commercial, you can employ one of the emerging breed that skillfully handles both roles. It is an interesting concept, coming full-blown from the ranks of professional still photographers. This combination reduces the chain of command on the set by one.

A director/camera person is a good choice if lighting and camera work are more important than directing on-camera talent. Food commercials are a good example. The key differences between a superior food commercial and an average one can be seen in the lighting and the movement of the camera; both are the responsibility of the director/camera person.

Moreover, there are difficult location commercials that can be "directed" *only* by the camera person. For instance, if you are shooting from a helicopter, a director/camera person is essential. This is also true for most other types of location shooting done from moving vehicles or great heights, where a person must work alone.

Traditionally, the drawback to using a director/camera person has been that he or she is the only person who sees what is being filmed. However, be sure to ask for a camera with "video assist," which allows everyone present to see what is being shot on a video monitor.

Do not expect to save one of the two fees when you opt for a director/camera person. Such a person is an expert in both fields and is paid for both jobs. But the results can be superior under the right commercial circumstances.

If a commercial depends on dialog direction, I would hesitate to hire a director/camera person. Directing the actors in their lines and movements requires complete attention, uninterrupted by the camera's physical necessities. In my opinion, it is wise to separate the roles of director and camera person in dialog commercials.

PRODUCER AND PRODUCTION ASSISTANT

Many directors use a producer production assistant (P.A.). One or both of these people, either on staff with the production company or hired as free-lancers by the production company, actually prepares the production for the director. If the commercial is a very complex one, an assistant director may also be brought in for a time. However, it is the producer or P.A., along with the director, who will assign such tasks as casting to a production company staff member or an independent casting director. The casting function, in either case, is done under the director's supervision.

However, the production company producer and/or P.A. will often follow through in setting up the casting schedules. The producer/P.A. may also scout for locations, or the company may hire an independent location manager who specializes in finding specific types of locations. The number of people involved in helping the director during the pre-production planning is in direct ratio to the complexity of the job. If there are many locations involved, the production company will probably have both a producer and a P.A. plus the other people mentioned earlier in the section on the pre-production meeting.

THE ASSISTANT DIRECTOR

If the job is complex, an assistant director (A.D.) is brought in for a specified number of days. Otherwise, the A.D. is brought in just early enough for the director to turn over all the details of the actual production to him or her. These details include setting up the time and place for cast and crew calls. Also, if a location is to be used, the A.D. will furnish maps to all drivers, along with estimates of how long the drive will take under normal and rush-hour conditions. The A.D. arranges with a catering service for the on-location lunch and also the crew's breakfast of coffee, doughnuts, bagels and cream cheese, etc. (It is possible to put on three pounds in three days on location, due mainly to those breakfast munchies.)

In short, the A.D. is in charge of the thousand-and-one details that surround a shoot. The A.D.'s phone book includes names, addresses, and phone numbers for everything and everyone connected with production. It includes both home and hotel phone numbers so the A.D. can call client and crew with last-minute location and shooting changes necessitated by weather conditions. It lists laboratory numbers for communicating specific negative-processing information. It includes phone numbers for screening rooms for either tape transfers or film dailies. With this information, screenings can be both set up and changed if production is running behind. There is a phone number for the government weather station to check on last-minute weather changes, plus a zillion other names and phone numbers of people and organizations who must be reached, often at the very last minute.

Another characteristic typical of the A.D., the producer, and the P.A. is that they always have change for a dollar—usually in quarters. They are so accustomed to making phone calls from remote gas-station pay phones in the middle of the desert that they automatically carry lots of change. And many of them carry cellular phones.

The A.D. carries out the orders given by the director during the shooting. He or she must have an immediate grasp of every possible problem the director may face and be prepared with a solution.

ASSISTANT CAMERA PERSON

The assistant camera person is solely responsible to the camera person. His or her duties are myriad, mostly having to do with being sure the right camera gear has been ordered and is in working condition and that backup equipment is available if needed.

The assistant camera person will prep the equipment only if paid for a prep day. Unless the company has a staff person to handle this function, it is important to add this cost to the total production cost. On an equipment prep day, the assistant camera person checks out all the lenses and their calibration, checks the zoom motor for smoothness, the zoom lens for possible shifting, etc. The assistant determines whether diffusion filters are needed on the set or location and whether diopters are needed for the zoom lens. He or she checks out the "legs" (adjustable tripod) and "high hat" (lowest platform for a camera, allowing shots from less than one foot above the floor).

The assistant camera person also checks camera supplies, such as batteries and film magazines, to avoid halting the shooting day. He or she will have prepared enough film magazines so there will not be too many trips to the "changing bag." The changing bag is like a portable darkroom. The assistant camera person can empty and reload a film magazine in this large black cloth bag, but it takes time—and time is money on the shooting day. By filling sufficient magazines with unexposed film negative before the shooting starts, this delay can be avoided.

The assistant camera person is one of the most important people on the shooting day, as well as the prep day, because the camera equipment and supplies are almost wholly his or her responsibility. The assistant checks the "gate" (the alternating shutter through which the film negative passes) to make sure there are no hairs or dust to cause film scratches. He or she checks to be sure all light meters in use are within a quarter of a stop of a calibrated light meter.

As the exposed film magazines are removed from the camera, the assistant puts "gaffer's tape" (a strong, all-purpose 2-inch tape) across the face and around the can to indicate that the film is exposed. He or she labels each can with all pertinent information for the laboratory, including the type of film used and the ASA number.

I have gone into some detail with this person's job to stress the fact that there are a great many specific assignments made to each member of a film crew, and each assignment is important to the success of the shooting day.

SCRIPT CLERK

It is the script clerk's duty to time all scenes before any shooting is done and to communicate these timings to the director. The agency producer should also confirm these timings from the timings the agency made earlier. The script clerk's information will have a bearing on how the director will lay out the action of each shot. Remember, a commercial exists in real-time elements of 30 seconds or 60 seconds, and the film won't "cut" (edit together) if any scene is too long. During the shooting, the script clerk times each "take." If any of them is too long, the clerk informs the director so the next take will be within the time allowance for that scene. His or her word on this matter is law.

When scenes are not shot in chronological order, then the duties of the script clerk become more important. He or she must be sure the storyboard is covered, that is, that all the agreed-upon scenes in it are shot, regardless of their order. Many directors have their own ideas of how certain scenes should be shot, but any additional interpretations are shot *after* the storyboard has been covered, and it is up to the script clerk to be sure those storyboard scenes are "in the can" (the exposed film can).

The script clerk must keep an eye open for filmic anachronisms, the sort of thing critics love to find and that drives the editors crazy. He or she must guard against props and gestures that don't match from scene to scene. (Examples would be a glass of water that suddenly switches from an actor' right hand in scene one to his left hand in scene two, or a woman's hat that is on in scene one and off in scene two.) One way to keep a constant check is by taking Polaroid instant stills of each scene. It is also possible to get a still-frame print-out from many video-assist cameras. In any event, the film clerk must be a combination of diplomat, film detective, and hawkeye.

THE SOUND PEOPLE: PLAYBACK, RECORDIST, AND BOOM PERSON

The number of sound people needed on a set or location is dictated by the type of sound involved in the shooting. Even when the shooting is done without sound, a sound person is often required.

Playback

For example, if the track has been prerecorded and will be played back during each silent camera take for rhythmic purposes, or if the director must refer to it between takes, a "playback" person and equipment will be needed. This equipment must operate at true speed so that the shooting done to its beat will be rhythmically correct when viewed in the screening room.

Incidentally, the term *MOS*, which you'll hear on the set, dates back to the early days of sound motion pictures and to a middle-European director who had some problems pronouncing the English language. When he was asked if the next scene would include sound, he replied, "No, mit-out sound." Ever since, silent takes have been referred to as "MOS."

Recordist and Boom Person

If live dialog is to be shot with the scene, then you will need a recordist and possibly a boom person. The recordist is a recording engineer whose responsibility it is to record all on-camera "lip sync" dialogue. The boom person controls a microphone over the actor's head on a long boom. On location shots where the boom would be seen by the camera, shortwave microphones are attached to the actors clothing instead, and the on-camera sound is fed (without wires) to the recording equipment.

Sound is captured on magnetic tape these days, and sound equipment is completely portable and light in weight. With further advances in printed circuitry and fiber optics, plus electronic chips, sound equipment will become even better and more portable in the future.

CHIEF ELECTRICIAN OR GAFFER

This crew member is in charge of all electricians on the set. Electricians move, mount, connect, and focus all the lights used in the production. The chief electrician, or gaffer, gets instructions from the camera person. (The term *gaffer* dates from the days when lights were hung from battens, and a long pole, or gaff, was used to move the lights rather than mounting a ladder.)

The gaffer continually listens to the camera person for the many slight adjustments that must be made with the lights, always aware of special devices that affect the intensity of each light (scrims, gobos, shields, nets, barn doors, and the like). All of these adjustments will be made while the camera person sets up and checks the upcoming shot.

If the production is complicated, there will be more than one electrician. The electrician next in seniority is called the *best boy*, because he or she is the best of the apprentices and is next in line to be a chief electrician. The best boy can help greatly in cutting down the time it takes to get the lighting ready. On the set or location the meter is always running, and time is money.

THE HEAD GRIP (OR KEY GRIP)

Grips handle all nonelectricial equipment, with the exception of hand props and set dressing. This includes nontechnical handling of the camera, such as lifting it and putting it on a tripod.

The first impression many neophytes get when they step onto a shooting set is that there are too many people in the crew. This is not necessarily true. The equipment involved in shooting is heavy and must be handled in precise ways to avoid damage. When a move from one setup to another is ordered by the director, strong, knowledgeable hands are immediately needed. I think the term *grip* must have come from the crew's strong hands and their ability to use them to move heavy equipment gently.

A specialized grip, the dolly grip, moves the camera dolly during the actual shooting. The dolly grip must know how to start the dolly without jarring it and stop it gently at precisely the right point on the dolly track. Another specialist is the crane operator, who operates the camera crane during setup and actual shooting.

OUTSIDE PROPS AND INSIDE PROPS

"Props" is short for "properties." Prop people obtain and move various properties on the set or location at the behest of the director or camera person. On the East Coast, "outside props" go out and acquire the props, and "inside props" handle the props in production. On the West Coast, a prop person primarily handles hand props used by the actors in their performance: bicycles, skis, and so forth. Although a prop person can handle small set dressings, a large location job requiring redressing would probably require an art director/set dresser, who would receive his or her instructions from the director.

Animals are handled by an animal handler. This is a field that requires very specialized knowledge and skill, especially when shooting dogfood or catfood commercials.

In the prop department, the chain of command is generally from director, to art director, to set dresser, to prop person. Generally, the director also works directly with the prop person. But all of these people coordinate their efforts to avoid duplicate rentals and so forth. This may sound like overkill, but if the production is large, every wasted moment costs you a lot more than having enough hired hands to do the job quickly and efficiently.

THE HOME ECONOMIST

If the preparation and photography of food are vital to your commercial, this crew member is key to its success. He or she will know enough about shooting to allow sufficient prep time. The home economist will be wise enough on the set to know that a lot of food must be ready in a hurry when the shoot starts. Cooking areas are needed close to the set so the food will arrive hot and on time in front of the camera. The home economist will most likely need one or two extra pairs of hands at such times; that help will come from an assistant, and from the prop person if necessary.

MAKEUP ARTIST AND HAIR STYLIST

If there are close-ups in the commercial, or if the product being advertised is a cosmetic or hair product, the importance of these two experts is obvious. In certain situations, these functions may be performed by one person. Again, this is a unionized job with skilled people available.

WARDROBE ATTENDANT

If the cast is large and involves costumes, or if the product being advertised has to do with fashion, the wardrobe attendant is needed to ensure that everything is pressed and looks as good as it should be on the actor or model. The wardrobe attendant will need hanger space as well as an ironing broad and iron. Complete sewing equipment is often advisable—and sometimes even a washer and dryer.

TEACHER-WELFARE WORKER

In Los Angeles County, if you have a minor on camera—anyone 18 years old or younger—you must also hire a teacher-welfare worker. This person is a teacher who holds proper State of California teaching credentials, is experienced in welfare supervision, and has been certified and assigned by the Work Permits Office of the Los Angeles Unified School District. The complete set of rules and regulations governing the employment of minors in the Los Angeles area entertainment industry can be found in Appendix Four. These rules followed abuses in early filmmaking, from 1910 into the 1920s. Here is how long the rules allow each age group to appear in front of the camera:

- 15–180 days old: 20 minutes of camera work; 2 hours on the set
- 6–24 months old: 2 hours of camera work; 4 hours on the set
- 2–5 years old: 3 hours of camera work; 6 hours on the set
- 6–18 years old: 4 hours of camera work; 6 hours on the set

If your commercial involves children on camera and you are shooting in the Los Angeles County jurisdiction, study the rules carefully. Not to do so could cost you additional days of photography, at considerable expense to your client. The use of children in commercials calls for very careful planning. If the child lives in Los Angeles County, there must be a teacher-welfare worker on the shoot, even if the location is outside Los Angeles County and even if school is not in normal session. These rules do not apply elsewhere in the United States.

SPECIAL EFFECTS

The special effects person is the set magician. You say you want rain? The special effects person will create it, either on a set or on location, from a drizzle to a downpour. That goes for snow, fire, and explosions as well. They can also rig people to fly, doors to open as if by magic, and any other bit of visual legerdemain.

SCENICS

The scenic artist paints the backdrops and sets, hangs wallpaper, and creates signs and other graphics.

VIDEOTAPE RECORDING

If you are playing back videotape as a reference during the filming session, a VTR person and equipment are needed. If you are taping and filming simultaneously, you'll need the VTR person and specialized equipment as well. If the taping is only for reference, the tape can be recorded on portable equipment, probably on 3/4-inch tape.

TELEPROMPTER AND OPERATOR

If your talent can't memorize, you will need a teleprompter that rolls the script by in large letters directly in front of the camera lens. And you'll also need an operator who will keep the script rolling by at the speed of the actor's delivery.

GENERATOR OPERATOR

The generator operator is a specialized electrician who operates a portable generator used for supplementary outside lighting or interior lighting on location when in-house electrical sources are inadequate. It is the operator's duty to constantly monitor the flow of electrical current. If this flow is not even, the lighting intensity will vary, which will adversely affect the way the film looks. And if the generator is on a truck, you will need a driver as well.

STILLS

If you will want photographs taken of the cast and/or crew during production for purposes of publicity, you need to hire a unionized still photographer. Don't count on using your own still camera. In the major film centers this violates union rules.

TEAMSTERS

Teamsters are the drivers of the various vehicles needed in production. If it's a location job, you will probably have an equipment truck, a generator truck, perhaps a crane, a Winnebago motor home (known as a "Winnie") for the cast to rest in, and a prop truck with the hundreds of little items that always seem to be needed at the location. Included of course will be many rolls of that great invention, gaffer's tape—the strong tape that virtually holds the production together. Incidentally, these drivers are members of the Teamsters Union, one of the strongest unions involved in filming.

The technical members of the crew report to the assistant director and camera person. The overall supervision is in the hands of the director. The chain of command is as follows: director, producer/P.A., assistant director, camera person. Each part of the crew has its own head of operations. Even the drivers have a captain.

The smaller the production, the fewer the people. You don't need all these crew members if the commercial features a fruit salad on a table. Also, the smaller the production city, the fewer union requirements there are to regulate personnel required in any type of production.

As with any operation involving people, a well-organized crew can get a great deal of work done during a shooting day. If it is not well organized and well directed, or if the chain of command is broken, all those workers can waste a lot of time and turn out a disappointing commercial.

The Client

Now that we've described the crew, let's turn our attention to the people who hired them: the client, or representatives of the advertising agency and the advertiser. (Both agency and advertiser are "clients" to the production company.) In too many cases, no communication system has been set up among the representatives of the agency and the client, all of whom watch wistfully in the background on the shooting day.

How Information Is Obtained During Production

If this is the first time the client has attended a production day, what is the proper protocol? What questions can the client ask? And whom does the client ask?

Let's take that last question first: Ask *only* the agency producer, or the person from the creative group who is in charge for the agency. This may be the writer, the art director, or the agency producer. This one person should be the agency voice on the set; we will call him or her the producer. The agency producer is the mouthpiece for the agency and its client on the set or location. If the producer doesn't know the answer to your question, it is up to him or her to get the answer for you. Don't ask the director, the camera person, or any member of the crew. They have their separate duties to perform. The producer should also be the only person from the agency or client to discuss shooting details with the director during production.

Now, let's get to the questions you should and shouldn't ask. Knowing a bit about how things work on a shoot may keep you from asking some embarrassing ones. For instance, many first-timers don't realize that the scenes for a commercial are not necessarily shot in chronological order. If the commercial opens with a shot of the product, this is probably not the first shot on the shooting day. Chances are it will be made at the very end of the day—and for good reason.

What Is the Usual Shooting Sequence?

Let's say the product shot is a relatively simple setup. In most commercial productions, the more difficult scenes from a lighting and logistics standpoint are shot at the beginning of the shooting day. Then, as the day progresses, the shooting order will go to simpler and simpler setups, maybe winding up with that product shot that opens and/or closes the commercial. If the shooting begins to run into overtime at the end of the day, it is a lot less expensive to go into overtime with a simple setup and a few crew members than an elaborate setup and a full crew.

Whether elaborate or simple, scenes involving on-camera dialog are usually done first. There are two reasons for this:

1. Most directors like to work with the actors who have on-camera roles while they are fresh. All scenes with actors, even the silent scenes, are usually completed most successfully when energy levels are at their highest, early in the day.
2. Once the sound takes are completed, crew members with only sound shooting duties can be dismissed for the rest of the production day.

After the major scenes are shot, the director will probably shoot a series of close-ups and reaction shots from each of the actors. Although this footage may not be on the storyboard, a competent director always ensures his or her production with these short scenes, called *pegs* or *turnarounds*. Close-ups and reaction shots will enable the editor to make a smooth transition from one scene to another, even if the scenes don't cut together too well.

Close-ups are also made of the product: by itself, in the actor's hand, being passed to another hand, being put down, being picked up. Again, the purpose of this additional photography is to aid in editing the commercial. There is nothing more discouraging than to hear a good editor say, "I need a good tight close-up of the product between these two scenes, but I can't find such a shot in the dailies."

Even during that first day on a shoot, it will be noted that some things are done to a set routine. For example, each "take" of each scene is written on the "slate." Each time the director is ready for a take, the assistant director will request quiet on the set. When all is quiet, the director will say, "Roll camera." When the camera is rolling at the normal rate of 24 frames a second (or whatever speed has been decided on), the camera person or recordist will say "speed," which means the camera and sound equipment are operating at the filming speed and all is in readiness for the take.

If it is a "sound take," meaning there is live dialog to be recorded with the filming, the sound person will call for "sticks" or "slate," saying, "Mark it." At this point, the assistant camera person (or whoever is holding the slate in front of the working camera) will read aloud the scene number and take number, which are recorded on film and sound tape. For example, the person might say, "Scene three, take six." Then he or she will drop the "clap stick" (the top part of the slate).

The sharp sound made by the clap stick as it is dropped has a very important function later, when the film and sound track are lined up. That clap stick picture allows the editor to "sync up" the picture with the sharp sound heard on the separately recorded sound tape. Thus the sound and picture will be synchronized.

After the clap stick falls, both the camera and the sound tape are rolling, and the take is ready to start. It is essential that everyone be absolutely quiet during sound takes. The assistant director will remind you just before the director calls for action, saying, "Quiet please," or "Let's settle down." In commercial production, most takes in a dialog commercial last only 10 or 15 seconds. A few commercial formats benefit from doing the entire commercial in one sound take from top to bottom, but they are the exception rather than the rule.

The formalized rolling of the camera and the beginning of the take apply mostly to sound takes. The silent scenes are not so formally announced, but observers should still hold conversations to a minimum while on the set. Off-camera conversations and laughter from those not directly involved with the scene are quite disturbing to the director and camera person. And whispered conferences between agency representatives and clients are even more disturbing. The director assumes that the shoot is not following the agency/client wishes, and "something's got to be done." If this occurs, the astute director will call a halt to the shooting and find out what (if anything) is going on back there.

A word about lunch on the shooting day: The director will decide whether the lunch break will be for half an hour or an hour, and when it will be. This could be any time between noon and 1:30 p.m. without penalty, based on a normal starting time for the crew. A word to the wise regarding lunch: Save your cocktails until the end of the day, after the shooting is over. Martinis don't mix well with production, even if you are only an observer.

If the agency/client representatives go out for lunch rather than eating with the crew, it is crucial to return to the set on time. All involved should be there to help with decision making as the first setup is being prepared after lunch. What I've said over and over applies here, too: Remember how much of the advertiser's money you're spending for every hour of shooting time, and how much of it you waste if you're not available when you should be, or if you're heard from when you shouldn't be.

CLIENT RESPONSIBILITIES

Now that we've covered the protocol on the set, let's talk about the duties of the advertiser who is present.

1. Make sure the product is properly handled and displayed. Someone who understands everything about the product should be at the shoot.
2. Make sure the intent of the commercial is being followed. This means that the actors' lines should be delivered as agreed upon in the pre-production meeting, and that the expression of the visual should be consistent with the pre-production agreements.

Monitor the Commercial's Intended Meaning

Don't panic if the director doesn't get the right reading from the actor in the first take. Many directors wisely let the actor work his way into the right reading of a line. On the other hand, if the direction seems to be going *away* from the intended inflection, something should be done about it. If you're the writer of the commercial, and this is your first production trip, what do you do when you hear readings that are straying from your intentions? Remember who your mouthpiece is. Don't talk to the actor, and don't talk to the director. Make your concerns known immediately to the agency producer, whose responsibility it is to represent the agency to the director.

Be Decisive

Another thing you must learn as agency/client representative is how to say yes or no without waffling. Decisions must be made on the spot. If you say, "No, it's not right yet," be ready to explain why it's not right.

Proper planning in the pre-production meeting should help resolve most problems that arise on the set. Constant attention to what is happening in front of the camera will show up difficulties as they occur, and you can pass on your comments to the agency producer while there's time to act on them.

Observe the Crew's Teamwork

If it is a fairly complicated production, there will be times during the day when several of the crew members will not be busy. They are not goofing off. These electricians, gaffers, and grips have completed their lighting and setup duties for the moment, but they will plunge into action when a change or new setup is called for. The way to tell how well they work together is to watch what happens when the next lighting situation occurs. You will see that several pairs of hands and feet work in unison to prepare lights, props, and camera equipment for an entirely different visual situation. Actual production is a hurry-up-and-wait business.

Be Aware of the Schedule

One of the toughest problems that can arise on the production day occurs when there is more shooting to do than there is time for. What can be done to keep from going into expensive overtime? The experienced agency producer and director will realize this situation is building up by mid-afternoon. At that time they can consider several alternatives that may allow production to end on time:

1. Do we need that additional angle to cover this scene? Can we go with the angle we're now shooting? (Each new camera angle calls for time-consuming light changes.)
2. Don't we already have a good take of this scene? Are additional readings really necessary? (Check the tape assist to see whether usable scenes are in the can already.)
3. Can the order of shooting be changed for the rest of the day so that overtime will only involve a small part of the crew? (Product close-ups, pouring shots., etc., can usually be handled by a skeleton crew, with the rest excused at the end of the normal shooting day.)
4. Is it possible to hold those small-crew shots over to another shooting day and combine them with some other insert shooting the studio must do for another client? (If so, all the remaining time can be concentrated on the bigger setups.)

The best plan is to get the big, talent-heavy, crew-heavy setups completed within the prescribed shooting day. Then, any overtime that is necessary will involve only a small crew and no talent except perhaps a hand model for product close-ups.

There is an unexpected benefit to be reaped from such a situation. With most of the people excused at the end of the normal day, the insert crew can concentrate fully and without interruption on the intricate job of lighting and shooting the product shots. And, as we should constantly remind ourselves, the *product* is what the commercial is all about.

VIDEOTAPE PRODUCTION

Although we have been talking about a film production day, the same considerations of time and money pertain when you shoot on videotape. Just because you can light more simply for tape and play back all your takes with even greater ease than when using a video-assist film camera, it does not follow that you will arrive at the ultimate performance any sooner. Unfortunately, there has been a tendency in tape production to settle for less than the best because of the immediacy of tape. That

Exhibit 9.2

Inexpensive Production

RichMarc Productions in Indianapolis, Indiana, accomplished this location
commercial for under $26,000 (through dailies) by using ingenuity instead of renting a
camera car. Rick Thompson rented a utility trailer used to haul lawn mowers,
mounted a stationary bike on the trailer, and pulled the contraption down the street
as the young newsboy pedaled a stationary bike. A camera dolly was also mounted on
the trailer so the camera could be moved back and forth to insinuate further
movement as the paperboy threw folded newspapers to nearby doorsteps. Says Rick
Thompson of RichMarc, "a camera car would have been more convenient, but the
tight budget forced us to improvise. The resultant scene came out the same—but
much less expensive to produce."
Courtesy RichMarc Films, Indianapolis, Indiana.

tendency starts with less complete pre-production planning and continues right through production day. (See Exhibit 9.2.)

So although the production modes vary in many ways and crew
sizes change according to production necessity and shooting locale, the
attention to production details should remain the same whether you
produce on film, videotape, or whatever they invent next.

In Summary

The production day is when all that pre-production planning comes together to film or tape the commercial. Although the advertising agency has sold the idea of the commercial to the client, on production day it becomes the responsibility of the production company to make the idea come alive.

A first-rate production company will be thoroughly organized, with definite responsibilities assigned to the various members of the production crew.

The person in charge is the director. The buck stops there, and all authority emanates from the director. There is a definite pecking order on the set or location, and it is the wise agency or client representative who understands that order and abides by it.

Only one person from the agency should speak to the director. All comments or suggestions from other agency or client people should be funneled through the one agency person who assumes or has been assigned the role of leadership for the client/agency team.

If all goes as planned, the production day should result in the film or tape footage that will be edited into the final commercial. This footage will become the "dailies," which will be discussed in the next chapter. The production day will remain as the ultimate search for a new, more effective expression of the selling force of an instrument called a television commercial.

10 PRODUCING IN LIVE ACTION

By definition, live-action commercial production used to mean that only live-action scenes were used. In today's computer-assisted world of commercial production, this definition is a bit simplistic. Live-action shooting is now frequently combined with all sorts of special effects, from simple computer graphics to complex animation. It is now possible to see a real bull walking serenely along a girder in a huge building under construction. (See Exhibit 10.1.) Merrill Lynch and its agency accomplished this using a cutting-edge combination of live-action elements. (We will discuss some of the more sophisticated applications of live-action shooting in Chapter 14.)

Most live-action commercials involve real actors with on-camera dialog in a realistic setting. They range from slice-of-life dialog to product demonstrations. The ability to show how a product can be used by the consumer is one of the best uses of live action. In general, live-action commercials mimic either the real or an idealized world. Perfume and cologne commercials would fall into that second use of live action. These live-action fantasy commercials make use of unusual lighting, sets, angles, and graphic treatments to invite the user into a new experience.

So before choosing to shoot in live action, determine whether the product or service would be best promoted by showing it in the real world. If it would benefit more from some form of graphics, animation might be a better choice. In many cases, a decision must be made between realism and fantasy, live action and animation.

Preparing a Live-Action Commercial for Bidding

Having decided to shoot in live action, the next decisions to be made by the creative department are as follows:

1. Should the commercial be shot on a set or on location? (Chapter 6 details the advantages and disadvantages of each.)
2. Should we shoot locally, or should bids be invited from top-flight companies on either coast? (Budget will be a major determinant.)
3. Which three companies should be asked to bid on this commercial (assuming a major production center will be involved in the bidding)?

Exhibit 10.1

Merrill Lynch Live Action

ILM (Industrial Light and Magic) uses computers to perform miracles in commercial production, including a bull for Merrill Lynch that seems to be walking along steel girders in the framework of a skyscraper, although it actually never left the ground. The live bull and miniature sets were combined in a computer.
Courtesy Industrial Light and Magic.

The answers to these questions are guided by several interlocking factors: budget limitations, time constraints, and creative objectives.

It is a fact that the harder everyone concerned works to answer these three questions, guided by these three factors, the better the final commercial will be. The more time, thought, and energy expended in preparing and pre-producing, the better a commercial idea becomes, and the less expensive its production. Why? Because the planning will become focused—and, quite often, less expensive.

SAMPLE REELS

In choosing production companies to bid on live-action commercials, one of the best guides is to look at their sample reels. These reels will display the production each company believes best represents its abilities. If your commercial calls for underwater photography, for example, the production company search will include camera personnel with this special ability. (See Exhibit 10.2.) If, on the other hand, the commercial is for a salad dressing, and the live action will consist mostly of making a salad and applying the product to the finished salad, you will look for an entirely different type of company. This company should have camera personnel whose pride and joy is lighting the smallest objects on a tabletop, and making them appetizing to the viewer. All this information is in the sample reels.

Because there is such a variety of production modes available, I will assume that the commercial we are discussing will be shot in 35mm for a large regional or national client. This type of production calls for the most preparation and planning, and local commercial production with smaller budgets can gain from this top-of-the-line viewpoint.

THE PRODUCTION PACKAGE

Once the three competing production companies are chosen, the production package is sent to each company. This production package includes scripts, storyboards or animatics, writer's production notes, and scheduling requirements for air dates or client meeting dates. There will be initial phone discussions with each company, in which the agency representative (nominally, the producer) will review the commercial's requirements.

Then, each competing company will submit an AICP form to the agency representative. AICP stands for Association of Independent Commerical Producers, and its importance is discussed in Chapter 4. There is also a copy of the AICP form in Appendix 3. The ACIP forms will be gone over carefully, and any adjustments that the agency thinks should be made are communicated to the production companies, thus asking for a revised bid for final approval.

In discussing a live-action shoot, some production companies may suggest shooting on a stage instead of a location, or vice versa. Very often, the agency's choice of production houses depends on which company has the best reasons for such a suggestion.

The First Production Meeting after Bid Approval

Every live-action shoot—whether stage or location—must start with a thorough Pre-preproduction meeting. This is held after acceptance of the bid, and it is the forum for discussing and agreeing on details of the production. This is a long list of "who is responsible for what." (Appendix 1 is a specification sheet from Leo Burnett that outlines these important responsibilities.) All of them must be reviewed and agreed upon in this first meeting between the live-action production company, the client, and the agency.

Following this first meeting, the various departments of the production company get busy: if it's a stage shoot, it is their responsibility to rent the stage; to arrange for set construction, including painting and props; and, in general, to get ready for the shooting day.

If it's a location shoot, it is the production company's responsibility to search out locations and take photos of them. These photos must be annotated with the direction of the sun, time of day picture was taken, and any limitations, such as "no shooting after 6:00 p.m." These photos will be shown to the agency for their eventual approval, and all time-and-place arrangements are then made to use the location, whether a house, a stadium, a store, a beach, etc.

The production company producer also makes arrangements for the necessary supporting services: police and/or fire protection; a teacher, if a school-age child is in the cast (see Appendix 4 for details); food to be prepared and delivered to the site for lunch and/or dinner; auxiliary lighting equipment to be ordered, after checking with the head electrician; and many other items listed in the specification sheet. Whether using a location or a stage, the production company will work with the agency in setting up casting sessions, wardrobe sessions for the cast, etc.

THE PRE-PRODUCTION MEETING

Chapter 9 covers pre-production in detail, but let me once again affirm how important this day is to the final success of the commercial. The original meeting with the production company, the pre-pre-production meeting, assigned responsibilities and set up casting sessions, discussed set designs or locations to be searched, and laid out a production schedule. The final meeting before the actual production is now at hand—a final check on all the details that go into the actual production.

There is nothing worse than a basic misunderstanding of any of the myriad details that go into the shooting of a live-action commercial. For instance, if there is a lack of understanding on wardrobe, the cast

Exhibit 10.2

Daredevil Camerawork

One of a series of commercials shot by daredevil camera people, this one for Coca-Cola was shot in Australia. The cameraman, with the camera mounted in his helmet, free-falls with the "sky surfer" before they separately parachute to safety. It takes a special type of camera operator to accomplish such a commercial.
Courtesy McCann Erickson, Sydney, Australia.

can easily show up in the wrong clothes, and several hours of the shooting day are lost trying to correct this mistake. The pre-production meeting's main purpose is to be doubly sure that all details—down to the very smallest—are completely understood by all concerned. Any time lost on the production day because of misinformation can be costly not only in money, but also in the energy of the cast and crew.

BENEFITS OF LIVE ACTION

To wrap up this discussion of shooting in live action, remember that in contrast to producing a commercial in animation, there is always a chance for an additional take of a scene. As a result, quite often the meaning of the scene can become more focused. Animation doesn't offer this opportunity for additional takes.

Shooting in live action takes concentration and a consistently high energy level, from the pre-production day right through the shooting day and right on into viewing the dailies. Every effort must be made to simplify rather than expand or complicate the expression of the idea. This effort should continue right into the final editing and finishing of the live-action commercial. Meticulous care must be taken in the editing. All too often, it is easy to settle for an edit that isn't necessarily the best edit because it happens to be the right length and seems to fit the track. The possibility that careful editing will lead to a stronger commercial is particularly true of live-action production, in which many takes of each scene are available to give a wide choice of editing rhythm and intent.

In Summary

Producing in live action offers you a variety of options, including the following:

1. Shooting on a stage for controlled sound and lighting
2. Shooting on location for realism
3. In either case, don't neglect the importance of agreements, down to the smallest detail. Live-action supervision takes constant attention and lots of energy. "God is in the details."

11

PRODUCING WITH ANIMATION

Animators have been called the "frame-by-frame filmmakers." This is because, whereas live-action commercials are produced in running footage at normal 35mm speed of 24 frames per second, animated commercials are drawn one frame at a time. These artists, who meticulously draw the still pictures that capture the illusion of life, have sold millions of dollars worth of products and brought enjoyment to viewers all over the world. In fact, some of the early drawings from animated cartoons have brought high prices as collector's items.

Because of its cinematic origin as theatrical short subjects, early cartooning became synonymous with the word *animation*. Actually, cartooning forms only a small part of the field of animation. Today, there are many more sophisticated applications of the art in other forms, using such materials as clay and pigment applied directly to the *cels* (a word derived from *celluloid*). The reason cels are used is that they are transparent, and they can be lit from underneath when filmed. This technique, perfected by Walt Disney's artists, is still used commercially, even though there are now more elaborate ways to animate drawings and photographs. (See Exhibit 11.1.)

The horizons of drawn art in motion are constantly being pushed ahead by the use of the computer, but currently there are four basic types of animation. The categories are separate but interlocking:

1. **Cartooning:** Character drawing in the frame-by-frame style; full animation depicting animals and humans, all drawn on cels. As many as 24 separate drawings per second are needed to create the illusion of life.
2. **Animated graphics:** Graphic types of frame-by-frame drawing, including metamorphic combinations that flow from one graphic to the next. These flowing graphics are often seen in show titles, such as "Monday Night Football" or "The Sunday Night Movie."
3. **Computer animation:** Characters entered into a computer in three dimensions to be manipulated and brought to life.
4. **Rotoscoping:** Frame-by-frame drawings added directly to live-action filming.

135

Exhibit 11.1

Stop-Motion Commercials

English humor prevails in this Talking Turtle stop-motion commercial. The series also featured talking pandas. These commercials were winners in the Mobius International Awards in 1992.
Courtesy GGK, London, England.

Even as this is being written, an artist somewhere is sitting down with a computer expert, and, between them, they will dream up the next exciting use of animation. This is truly an explosive part of TV advertising production.

Cartooning or Character Drawing

In the production of traditional cartoon animation using frame-by-frame drawings, seven steps are required to produce the finished product:

1. Preparing the storyboard
2. Creating key drawings
3. Preparing layouts
4. Recording the sound track
5. Reading the sound track
6. The pencil test
7. Inking and painting

PREPARING THE STORYBOARD

First, the advertising agency draws a storyboard that depicts the type of characters to be animated. The storyboard also gives a general feeling for the characters' style of movement and a written story line for the commercial. An example of such storyboard preparation would be seen in the development of commercials for the Keebler Elves or any number of breakfast foods seen on Saturday morning television.

Occasionally, storyboards are done by the animation studio, but in most instances the original storyboard and commercial idea come from the advertising agency. Storyboards shouldn't be so complete that they are locked in cement and cannot be changed. The professional animator should be able to suggest improvements.

CREATING KEY DRAWINGS

From the storyboard, five or six key drawings are made to set the style of the commercial. These drawings are usually done by an outside illustrator or someone from the animation studio's staff, not by the advertising agency.

Many well-known illustrators can be hired to make key drawings that will give your commercial a "look" stamped with a unique drawing style. These drawings will determine not only the look of the characters, but also the background style and colors.

Preparing Layouts

Next, working with tracing paper, the animation company makes layouts that spell out the entire action of the commercial. If it is a 30-second commercial, usually about 30 drawings are made at this stage. These pencil layouts follow the illustrator's style and suggest the final movement within the commercial.

Recording the Sound Track

At this point, the sound track is recorded. When recording the sound track, be sure the animation director is present. Because of years of experience in timing drawings against a sound track, this expertise is basic to the success of the commercial. During the session, the animation director may suggest speeding up a reading to fit the animated movements, or elongating a chord of music to allow more time for the action. To leave the director of animation out of the recording session is to court disaster in the final animation.

Most animators feel that an effective sound track is just as important as good visuals. If the sound track lacks rhythm or is hard to understand, the visuals will suffer. Keep in mind that when a TV program ends and a commercial comes on, the home viewer has several choices, only one of which is to watch your commercial. If your sound track doesn't grab the viewer from those other options in the initial two seconds, you've blown your chance to hold the viewer's attention through the rest of your commercial. When you capture attention with the opening of the sound track, the visuals will keep it through the balance of the commercial.

Reading the Sound Track

If the character speaks in synchronization with the sound track (called *lip-syncing*), the animator will be able to tell you whether the reading in the recording session is too fast or too slow. Remember, the drawings will be made from a reading of the track. This reading is a charted breakdown of each twenty-fourth of a second of the sound track. An exposure sheet with timings will be made by the animator as the frame-by-frame guide to what will happen in the final animation. In some cases, the editor does this for the animator.

The Pencil Test

The next step in frame-by-frame animation involves between 300 and 400 drawings made on tissue sheets from the original layouts. In the final commercial, up to 700 separate drawings will be needed for a 30-second commercial. These are now done in rough pencil form, and this shows overall movement. Held for two frames each (called "shooting in twos"), these rough drawings are filmed and become the next step in the animation process.

The filming of the rough pencil drawings becomes the "pencil test" that will be shown to the agency for approval or changes before the final animation is done. If changes are to be made, this is the stage to make them without great expense or loss of production time. In a way, the pencil test is to animation what a choice of takes of a scene is to live-action filming. It is the only stage at which changes of action or sequence can be made without great expense.

INKING AND PAINTING

Upon approval of the pencil test, the final animation begins and the inking starts. "Inkers" are meticulous copiers who trace the animation drawings onto transparent cels. In this process, the cels are lit from underneath. After the inking is done, the opaquer paints in the colors on the reverse side of the inked-in cels. We now have a series of painted layers, and each camera shot will be made with top light.

APPROVAL OF ANIMATION

After about ten weeks of intensive work, the animation is finished and ready for approval. To allow less time would mean working the animators over weekends at additional expense, as well as chancing a lowering of the quality of their work. This type of work can be quite tedious, and concentration begins to lag after normal working hours.

As with live-action production, there are less expensive ways to achieve full cel animation. It is not necessary to use a Hollywood source. Believe it or not, there are similar companies in other parts of the country, including Hellman Design Associates in Waterloo, Iowa. If the animation is quite simple and direct, considerable dollars can be saved by going to Iowa instead of California for full animation. I use them as an example of companies that do well and prosper for local and regional advertisers who can't afford the full Disney touch.

While New York and Los Angeles boast the most originality in animation design and style, they also have the highest prices. And while there are fewer companies producing animation than live action, you can find competent animation in many of the secondary cities.

Animated Graphics

Animated graphics takes a visual—any graphic, whether photographic or artwork—and brings it alive with frame-by-frame changes in the visual. If your idea can work without a lot of separate drawings within each frame, and if your basic art elements are already established, you won't need the expertise of a top-drawer designer and director of animation.

EXPLORATONS IN ANIMATION

"The Natural" was produced by Leo Burnett USA for United Airlines through Will Vinton Productions, Portland. A talented artist/animator, Joan Gratz, mixed clay with an oil-based thinner to a consistency similar to paint. In this state, it does not dry out. The technique then follows stop-motion production techniques. The original frame is created or "painted" and is then manually altered, frame by frame, 24 frames per second of finished film. Visual changes from landscapes to airplanes to the faces of United Airlines employees are made in a continuous flow. The sections of the commercial featuring human faces were created by working with SAG performers who had been photographed. Shooting took place over a four-month schedule. There were only two breaks built into the continuous flow, primarily to accommodate changes or client concerns if necessary, without the need to go back to the beginning and reshoot everything. This metamorphic animation in colorized clay represents a true breakthrough in the look and feel of a commercial. *Director/Artist/Animator: Joan Gratz/Will Vinton Productions, Portland. Music: Warner Chappell, Inc., arranged by Manny Mendelson/Comtrack, Chicago. Courtesy Leo Burnett, Chicago.*

Which takes us back to Waterloo, Iowa. Hellman Design Associates took one agency's idea and did a simple but effective job of animating a credit card for a chain of hardware stores. Staying completely within the artwork of the credit card itself, Hellman animated it into a tooth-edged saw to demonstrate that you could buy lumber with it, and into the head of a hammer to show that you could buy other building materials with the credit card as well.

There was relatively little movement to be drawn in each frame, and since the basic design of the credit card already existed, Hellman merely drew the cels to change the card into building tools. Other smaller cities have similar graphics companies. In these cases, you are not limited by the size of your budget, but by the size of your simple animated idea.

METAMORPHIC ANIMATION

Another type of animated graphic is referred to as *metamorphic animation*. It consists of using visual symbolism for words and thoughts. This offers the viewer a certain freedom to interpret the image in an individual way. Ironically, metamorphic animation is a throwback to the very earliest days of filmmaking. In 1910, a man named Windsor McCay used a series of sequential drawings to suggest a flow of motion. In so doing, he became an innovator long before character animation was developed and perfected by Disney artists.

This continuous visual flow is a frame-by-frame sequence that shows continual structural change, or change in form, with one graphic flowing directly into the next. Thus, there is a constant movement in the

LEO BURNETT COMPANY, INC.

UNITED AIRLINES

AS FILMED AND RECORDED (4/92) "Natural/Non-ESOP/CC" :60 UAPF1736

1. (MUSIC: UNDER THROUGHOUT)

2. ...

3. ...

4. ...

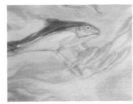
5. ...

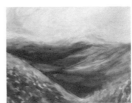
6. HACKMAN (VO): What is it that makes the world so great?

7. Is it the beauty we see everywhere we go? It is.

8. But probably, what really makes the world so great...

9. is people.

10. We think the same way about our airline.

11. United.

12. Come see what dedication is all about.

13. Come fly the friendly skies.

14. ...

15. ...

art elements from frame to frame. In the hands of a talented artist, this technique can be most interesting and highly individual.

One of the most stunning examples of this metamorphic approach to animation was achieved by Will Vinton Productions in Portland, Oregon. The commercial for United Airlines is called "The Natural." Using clay mixed with pigments of paint, small changes are made in every frame—24 frames per second—to flow from the face of one employee of United Airlines to another, and from the earth to the sky to a United Airlines plane in flight. The entire clay-and-pigment process took a full six months to accomplish. This is a long time, but the results are a monumental example of the modern use of metamorphic animation.

Computer Animation

There is a "newness" to old-style animation, which has been brought on by the wonders of combined movement within a computer. The computer animation process is referred to as CGI (Computer Graphic Imaging). Here is a description of how it works. The details apply specifically to Rhythm and Hues in Hollywood, a top practitioner of computer animation.

THE DESIGN PHASE

Most CGI projects start with a few color drawings or a storyboard. Character sketches and color drawings are passed back and forth until the entire storyboard is agreed upon. These commercials are usually not bid to more than one production house because of the necessity to work together from the conceptual stage right through to the finished commercial.

MODELING

When the design phase is approved, the characters must be entered into the computer in three dimensions so they can be manipulated and brought to life. Modeling can take a few minutes for a simple sphere, to as much as several weeks for a complicated figure like a dinosaur, which will have to be researched, sketched, and sculpted before it is entered into the computer.

Some types of flat elements can be traced using a sophisticated "mouse," which acts almost like a pencil. An animator will place the drawing on a mouse pad and actually trace the drawing using the mouse. This process is called *digitizing*. The information is then electronically transferred to the computer, which sets up rough coordinates for the element (e.g., a chair). The animator will then fill in the three-dimensional (3D) coordinates so that the chair looks like a 3D white line drawing on a black background. This is known as a "wire-frame" drawing.

THREE-DIMENSIONAL DIGITIZING

More complex figures may have to be entered into the computer using a process called three-dimensional digitizing. In this process, the entire figure is sculpted to its correct and exact proportions. The sculpture is then divided into segments using lines actually drawn on the sculpture with a pencil or pen. The animator painstakingly traces these lines and their coordinates into the computer, using a type of electronic pencil.

THE SHAPE LIBRARY

An animator can also build objects interactively in the computer using various proprietary software in what is referred to as a "shape library." A shape library is a form of storage where basic geometric shapes (spheres, squares, triangles, etc.) are already in the computer and can be used like line drawings, then built upon to create more complex figures.

The entire scene can thus be created using the wire-frame method, manipulated and moved about through space, then shot on film or videotape so the animators can see how the characters are placed and how they will move. This drawing in motion is referred to as an *animatic*.

CHOREOGRAPHY AND ANIMATION

The animatic is created using specialized software that can draw lines very quickly. The animator can instantly specify playback and change simple motion so it can be seen how the project will move and flow. Usually, several of these wire-frame animatics are viewed before approvals are finally given for the next step.

The rotation and translation of cameras and rigid objects is called *choreography*. Choreography shows the movement that will be filled in later. Usually, there is a beginning look at movement, in two or three jerky motions to sketch out the scene. This beginning choreography is used in creating the animatic.

The next step, animation, is where it really happens. This is where the characters are made to bend, flex, squash, and in other ways move to reflect the subtlety of living things.

CGI allows the animator to play with three-dimensional images. A realistic fighter jet can be made to fly, dive, and roll above a miniature city with no supports or restraints; a toaster can hop onto a kitchen counter. Or the computer animator can devise an absolutely photoreal 360-degree circlevision view of the city of Paris 200 years from now.

COLOR, LIGHTING, AND RENDERING

Now the scene is ready for color and lighting. The animator must tell the computer whether an element is red, blue, gold, or marble; opaque or transparent; shiny or dull. Certain aspects of lighting, such as highlights, reflections, and shadows, are sensitive to the positions and movements of cameras and elements in the scene. For that reason, most color and lighting decisions cannot be made until choreography and animation are finalized. Throughout these processes, low-resolution motion tests are presented for agency approvals. These tests show how various elements—reflections, transparency, liquids, and so forth—appear in motion.

Once the computer has the information on materials and lights, it can calculate what the colored, completed images will look like. Rendering is the process by which the computer takes all the information about a scene or object, performs all the calculations, and creates the image. From this point on, the images are referred to as "rendered" images. Because these calculations take time, the animator will choose a few key frames for color and lighting tests for agency approval. These frames are shot to film, with a variety of brightness and contrast choices to be made. When the color key frames are approved, the computer can calculate the lighting for the rest of the frames, based on the approved rendered image.

DIGITAL COMPOSITING

Compositing is the process by which various elements of a film are put together in order to create a coherent and fluid whole. In the past, elements of a commercial were composited by means of an optical printer, and that is the method that is traditionally used today. But it has its drawbacks. Essentially, an optical printer consists of a camera and one or two projector heads. Within the heads, two pieces of film can be sandwiched together to create one new image (e.g., a live-action basketball player and an animated basketball). The camera then shoots this new image onto another piece of film. Many of these passes may have to be made, depending on the complexity of the commercial.

With digital compositing, all the elements can be entered into the computer, manipulated, and combined any number of times, without any loss of quality. For instance, Rhythm and Hues did a commercial for Citibank called "Shrinking House." In it, the live-action scene of the house was made small, then larger, using animation techniques in the computer. This also allowed a live-action painter on a ladder to relate to the house in a real way as it changed in size and shape, without any degradation of the original image.

This is the magic of CGI: Once an element has been translated into numbers in the computer (the second generation), it can be combined any number of times without loss of quality. However, this can be an expensive process, requiring a very expensive film scanner and excellent proprietary software. But the results of a CGI commercial can be an amazing blend of any elements you might want to use, to create a world that has richness, color, diversity, and movement. (See Exhibit 11.2.)

To this point, the CGI discussion has related directly to Rhythm and Hues on the West Coast. But the geographic location of animation houses is also changing. In Minneapolis, Larry Lamb has been a leading innovator in computer-animated characters that have real personality and that combine in new ways with live-action footage.

In a commercial for General Mills Fruit Snacks, Lamb & Company took two-dimensional still photographs of children walking and talking; as they ate Fruit Snacks, they were transformed into 3D people. In order to accomplish this, Lamb & Company had to write new software and do a fair amount of experimentation. The new spirit that goes with these new techniques was described this way by Larry Lamb:

> Computer animation is such a collaborative process. It is not like a Cecil B. DeMille production with an autocrat at the top. It requires the best efforts of the lowliest and the highest person. They all have to work in harmony. In that regard, we are a "collective."

The use of computers with various types of animation has brought other cities into the production business. In Denver, Celluloid Studios uses computers to assist their cel animation. For Foote Cone & Belding, Chicago, Celluloid Studios produced commercials for Raid (a bug spray) that were based on cel animation but completed in computers. First cel drawings and animations of bugs were created, and to these were added layers of information in the computer, including a shadow layer and highlight layers, which are animated differently. Then all of this was shot on film and put together in the computer. It's a perfect marriage of live action and animation achieved within a computer.

Rotoscoping

The motion picture *Roger Rabbit* owed a great deal of its box-office success to a sophisticated combination of cel animation with live action. Animated characters appeared to go behind, around, and even through live-action characters. The combination of real people, real sets, and the animated Roger Rabbit cast was achieved by digitizing all the pictorial elements and combining them in a computer. This saved a great deal of time over the former way of combining such disparate elements. It also gave a remarkable clarity to the end product, thanks to the digital ability of computers to keep the elements in the "first generation." This

Exhibit 11.2

Computer Animation

Animation that originates and is developed in the computer represents a cutting-edge look at the animation process. Rhythm and Hues in California developed very individual commercials for Lexus, Reebok athletic shoes, MatchLight, and Miller Beer, shown here.
Courtesy Rhythm and Hues/Los Angeles.

particular combination of animation and live action saves more time than it does money. Be sure to price out your production before getting under way.

In Summary

Be aware that some of the examples in this chapter are quite expensive to produce, while others are relatively inexpensive. In the bargain basement of animation are the logos, packages, and credit cards that can be manipulated using known art elements, with cel animation added only as needed.

Going up the price scale, straight cel animation without complicated backgrounds or complex pictures is next in line. When the commercial is combined with disparate elements, such as live action that must be specially shot and full animation that must be drawn frame by frame, the price takes a sharp upward climb.

If you use new applications of various techniques (like the clay-and-pigment commercial for United Airlines), boundaries are being challenged, and you will invest both more time and more money. This would include today's CGI techniques, which may come down in price in the future as new software becomes available.

In any case, animation is improving in its variety and scope as more and more computer-minded artists come into the production picture. However, just because a commercial is a technical breakthrough does not automatically guarantee its success as a selling tool. The advertising business is not about camera tricks; it's about involving the buying viewers in a purchase situation. Often, this can be best accomplished with simplicity rather than technical derring-do. Keep this in mind when budget restrictions must be met.

12 VIEWING THE DAILIES

The production day is now over. Everything went well and there's good footage "in the can" (exposed negative film can, that is). It's the day after production, and it is now time to see whether or not the production day was a success. It's time to view the "dailies."

Viewing the dailies is the first time you will see the scenes filmed or taped during the production day. The purpose of dailies is to check on the photography, action, and lighting and to choose the "selects" (selected takes of each scene) from which the final edit and finished commercial will be made. There are two ways to view the film dailies:

1. By looking at prints from the film negative, either in a projection room or on a Kem flat-bed editing table. A Kem is the more personal viewing method. The film print is viewed on a monitor about the size of a small television set, and the film can be easily stopped and rolled back or forward for more detailed viewing.
2. By viewing a tape cassette made from the developed negative, which is then viewed by the editor and agency personnel. From this viewing, selected takes are chosen and then fed into a computer. The final editing is then done from the selected takes in the computer.

One advantage of producing on videotape is the opportunity during the production day to stop after each take, rewind the videotape, and check the take instantly. You can see immediately whether the scene has been taped to your satisfaction, However, a take that seems satisfactory right after shooting may not be ideal when viewed as part of the entire commercial. To see each take in context of the complete commercial, the entire day's taping is often viewed at the end of the day, obviating the need for a separate day to review the dailies.

This advantage of videotape production also exists to a certain extent when producing on film. Although the film negative will have to be developed before the take can be viewed and judged, most film productions include a video-assist camera, which records a tape copy as the scene is being filmed. This tape copy can be checked between takes. It is not a clean copy, but it is good enough for rough reference. In either instance, the film or tape must be examined so that choices can be made for the final edit of the commercial.

Looking at the Print from the Film Negative

Traditionally, the dailies are viewed from a one-light positive print from the camera negative. "One light" means that the film negative has been developed at one printing light, paying no particular attention to lighting effects that may call for special printing. This is done to speed up the process of preparing the dailies. This viewing will usually lead to a film edit. After the positive prints of the dailies have been viewed and takes selected, the editor physically edits the print into a rough-cut of the commercial, splicing each print scene to the next. The term *rough-cut* means exactly what it says: it is a fairly rough idea of how the commercial scenes should be cut together, in their proper length and correct order. Often this rough-cut film is then transferred to a 3/4-inch cassette for agency and client viewing.

Looking at Dailies on Videotape

The second method of viewing dailies is to develop the film negative and then transfer the negative picture to a videotape cassette. This 3/4-inch cassette is then viewed by the editor and agency creatives, and the selects are chosen. The editor types into the computer a log of the selects, and the selects in turn are fed into a computer. In this current mode, dailies are viewed on a monitor about the size of TV screen. This is the first step in using the computer to edit the scenes into a final cut. We will discuss this mode later in this chapter.

In either method, the original film negative is then put aside, not be touched until the final steps of finishing the commercial. Now back to viewing the dailies, in either mode.

The Script Clerk's Log

The script clerk has made a complete log of everything that has been shot. This log also records the "takes" the director considered to be best. This log is used as a guide in viewing the dailies.

There is one cardinal rule to remember: If there is a question about whether a particular take should be considered, hang onto it. The time involved in looking at an additional take for the final edit is well worth it.

In the case of sound takes, the script clerk must also match the log with the sound operator's log for "accepted takes." The sound at this point is separate from the picture if film was used during the production day. If the dailies are viewed on film, the sound track will have to be synced up (i.e., synchronized) with the picture so the sound can be checked as well as the accompanying picture.

The script clerk's log should include the following:

- Names of the production company, director, and camera person
- Title of the spot
- Names of the agency and agency producer
- Camera roll number (motion picture film comes in 100-foot and 400-foot rolls)
- Scene number and sound slate number
- Length of scene and footage of the shot
- Basic action and comments of the director

These comments might be written as "Looks like a good take," or "The action was different but it might be interesting." These comments will become important in making choices in the screening of the dailies. The script clerk's main function is to keep track of all the director's comments and to write them down, as well as to write down the take number, scene number, etc.

Who Attends the Screening of the Dailies?

The editor is there. The editor does the work of putting the various takes in their proper order and editing them to the exact length for the finished commercial. The editor will have the script clerk's log and notes.

The director also attends, unless already on a new production assignment. The director will want to see the results of the shooting day and make comments about which takes he or she prefers. Some directors (bless their hearts) will stay with a commercial right through to the final edit, putting a stamp of approval on the final result.

The agency producer is present, as well as the writer and/or art director. But there is usually no one representing client or account management. Again, because every agency functions differently, this lineup at the screening of the dailies varies. The number should be kept at a minimum. As the old saw goes, "Too many cooks spoil the broth." Too many opinions are not needed here.

What to Look for in the Dailies

Screening the dailies for the first time can be a very confusing and somewhat frustrating experience. The following pointers may allay some concerns.

The scenes were probably not shot in a chronological sequence, for all sorts of practical production-day reasons. Therefore, the dailies will not be seen in their correct order. The takes of each scene must be looked at for their own worth. This will take a bit of practice. Also, the takes will be much too long. (Once more, a "take" is the filming of a particular scene. Each scene may have three or more takes, so the effort is to choose the best take in looking at the dailies.)

Because the scenes are not viewed in order, it is a good idea to have the storyboard handy. Be sure the scenes on the storyboard are properly numbered, and then check them off against the slates at the beginning of each new scene. This will be a reassurance that all the scenes have been shot and nothing has been left out.

Each take will be seen from camera start to camera stop. This means that everything seen by the camera and heard by the sound equipment will be up there: the slate, the voice of the assistant director reading the slate (if it is a sound take), all the camera work before the scene begins, and the run-out footage after the scene ends, right up until the camera is turned off. Because of this overshooting, many things look like they won't fit together.

That's where the editor comes in. The editor determines whether, within the selected takes, there is the action necessary to complete the commercial. If there is any doubt, the editor should be asked how it will work. The editor can usually do this verbally. As the dailies are viewed, the editor makes notes on what is seen and heard. For instance, if the director says, "Did you see that head-turn? I wonder if that would help emphasize the copy line?" The editor will duly mark that take for possible use in the final edit.

A good editor knows many tricks. Starting with the overall viewpoint and objective of the commercial, the editor will match the editing style to that objective. It is possible that, after viewing the dailies, the editor will suggest a retake in order to make the action fit together perfectly from one scene to the next. If the director and agency agree, such a retake can be obtained on a "down" day (i.e., a day when there is no production scheduled). Or that retake might be made on another short shooting day. Retakes are expensive, particularly if on-camera talent is involved. They shouldn't be taken lightly. But if improved action demands it, then a retake is advisable.

As you look at the dailies, you will learn the importance of all those close-ups and reaction shots that were made. Time after time, you will see a move, a smile, a hand movement that would enhance the commercial, but it won't "action-cut." (The action from one scene won't match the action going into the next scene). However, by using those close-ups and tight reactions, it may be possible to insert a reaction shot or a product close-up, and, in the following scene, return to the original edit. If done carefully, this can smooth out the edit without doing violence to the overall action or necessitating any reshooting.

The dailies are the first chance to see everything that was printed or transferred. From this point on, the steps will represent fine-tuning the finished edit. It is important to be sure that the dailies are complete.

It is customary to run through the dailies at least twice to double-check your selected takes. Following the screening, the editor packs up all the dailies and goes to work putting the final 45 feet of 35mm film together for a 30-second commercial (or 18 feet if shot on 16mm film).

Viewing the Film Dailies in a Computer

The development of computerized editing and finishing reaches back into the actual screening of the dailies. From this point on, we will be using new buzzwords having to do with the use of the computer in viewing the dailies and in editing and finishing the commercial. To cut down on the confusion of technical names and systems, let me define a few of these buzzwords.

DIGITIZING

The ability to take both picture and sound elements and store them in a computer to be retrieved as computerized elements instead of physical film or tape elements is known as digitizing. The digitized dailies are edited in the computer via commands typed by the editor.

RANDOM ACCESS-NONLINEAR

Digitized elements can be instantly retrieved and brought up on a screen in any order, simply by typing commands into the computer from a keyboard. This is *random access* to the pictures and sound tracks, and editing is done in a *nonlinear* mode. Different takes can be instantly viewed in any order desired.

D1, D2, D3, ETC.

D stands for digital (computerized) video. The developed film negative can be transferred to these various systems, but for differing reasons.

D1 is similar to the 35mm negative: All the information, including all the colors, are there in their most original form. D1 is what you will need to do visual effects. To compare it with film editing, D1 is where you would start (with a film negative) for a film optical. These effects and opticals can be added, changed, and amended, all in the first generation, D1 is *not* a copy, it is the computer's version of the original negative.

D2 is like a 35mm film print. You get a good representation of what is on the negative, but it is not the negative. D2 is great for editorial work where the artistic element is in the editing of the original filming, not in the addition of visual effects.

The additional "D" numbers are further refinements and variations of D1 and D2. For example, D3 is like D2, except on smaller tape. It is wise to consult your editorial house for further counsel and clarification, because new equipment continues to be developed. The wise editor is the one who doesn't speak in computer jargon. If there is any basic problem with this computerized method of editing, it is the confusion of terms as new equipment and computer programs continue to be developed.

LOADING THE FILM NEGATIVE INTO THE COMPUTER

Step 1

The 3/4-inch dailies are transferred from the original developed film negative onto cassettes. The sync audio is also transferred.

Step 2

The original 3/4-inch videotape dailies are viewed by the editor and client (agency creative personnel), and the selection of preferred takes is made.

Step 3

The editor types this information (scene and take number) into the computer to create a log file of preferred takes. This log file can be printed out, and it becomes the running record of the various take options available for editing. Using this log file, the editor can call up specific scenes and takes from the computer.

The computer system then automatically loads in the select material from the 3/4-inch dailies cassettes, playing back each scene as its video and audio elements are fed into the computer and captured in real time. (If the take is 15 seconds long, it will take 15 seconds to load the take into a hard disk in the computer.)

This loading into the computer (or digitizing) is rather time-consuming. It is one of the few current drawbacks to the nonlinear editing process. Future developments will probably correct this flaw.

In this procedure, the selected takes from the original developed negative have been loaded into the computer *but not edited*. All editorial decisions will be made from the computer's first-generation copies of that negative. The original developed negative is stored away in its original, pristine state.

In Summary

The screening of the dailies is a most important step in producing a commercial, whether done with a one-light film print from the developed camera negative or from tapes transferred from the developed negative and then fed into a state-of-the-art computer system. Viewing the dailies will answer these vital questions:

1. Do we have all the footage we need to edit the commercial?
2. In the opinion of the editor, is there sufficient picture and sound coverage to make a smooth edit?
3. If not, is a reshoot of some of the material necessary?
4. Is the product handled and photographed correctly? If not, should there be additional insert photography scheduled?

The next step in the production process is working with the editor to achieve either a rough-cut on film or, if working with computers, an almost-finished edit of the commercial. It is at this point that the art of commercial-making really takes over, because the feeling, intent, and overall selling force of the final commercial is achieved in the editing and finishing of the picture and sound track.

13 EDITING THE COMMERCIAL

In this chapter, we will first discuss briefly the traditional method of editing film. Most of our attention, however, will be directed at the changes that have revolutionized editing processes and have shaped the future of editing TV commercials.

Editing is the selection, assembly, and rearranging of the best footage that comes from the shooting day. How much footage is shot for the average 30-second commercial? The answer depends on the type of commercial being produced. For example, a commercial consisting mostly of dialog will obviously not represent as many feet of film as one composed of impressions and vignettes edited to a prerecorded music or sound effects track.

Typically, for a 30-second dialog commercial on 35mm film, the production company normally budgets between 4,000 and 5,000 feet of original negative to be shot and developed. This allows for many takes of each scene, and the camera runs much longer than each scene will run in the final edit. For a commercial with many scenes that will be edited to an existing sound track, as much as 16,000 feet of film negative may be estimated. A montage shoot may include many scenes that will never be used in the final edit. (A *montage* is a rapid succession of film images to express a selling idea.) Do you realize what this means to the editor? From all that footage, the editor must condense the film down to 45 feet for a 30-second commercial! (In 35mm film, 45 feet equals 30 seconds of time.)

Productions shot on videotape rather than on film use far less footage. The reason is that each scene can be played back immediately after shooting and rejected if not acceptable. Only acceptable takes are needed in post-production. Unacceptable takes can be erased and the tape reused for the next take, if economy is key. This makes the final assembly a much easier task with videotape as compared to film.

Traditional Film Editing

In a film production involving up to 16,000 feet of film, the traditional method involves developing as many scenes as are deemed worthwhile and physically separating the selected film takes from the rest of the

157

footage. The outtakes (takes not used in the original edit) are not thrown away, but are saved for possible later use. A trim (a short piece of film from the head or tail, or beginning or end, of a take) may be used.

Once the positive film clips are selected, they are arranged visually on pins that feed down into a cloth bin, where they are labeled. Editors then cut the selected section out of the clip, splice it to the preceding scene of film, and trim it. This process is time-consuming because of the physical handling and editing of each piece of positive film.

In this traditional method, the various takes are hung up, pulled down, viewed, spliced, assembled, projected, and checked on an editing device such as the Kem. The Kem is a flatbed editing table with the positive film running laterally and viewed on a rear-projected screen slightly smaller than a TV screen as the scenes are spliced together.

Although this method is labor-intensive, it is still relatively inexpensive if the commercial is a straightforward picture edit. For this reason, many commercials will continue to be edited in this manner.

The major disadvantage to traditional editing occurs when the commercial includes special visual effects. Not only is this type of optical work expensive, it is also time-consuming. In this mode all special visual effects must be achieved in a separate optical house or video post-production facility after all physical film editing is completed.

Editing by Computer

The introduction of computers in the editing process has opened up an entirely new way of achieving an edit—and a finished commercial. Basically, once the developed negative film images have been processed into the computer, the actual negative is not touched again until the final assembly, after all the editing and finishing decisions have been made.

In Chapter 12, we defined such words as *digitizing, random access, nonlinear, D1,* and *D2.* I will do my best to keep the computer jargon to a minimum and explain the operation in basic English. Toward that end, whenever a new trade-name is brought up, I will define it. I hope, this will make it easier for you to enter the computerized edit suite and contribute to the editing and finishing of the commercial.

The first step in computer editing is to take the original camera negative, have it developed, and then have 3/4-inch videotape cassettes made of that footage. Next, the agency and editor sit down in front of a TV monitor and view this footage. As acceptable takes are viewed, the editor types code names into a host computer, and that footage is thus converted from the 3/4-inch tape copy of the original negative into the computer's memory.

This is the beginning of editing your material in a mode that will not disturb the original negative (which will not be involved in the edit).

Because of the computer's ability to retain all the clarity of the original film negative, layer after layer of visual and sound information can be added to the edit within the computer without affecting picture or sound quality.

At this point, the newcomer to computerized finishing should feel free to ask any questions that come to mind. More and more of the editing and finishing houses that rely heavily on the random-access abilities of the computer are taking the time and energy to explain to the neophyte what is going on. Without the helpful advice of these technical experts, the whole process can become mumbo-jumbo to the uninitiated.

Before editing begins, it is a good idea to actually schedule a "prepro" meeting with the editor so time can be spent discussing the best way to approach the edit for that particular commercial. When an editor uses technical terms, ask for a translation. Buzzwords often get in the way. It is better to explain to the editor what the hoped-for end product will be and to let the editor figure out how to get there.

The editing of many commercials can benefit from the marvels of nonlinear editing, with the ability to quickly change scene sequences (random access). Such commercials should be edited and finished on an Avid Media Composer or an E-Pix. (See Exhibit 13.1.) These and similar systems are able to manipulate the video and audio information in the computer. The editor types in edit commands in a manner similar to using a word processor. Also, rather than punching time-code numbers into a keyboard, the editor may work with actual frames of video on a preview screen and manipulate them by pointing a light pen.

The editor should work with the machine he or she is comfortable with. Agency creatives don't have to understand the difference between an Avid and an E-Pix. The choice of systems should be at the editor's discretion. All the nonlinear systems are similar. There are minor differences between systems, and they continue to become more sophisticated as time goes by and new computer programs are added.

An interesting aspect of this computer revolution in editing is that the finishing of a commercial becomes a continuing part of the edit. Rather than achieving the edit then turning the materials over to an optical house, the entire process from edit through to finished commercial is becoming part of a one-stop operation. This is particularly true in the major production centers of New York, Los Angeles, San Francisco, Chicago, Atlanta, and Miami.

It is possible to walk into such editorial houses with the developed camera negative and walk out a few days later with fully realized, high-quality, ready-for-broadcast videotapes. Thus, the process of editing, mixing, and finishing, which used to take weeks, can now be accomplished in a few days.

Exhibit 13.1

The Avid in Use

Foote Cone & Belding Executive Producer Jim Martin watches as the editor for
Avenue Edit in Chicago works editing magic with the Avid Media Composer. Using
such a digital editing system, a finished edit that formerly took days to produce can be
completed in less than an hour. All visual and audio materials have been entered into
a computer, and the edit is accomplished and played back in real time.
Courtesy Avenue Edit, Chicago, and Avid Technology.

THE COMPUTERIZED EDITING/FINISHING PROCESS

Editing begins with the making of 3/4-inch videotape transfers of the
developed film negative and the transfers of sync audio (the on-camera
dialog that must match the picture) from the original 1/4-inch tape to
DAT (Digital Audio Tape).

The videotape cassettes of the dailies are then screened by the
editor and agency personnel, and the editor types in the information
to create a log file of the selected material. This material is then
automatically loaded into the computer, and both picture and sound

are ready to be played back from their stored position on hard disks. Voiceover tracks and all other audio elements are also entered into the computer system in the same manner.

A SET OF DAILIES FOR THE FILM CONFORMER

Often, a second set of dailies cassettes is made at the same time with "window burn-in" of the time code. The window consists of a series of rolling numbers in the lower part of the visual which represent the time code, similar to edge numbers on negative film. These windows help the negative conformer to find the exact matching picture and track. The conformer only enters the process near the very end, when the original negative is re-introduced to make the final picture composite.

These duplicate time-coded cassettes are not used by the editor, because the burn-in windows obscure too much of the visible picture. Again, they are used by negative conformers to cross-reference negative material during the final compositing process.

THE EDITING PROCESS WITHIN A COMPUTER

Back to the editor, who has now entered the selects, or preferred takes, into the computer system. This loading-in, or digitizing process, is time-consuming. It is currently one of the few drawbacks of the nonlinear editing process. As time goes by, this process will also be speeded up, as new programs are added to the computer.

From here on, the editing process is quite straightforward. The editor types in commands from a keyboard (or using a mouse, light pen, or trackball). The edit is now seen on a screen, with the scenes in the desired order. You now have what amounts to the first edit. (Sound elements are synced in the same manner).

At any time, the system can play back the edited material in real time on the computer monitor, although presently the picture quality is not the very best. Future refinements will undoubtedly correct this shortcoming.

The edited material, or sequence, is really just a collection of typed-in instructions to the system to play certain scenes in a certain order, and this can be amended and changed at any time. Whenever the editor wishes, this sequence can be brought out of the computer and onto a 3/4-inch videocassette for presentation to the agency or client. If it has been approved, the cassette can also be used for music post-scoring or track-mixing sessions.

Because of the sophistication of these computer systems, the rough-cuts don't have to be rough. The editor can include dissolves, picture speedups, picture slowdowns, graphics, titles, and sophisticated sound and music mixes, all created within the computer.

If a very finished rough-cut is desired for client presentation or focus-group testing, the system can produce an EDL (Edit Decision List) disk of the requested sequence. The editor may take this disk to an online editing suite and go directly online to the original material on 3/4-inch cassettes. There, a test version of the commercial can be conformed from the 3/4-inch dailies cassettes. As the picture quality of the digital offline system improves, this intermediate rough-cut will not be necessary.

It is possible to create a variety of rough-cut edits for client presentation. This can be done directly from the computer system onto 3/4-inch cassettes without optimum picture quality. This is both a blessing and a bane. The blessing is that these additional versions can be achieved in a matter of minutes. The bane is that, in post-production, too many cooks spoil the commercial, and each additional edit may weaken rather than strengthen the end result.

Once a cut is approved in a one-stop editing/finishing house, the editor will make one or more 3/4-inch videocassettes of the approved rough-out for use in the final mix sessions. In such a facility, these mixing sessions can be accomplished right down the hall in another editing suite. If the editing is done with a separate company, you would then take the cassettes to a recording studio, which would mix the tracks.

In either case, floppy diskettes will be prepared containing the picture and sound Edit Decision List for use by the negative conformer and the online editor during the final picture and sound conforming. Remember, this is the only time the original negative comes back into play.

If the commercial has been edited to a prerecorded and premixed audio track, the sound conforming will not be necessary. The finished track will be striped (transferred) directly to the master videotape during the online video session. Otherwise, the editor will present the original audio elements to the audio mixer. The editor will fill out a chart listing the various sound tracks and when they are introduced into the final mix. Usually, the music will precede the voice audio, and the chart gives the exact point (in real time, or film length) when the various tracks enter and leave the audio mix.

As the computer systems become more sophisticated, edited sound elements are transferred onto DAT (Digital Audio Tape) or 1/4-inch sound tape, directly from the computer offline system. The mixer will also get an EDL (Edit Decision List) disk of the commercial, a paper printout of the EDL file, and a 3/4-inch cassette of the rough-cut.

Chapters 14 and 15 will cover the computerized effects that have become such an integral part of some commercials, including the use of the computer in live-action filming, cel animation, and various types of computer graphics.

Exhibit 13A

AVID MEDIA COMPOSER 2000

The editing and finishimg of commercials has been collapsed into one operation with the advent of computer-driven equipment like the Avid Media Composer 2000, shown here. This equipment runs in conjunction with the Macintosh Quadra computer, and both picture and sound can be edited from digital information that has been entered into the computer.

Not only can you preview both picture and sound (using either a mouse, a track ball, or the keyboard), but also editorial changes can be made swiftly, without in any way affecting the original materials entered into the computer. The edit-and-assemble monitor on the left includes a visual timeline, providing a graphic blueprint of the commercial, with tracks for video edits and graphic and audio elements. The screen on the right is the "bin monitor," showing frames from film or tape clips to be edited. They can be dragged over to the edit-and-assemble monitor.

Courtesy Avid Technology, Inc. Tewksbury, Massachusetts.

Finishing the Audio Elements

Although Chapter 7 covers music in detail, some mention of audio post-production is necessary here. Most of the audio post-production is achieved using digital audio workstations. They bear such names as AMS Audiofile and Solid State Logic ScreenSound.

These workstations store audio information on computer hard disks; access to their multitrack audio information is achieved by typing in commands on a keyboard. The latest generation of workstations also provides mixing and processing functions. However, many sound studios still use traditional analog (undigitized) sound mixing consoles for multitrack mixing to a final sound mix.

Digital sound workstations can store several hours of sound, with the ability to play 16 or even 24 simultaneous tracks with sound quality superior to a compact disc. This allows a one-stop editing finishing facility to finish the track mix as well as the final picture edit. Stereo-mixing is commonplace, and multichannel surround-sound mixes are often produced for special-event telecasts such as championship baseball or football telecasts.

An EDL (Edit Decision List) is originated for all audio elements, and that EDL disk is fed into the digital machine. This instructs the machine to load all the necessary material from the original audio elements. They will be correctly synchronized (timed) from the information on the EDL.

As you can see, whther working with visual or sound elements in the computer, the Edit Decision List is the key element in the whole process. This list has all the salient information needed to instruct the computer.

The audio workstation can be quite sophisticated. In addition to synchronizing the playback of the 3/4-inch picture rough-cut with the playback of the conformed audio elements, it is also possible to slide the sound elements in relation to the picture. Also, in the mixing console, the mixer will adjust levels, giving equalization and perspective as wished to the various sound elements.

The audio mix is repeatedly played back against the picture until all desired adjustments have been made. Then the final copy of this composite sound mix is laid off to Digital Audio Tape (DAT), 1/4-inch tape, or some other audio master.

If the final video master is available at the audio mix session, then that master may be striped to the video master directly from the audio workstation. In order to save wear and tear on the video master, it is never used as the picture reference during the audio mix session. If a digital videotape format is used for the master (i.e., through a computer editing system), the final mix will thus effectively be of first-generation quality.

Conforming the Picture

Conforming the picture means to go back to the original, exposed and developed camera negative and to separate out the negatives of scenes that will be used in the final edit. KeyCode, Kodak's new barcode standard for printing machine-readable key numbers on film stock, can greatly speed up the process of negative conforming. There are also software programs (OSC/R is one) that help conformers translate the Edit Decision List information that has been supplied by the editor.

Using the key numbers thus supplied, the selected takes can be quickly found. In TV commercial work, selected takes are usually pulled flash-to-flash (from the very beginning to the very end of the take). This is done for safety's sake, because there may be later revisions that will lengthen the scene.

If you have not used computerized editing and finishing, after conforming the picture, the opticals and effects would be added in a video post-production room. This method adds at least a generation to the picture and sound track.

In Summary

There is, in my opinion, a big drawback to the digital editing and finishing of a commercial: Just because you can achieve an edit quickly, the temptation is to come up with three or four other additional edits. Suddenly, instead of a "recommended" edit, you have a "take-your-pick" situation, which, in my opinion, tends to water down the final commercial. I urge you not to fall victim to the unfortunate syndrome in which everyone feels entitled to do an individual edit. I have seen productions where there were as many as six different versions of the original edit: one each from the director, editor, producer, creative director, art director, and, yes, the client, (to say nothing of the client's upstairs boss!).

Unfortunately, as each edit evolves, there is often a diminution of selling effectiveness. To my mind, editing is not a democratic process. It is not to be voted on by everybody, with each vote counting equally. Editors are truly talented individuals who understand not only the flow of action, but also the advertising thrust of the material.

In almost every instance, the first thoroughly thought out edit is the best. From there on, the road often leads downhill to conformity. So whether you edit from a one-light film print, splicing each scene and adding opticals and effects later, or do it all in the computer, the main person in the scheme is the editor. The editor is not only a trained techician, but also an artist. Editors are well worth consulting during the editing and finishing process of your commercial.

14 COMPUTERS AND SPECIAL EFFECTS

As I have mentioned in several previous chapters, the most important new word in today's commercial-making vocabulary is *digital*. Digital technology is used in commercial production to simplify the editing and finishing process for both images and sound. Traditionally, both the picture and sound elements were physically edited and spliced by a film editor. In contrast, the digital technique involves transferring the original photographic and/or sound elements (whether on film, videotape, or sound tape) into a computer, where they can be stored and retrieved as computerized elements instead of as physical segments of film or tape.

The tremendous advantage to digitizing the production elements is that all the picture and sound information that has been so transferred will stay in the "first generation." That means there will be no loss of clarity or definition, no matter how often the images or sounds are duplicated into the computerized material. What you will see is not a copy; it is the original generation of the material, over and over again. This ability is the one factor that has made the computer vital to all aspects of commercial production. Furthermore, the elements can now be put in any sequence or altered in any fashion without damaging the original digitized material stored in the computer.

As a means of explaining the specific applications of this digital technology in the production of commercials, let's discuss some commercials that have used it to tremendous effect. Bear in mind that these are merely examples of a continually expanding list of visual and sound possibilities. New software is continually being written to create specific shooting and editorial effects.

Use of First-Generation Elements in Commercial Production

Henry Sandbank is a true pioneer of commercial production. With an outstanding background as a still photographer, he continues to use his knowledge of the craft and his respect for light in the making of TV commercials.

Sandbank is also on the leading edge of computerized production technology, but he qualifies such use with this statement: "The ultimate goal is to make people believe what they see." Digital production is truly the art that conceals the art.

In a series of commercials for Purina dog foods, Sandbank filled the screen with 30 dogs running, sitting, and turning their heads in perfect synchronization, but only one dog was filmed. (See Exhibit 14.1.) Sandbank described the production process as follows:

> The process was shooting a single take of a dog doing whatever we wanted him to do. The dog was filmed by three cameras set up in this particular situation at the middle, back and foreground, so that there were three points of view. We predesigned each scene to know where each dog would be.
>
> The whole trick in reproducing 30 dogs in one scene is to add one dog at a time. It is an additive process done digitally. In an analog situation [without using the computer's ability to stay in the first generation], the images would have deteriorated as we repeated them in final assembly. But digitally, you lose nothing.

Sandbank worked in conjunction with a company called CIS (Composite Image Systems) in post-production. During production, the dog was shot against a blue screen, which cancels out the background, so that the process of adding the other dogs could be achieved. Lighting also played a part. The dog was backlit to keep the blue screen from reflecting on the dog.

A tremendous amount of preplanning went into this commercial production but, as Sandbank said, "Once we had filmed the dog, it was just repeat, repeat, repeat." And because of the computer's ability to keep this material in the first generation, one dog eventually became 30, each doing exactly the same thing, in original photography, and as clear as a bell. Without the ability to digitize the filming of one dog, each additional layer of images would have been slightly worse than the last. In other words, the image of the 30th dog would be 29 film generations away from the original photography.

Morphing and Motion Control

The word *morph* is a contraction of the word *metamorphosis*, which, according to *Webster's Collegiate Dictionary*, means "a change of physical form, structure, or substance esp. by supernatural means." In nature, the physical change of a caterpillar into a butterfly or a tadpole into a frog are types of metamorphoses.

In commercials, this magical quality was first found in the artist's ability to draw an object and, in a series of drawn cels, make subtle changes to create another object in a continuous flow of images.

Exhibit 14.1

How to Make One Puppy Look Like a Bunch

The task before Henry Sandbank was to film a single puppy for Ralston Purina Puppy
Chow and turn him into a screen full of puppies all doing the same thing. Sandbank
says, "The whole trick in reproducing 30 dogs in one scene is to add one dog at a time.
It is an additive process, done digitally." Three cameras were used, running in sync. In
an analog post-production situation, each dog image would deteriorate. But, done
digitally, nothing is lost. All dogs (really one dog multiplied) stay in the first
generation of film footage.
*Director: Henry Sandbank. Editor: Stuart Waks. Compositing by CIS (Computer Image
Systems). Courtesy Fallon McElligott.*

With the computer's ability to digitize all sorts of visual information, morphing is now applied to live-action images. Cars become
running tigers; trucks become race cars; and, yes, a small boy's face can
be aged to that of an 80-year-old man in two seconds.

One of the most striking early examples of morphing was seen in
the Michael Jackson MTV video "It's Black—It's White." Close-ups of
young people singing the song would morph from a girl to a boy, from a
man to a woman, from a black to a white. The faces were in perfect
register, and the transitions were seamless and striking.

Motion control is used in combination with morphing. Again, thanks to the computer, the exact camera exposures, shooting speed, focus, zoom, and dolly moves can be duplicated from one live-action shot to another. This motion-control capability allows the footage of the two separate but perfectly matched sequences to be fed into a computer, combined, and changed in a manner never before possible.

This synthesis can combine real actors with animated characters (as in the feature film *Roger Rabbit*) and real sets with artificial environments. But by introducing morphing into this motion-control process, even more amazing combinations can be realized.

Pacific Data Images, using this combination of motion control and morphing, was able to symbolize the power of Exxon gasoline by having a car, driving up a mountain road, transform itself into a running tiger in a little more than two seconds. The only problem with effects like this is that they become fads, and, as fads, they quickly fade from the public consciousness. Too often, such commercials become all form and no content. It takes fresh and new ideas to apply these techniques without the techniques taking over or becoming jaded.

When the idea is strong, the techniques fit into the commercial and explain the idea even more vividly. Such was the case with a production from ILM (Industrial Light & Magic), a division of Lucas Films (remember *Star Wars?*).

ILM's executive producer, Tom Kennedy, says ILM always looks for the best way to produce a project, based on its knowledge of the concept and the equipment available. Take, for example, the case of a commercial for Reebok tennis shoes, called "Talking Tennis Balls." The creative idea was to show a tennis player hitting practice balls propelled from a practice machine. Each of the balls would have the face of an unpleasant person she had encountered recently. Kennedy said that two options were considered: (1) using live-action actors who could shape their own performances and (2) using computer control, which would take a lot of rendering time to shape less-than-human performance.

The decision was to go with the first option, using live actors' faces on the various tennis balls. As each ball came toward the racket, the actor's face continued to talk, and the tennis racket smashed each in a freeze-frame of facial surprise. (See Exhibit 14.2.) It became a classic example of working with various pieces of running footage and auditory material, all manipulated in real time in a computer.

Imaging and Imagination

The Eastman Kodak Company further expanded the digital horizons with a commercial for the Olympic Summer Games of 1992. The creative idea was to show 20,000 people in a stadium flipping up photographic cards, which combined to make huge photographic murals. But to

Exhibit 14A

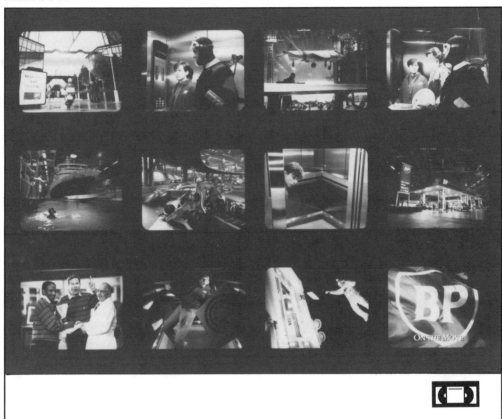

ANIMATION — GOING UP

A most spectacular application of motion-picture effects in today's digital world involves a 60-second international commercial for British Petroleum. The commercial is seen through the eyes of a delivery boy who is delivering a pizza to the BP Research Center. As the elevator rises, it stops at several floors, where he sees unbelieveable tests going on.

The elevator door opens at the "Marine Fuel Research" floor to reveal a full-scale ocean liner steaming along, as well as speedboats and a deep-sea diver. When the door opens on the "Aviation Fuel Research" floor, the huge area is filled with zooming jet-propelled helicopters.

He delivers the pizza to the top floor, labeled "Space Research," and a weightless astronaut catches the pizza box as it floats by.

These space-age visuals are achieved with matte paintings, which make a small building appear 10 stories high and each floor seem cavernous. Three or four layers of live-action photography are composited to show a complete auto racecourse, with live-action race cars.

Director: Matthew Robins, I.L.M. West Coast. Creative Director/Writer: John DeCerchio. Creative Director/Art Director: Gary Wolfson. Producer: Sheldon Cohn. Associate Producer: Allyson Raynes. Courtesy WB Doner, Detroit.

Exhibit 14.2

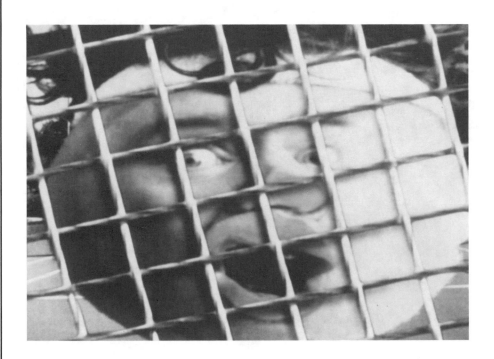

Talking Tennis Balls

Industrial Light & Magic in San Rafael, California, turned to the computer for a
Reebok commercial to combine a tennis ball flying toward a tennis racket with the
faces of obnoxious people on each tennis ball. The faces react violently when hit by
the tennis racket.
Courtesy Industrial Light & Magic.

actually photograph such a huge crowd at night would pose some in-
surmountable financial and logistical problems. First, the cost of hiring
20,000 extras would make the commercial cost prohibitive. And finding
a stadium that could be taken over for more than a week at dusk was in
itself a logistical nightmare.

To help control talent costs and get a good worldwide ethnic mix
in the crowd, the filming was done in an empty stadium in Argentina.
And thanks to the futuristic abilities of R/Greenberg & Associates of
New York City, the spectacular commercial was accomplished with only
200 card-flippers in the stands.

To achieve the illusion of the huge crowd, R/Greenberg shot
still photographs of various athletic events. The negatives were then
recorded onto a photo CD (digitized picture information on a compact

Exhibit 14.3A

Kodak's "Let the Memories Begin"

How do you make 200 extras in an empty stadium in Buenos Aires, Argentina, look like a football crowd of 20,000? Here are about 100 of the actors holding up flip cards, from a much larger computer-generated flip-card scene.

disc). This put the still photographs into a digital format. By taking this computerized step, the film's tremendously high resolution was maintained. The photographs could not only be enhanced, but also altered. For instance, the smiling face of a little girl was substituted for a more serious look, and the alteration was absolutely unnoticeable.

When each photo in the photo CD was finally approved, the negatives were enlarged eight times and made into a huge mural print, each enlargement being 4 feet by 24 feet. Recall that each photo originated on 35 mm film. Thanks to digitizing, all the detail and richness of color was maintained in the huge enlargement.

The enlargements were then processed, mounted, and laminated. They were then cut into pieces 2 feet square, and seat and row numbers were written on the back of each. These 200 pieces were given to the

Exhibit 14.3B

This is the entire group of 200 Argentinian film extras, which formed a crowd of 20,000 in the computer.

200 people sitting in the otherwise empty stands, and the card-flip rehearsal began. Eight different photographic blow-up scenes were thus filmed in the stadium. The negatives of the running footage were sent to the CGI (Computerized Graphic Images) department at R/Greenberg. The original flip-card negatives were recorded into a computer. This digitized format meant that all images could be altered, enlarged, and repeated. As a result, insead of 200 people in an otherwise empty stadium, the stadium was now filled with 20,000 people!

It was not as simple as I have just stated; many hours were spent to get the final picture. However, none of it could have been accomplished without the combined abilities of a new breed of young filmmakers and the first-generation abilities of digitized video material.

An interesting sidelight to digital production is that, if anything, the computer is too perfect. Digital images border on being cold and

Exhibit 14.3C

Here the extras hold up flip cards cut from a huge Kodak enlargement of a runner breaking the tape.

without emotion. With that fact in mind, as R/Greenberg built the card-flipping scenes, some of the cards were delayed in the computer, or even not turned at all, so it would look "human" and not mechanical. (See Exhibit 14.3.)

If you opt to go the computerized direction, bring money. Lots of money. As with most production techniques, there is a right way and a cheaper way to go. The right way is expensive; there is usually an inexpensive way to achieve a similar result, but with an overall loss in quality.

For example, before the advent of computerized and digitized images, I produced a similar commercial for Kentucky Fried Chicken with a group of 75 extras filing into the empty Rose Bowl Stadium. I had purchased stock footage from the National Football League showing a stadium full of people. Colonel Sanders walked into the stadium (in a

Exhibit 14.3D

This is the long shot of that same card flip, which has been multiplied in the computer.

close-up shot) and waved to the crowd (from stock footage), and a card section spelled out the words, "Thanks, Colonel." I achieved my card-flipping section by having an animator rotoscope flip cards on top of that piece of stock crowd footage. Compared to the Kodak commercial, my Kentucky Fried Chicken commercial was crude indeed. However, it did the job before the invention of digital possibilities, which were new as recently as 1990.

I use these two examples to illustrate the wide divergence in production costs and production time between two methods of achieving a special-effects commercial. The most expensive, the most time consuming, and the most perfect way to combine live-action and computer-generated images requires hours of painstaking effort on the part of many talented people. If the money is available, and the product is national (or in the case of Eastman Kodak's commercial, global), the "perfect" way to produce makes sense. If not, there are variations on this production theme that can achieve a similar, less perfect, and less expensive result for a local or regional advertiser.

Exhibit 14.3E

This is the final scene from the Kodak Olympic commercial, "Let the Memories Begin." A computer-generated star field and fireworks were added, and a city was compositied into the background.

Estimating Costs of Computerized Special Effects

One elusive element of producing a commercial that relies on the computer for much of its origin is estimating its cost. Because so many of these commercials are dedicated to breaking new ground, putting a dollar figure on the effort is a very difficult chore indeed. The only consistent element is the actual running time of the commercial—usually 30 seconds of real time. But what happens in that 30 seconds can cost as little as $500 to produce—or more than $1 million.

The production-cost problem must be addressed. When it is not thoroughly understood, cost overruns can exceed 100 percent of original blue-sky estimates. These overruns are usually caused by poor communication among the three groups that are important to all commercial productions: the advertising agency, the advertiser, and the production company.

So how does an agency budget for a special-effects commercial? Chances are that many of the visual and sound effects hoped for will have to be originated during the production process, so there is little advance knowledge of hard costs. Estimating costs faces two problems from the beginning:

1. The traditional storyboard may be obsolete because it cannot fully picture the moving visual effects hoped for.
2. There is no way of reliably estimating how many hours of computer time it will take to fully achieve the desired visual effect, if that effect is brand new.

In an effort to help solve this budgeting problem, one successful graphics-oriented production company, R/Greenberg of New York, has some suggestions to make. Robert Greenberg believes that one production house should have complete control from conception to final completion. In other words, the agency should not bid out the graphics to a graphics house, the live-action photography to a live-action house, and the editorial finishing to an editorial house. In staying with one graphics production source, the style and mode of the commercial can be discussed before bidding, and the graphics house can thus be more accurate in estimating the cost and more helpful in describing how the final visuals will look.

R/Greenberg & Associates has gone a step further. It has originated additional graphics estimating sheets to go with the usual AICP form. These sheets include the costs of computer time and the other special equipment used on an hourly basis in such a commercial production. A copy of this estimating form is shown in Appendix 3. The advent of computer graphics has not only indicated new visual and auditory horizons but also has caused unique cost and production problems.

In Summary

To summarize the role of the computer in keeping both picture and sound elements in the first generation while enhancing and manipulating them at will, a few rules should be followed at the pre-production stage:

1. The person at the advertising agency who is in charge of the production of a high-tech commercial should be armed with an understanding of how the "new look" can be accomplished. In many cases, this brings the art director into new prominence in production. It's a brand-new production ball game with new rules and most of these rules are visually oriented.
2. New methods of presenting creative ideas to both the client and a production company will continue to be developed. For instance, it may be that small models of visual elements will have to be assembled

so they can be turned and moved in three dimensions during the creative presentation to simulate the final look.

3. A closer working relationship is needed between the agency and the production company. The production company should be brought into the planning loop at an earlier stage. And it may very well be that your idea will require a multi-talented production company that can take your idea from inception right through the digitized combinations to the finished commercial.

4. Finally, the whole area of production cost will have to be considered carefully so that the new methodologies will not result in exorbitant overruns.

Clearly, the technological advances in commercial production impose new responsibilities on agency personnel and require changes in some advertising agency practices.

15 THE FUTURE OF TV COMMERCIAL PRODUCTION

Change is sweeping the future of commercial production. Not only is the introduction of digital technology in the production of commercials urging these changes along creatively, but the roles of production companies and agency creative departments are also changing.

In the 1980s, editorial houses were separated from film optical houses. However, the optical film finishing technique has largely been superseded by the computer, and traditional film optical houses are becoming history. Their optical role is superseded by the added digital duties performed by editorial houses. In the future, once the production materials—film or tape, plus audio tracks—enter the editorial/finishing houses, they will emerge as fully realized, ready-for-air commercials. They will truly be one-stop operations.

Within the creative departments of advertising agencies, the roles of producer, writer, and art director are also being redefined. With the visual possibilities brought about by the digital revolution, the desires of an art director to produce a series of images never before seen in a commercial can be satisfied in amazingly short time. As a result, many agency art directors have become leaders of the creative production team. Writers may still have the original idea, but the art director is often in charge of its expression. As a further change in the advertising agency production hierarchy, in many ad agencies the producer's role has been reduced to merely a financial one. The producer is in charge of production dollars, not of the creative aspects of production.

Another new trend is the rise of the "infomercial." The 30-second TV commercial is being challenged by lightly veiled, 30-minute commercial messages couched as straightforward information. In the presidential campaign of 1992, Ross Perot convinced more than 11 million Americans to vote for him, largely due to his shrewd use of half-hour infomercials on both cable and network stations.

The changing work and leisure habits of the viewing public are also having profound influences on the media itself. Because two-career families have limited time for shopping trips, the interactive use of television is coming to the fore. More and more goods and services are being sold through television without using traditional commercials. Already, many direct-response cable outlets are using this approach to sell directly to the viewer and taking orders using an 800 phone number. The interactive possibilities of television are reinventing the entire communications industry.

Whereas the three major TV networks had until recently been the kingpins of communication, the myriad of cable channels has now given instant access to the viewing public in new and exciting combinations. And the audience shift continues in that direction. There are more choices of what to watch and new ways to involve the viewer in variations of two-way communication.

The Film Is Changing

A basic ingredient of commercial production—motion picture film—is also undergoing improvements. With new emulsions constantly being developed, it is now possible to shoot either 16mm or 35mm film in the brightest light or in the darkest night.

Eastman Kodak is taking the lead in many new film directions. John Spence, Kodak's Manager of Worldwide Marketing Communications of Motion Picture/Television Imaging, puts it this way:

> Film-makers realize that film is 'future proof.' Because film is already the highest resolution image-capture media, film images are transferable to any present or future HDTV [High Definition TV] system without loss of quality. It is also possible to take film images that have been transferred to a digital format, and read them back to film with film resolution using the Cineon Digital Film System from Kodak. This is very important to commercial producers who also want to make full film-resolution commercials for theatre projection. [Many advertisers show commercials in theaters around the world.]
>
> Finally, Kodak is working to develop other technologies that allow film to merge easily with the digital and video world. Kodak Keykode Numbers, for example, provide a separate barcode number on each film frame, to allow film to interface seamlessly with electronic editing systems.

This gives commercial producers the option of editing video without compromising the image quality inherent in transferring directly from negative to low-contrast print. In addition, 35mm film prints of commercials that are shown in theaters can be made from the same first-generation cut negative.

These new film stocks are being utilized in a high-resolution electronic intermediate technology. This means that editors, utilizing new computer workstations, will be able to scan film in the digital format for all types of image processing, compositing, and electronic "paint" applications. These workstations will be able to transfer the digital images back onto various types of intermediate stock, for current TV projection, theatrical projection, or HDTV.

As the projection systems become more sophisticated, these applications of film will guarantee the highest quality picture and sound, not only for over-the-air telecasts, but, as noted, for theater projection as well. The Kodak system is geared to scan a single frame of film at 3,000 lines or 4,000 electronic pixels of resolution—much finer quality than even the most advanced HDTV systems are geared for. ("Pixel" is the abbreviation for "picture element." Pixels are the electronic dots that make up a videotape picture and are the smallest unit of raster graphics. A "raster" is the electronic equivalent of a frame of film.)

These advances in definition are of the utmost importance as new projection systems are developed that can accept and telecast pictures and sound of much higher quality than is now accepted by conventional TV transmission. When HDTV becomes a dominant projection system, these film stocks and the electronic intermediate workstations will deliver a product that will fit the new systems like a hand in a glove.

Another innovation that will affect film and HDTV is the Super 16mm format, which offers a larger picture area. Super 16mm is gaining popularity because of its low cost and its wide aspect ratio for tomorrow's wide-screen televisions. The Super 16mm format has 46 percent more image area than conventional 16mm film, because the film is perforated on one edge instead of two. As a result of this wider image and higher picture quality, it becomes compatible with HDTV requirements. By contrast, commercials or programs originated using conventional 525-line or 625-line videotape will have limited commercial use in the future. The picture and sound quality will seem fuzzy and grainy by comparison.

To summarize, commercial producers will shoot on film, either 35mm, 16mm, or Super 16mm, then transfer that exposed film negative into a high-resolution digital intermediate system. Here, the images will be edited, manipulated at will, composited, and then returned to a wide choice of projection formats: film, videotape, or HDTV.

The Future Is Full of Tricks

It is difficult to predict the various directions that communication will take in the future, because so many forces are at work simultaneously. Not only are TV channels increasing in number, but the use of interactive video cassettes also adds new dimensions to the projection and use of commercials.

Topping the list is the addition of three-dimensional (3D) images generated within the computer. This innovation is called *virtual reality*. By donning a helmet equipped with special goggles and headphones that provide computer-generated sights and sounds, you can enter a new

3D world. The possibilities of virtual reality appear limitless, including walking you through your own house to look at "new furniture."

On top of all this, the various telephone companies around the country are wired directly into millions of homes. In the near future, new technology will allow them to interact directly with television. As you can see, the view of the future becomes crowded with possibilities for all types of commercial applications, as well as new definitions of the words TV *commercial*.

The New Commercial Production Company Creatives

An interesting aspect of the new way of visualizing commercials is the type of young people who are attracted to its techniques. They are a different breed from the motion-picture people of the past. Most of this new breed has found a home in the production companies geared to the new computer techniques.

Their academic credits include advanced degrees in architecture, environomental design, computer graphics, mathematics, philosophy, and aesthetics. They are a highly intelligent, highly motivated group of people who possess the knowledge to tell a computer what to do— and the artistic ability to create fascinating visual problems for the computer's memory to solve and display. In many ways, they are closer to being scientists and mathematicians than traditional filmmakers, but the end results of their efforts are opening new vistas of sight and sound.

Robert Greenberg of R/Greenberg & Associates has this to say about the future of commercial production: "We are getting a convergence of technologies: film, videotape, and computers will essentially be one in the future. As long as we have systems which can work in several different resolutions, you can choose the resolution you want to fit the medium you want." In other words, if you wish highest resolution for a 35mm theatrical release print, these intermediate systems will cooperate with your desires, eventually returning your commercial material to 35mm or 16mm film negative form. The same choices will hold true for HDTV or any other mode of videotape projection and reception.

Traps to Be Avoided in the Computerized World

I would be remiss if I didn't point out some of the pitfalls lurking in the computerized future. One is the ability of the computer to be absolutely exact, to the point of being mechanical. The result can be dehumanizing, cold, and emotionless. This drawback is understood by many of the talented people working in the computerized mode, and they actually introduce "mistakes" in order to remove the stigma of absolute perfection. In computerized music tracks, that might mean a slightly off-key addition to the final mix. With computerized visuals, like the

Kodak flip-card extravaganza that turned the efforts of 200 people filmed in a stadium into more than 20,000 fans flipping cards, the computer was programmed to neglect to turn up a few of the cards and to slightly delay the turning of others. In this way, the final result looked real because of these added miscues.

ADVANTAGES AND DISADVANTAGES OF COMPUTERIZED EDITING

One advantage of editing within the computer can also turn into a disadvantage of great importance. It is possible to achieve a picture edit very quickly and to make all sorts of changes to that edit, without in any way disturbing the original edit. The disadvantage is that this immediacy invites too many editorial opinions. In my experience, re-edits by several different people can weaken the final commercial rather than strengthen it. In the end, editing is not a completely democratic process. You don't vote on which edit is best. The editor, the creative director, and the client are the three people whose combined opinion should guide the final edit.

It must be remembered that the sole purpose and duty of a TV commercial is to help promote the sale of products and services. This depends on creative ideas, not digital trickery. The danger of "form without content" lurks forever in the background.

Jerry Brady, of the West & Brady advertising agency in Greenbelt, Maryland, puts it this way:

> If it doesn't communicate, it's not advertising. That's the basic litmus test . . . . If it doesn't communicate, no matter how pretty or cute or funny or artsy the message is or how it's presented, it ain't advertising. It may be art; it may be comedy; it may be theatre, but if it doesn't communicate quickly, clearly and fully, it's something else besides advertising.

WHEN NOT TO USE A COMPUTER

As you decide on your production mode to communicate your sales message, you should consider this: Do I hope for an emotional response to this commercial? If so, it may be advisable to stay away from the computer and use more traditional production techniques.

For instance, in a commercial promoting the idea of taking baby pictures, targeting young parents as well as grandparents, Kodak opted for a single, 30-second close-up commercial of a very cute little baby. The result was stunning in its emotional simplicity. No amount of computer trickery—or additional production cost—could have improved on the selling proposition guaranteed by a single, beautifully lit 30-second look at a very young baby.

Another trap to be avoided is to think that the computer is a creative force. Computers react only when told what to do, and they follow directions exactly. However, the more information you put into the computer, the more interesting the results can become. The computer isn't creative; *you* are creative. And when the computer is used to support and illustrate a creative thought generated by a human being, that is a wonderfully different story.

For example, the creatives at Backer Spielvogel Bates in New York originated a commercial for Magnavox with the talented John Cleese on camera. Using the computer wisely to show a diversity of electronic products, we see Cleese appearing in live action inside each new product. We first see him holding up the Magnavox Notebook Computer, then we see him in the lens of the 8mm EasyCam, and, when the scene widens, we see that he is actually in the picture projected by the Magnavox TV/VCR, and so on. (See Exhibit 15.1.) This is a brilliant use of the computer's ability to repeat scenes within scenes— all in the first generation.

As we discussed in the chapter on original music for commercials, this computerized sophistication spills over into the origination of sound for commercials as well. As the talented modern composer Vangelis puts it, "Synthesizers work like a magnifying glass. With them you can be deeper into sound than you can with an acoustic instrument."

Composers believe they are not giving anything up by using synthesizers; they are only adding to the possibilities of space-age sound colors. And how will these new electronic devices help tomorrow's commercials? By separating them from their competition, not only in the way the commercial looks, but also in the way it sounds.

Where Do Commercials Go from Here?

As your TV screen becomes interactive and allows two-way participation with sights and sounds projected into your living room, the whole mode of human communication will enter another exciting phase. Although George Orwell warned of the danger of "Big Brother" taking over by using such media in his futuristic novel *1984*, so far we continue to express individuality despite the continuing possibilities of mass thought-control.

There is every reason to believe there will be more and more tools and techniques available to express advertising ideas. The challenge will be to originate new and different ideas in the first place. Technique without a basic idea is a beautiful but completely empty experience.

Is Advertising Persuasion Or Manipulation?

I was lucky enough to spend more than 18 years working for Leo Burnett Company, 11 of those years while Mr. Burnett was alive and

Exhibit 15.1

MAGNAVOX
"YOU KNOW WHAT'S SMART" :45

SPOKESMAN #1: Y'know what's smart? This Magnavox 386 Notebook Computer that fits in your briefcase and...

SPOKESMAN #2: But what's really smart

is this Magnavox 8mm EasyCam that shoots incredible videos yet weighs less than two pounds and...

SPOKESMAN #3: But what's brilliant is

this Magnavox 13-inch TV that has a VCR built right into it so...

SPOKESMAN #4: But what's really brilliant

is this Magnavox 3-inch LCD TV that even has an AM/FM...

SPOKESMAN #5: But what's truly ingenious is this 31-inch Stereo TV

with a Smart Window that lets you see what's on other channels and swap the picture.

SPOKESMAN #1: Y'know what's smart? This Magnavox...
SPOKESMAN #5: Oh, not him again.

SPOKESMAN #5: Go away!

ANNCR(VO): The ingenious products from Magnavox. They're smart. Very smart.

John Cleese For Magnavox

A stunning example of digital technology is this commercial, featuring multiple images of English humorist John Cleese, all in running footage with on-camera sound and first-generation clarity. This commercial has become the first of a continuing campaign for the family of Magnavox products.
Courtesy Backer Spielvogel Bates, New York.

running the show. Each December, Leo would gather his troops for the yearly review. This was an emotional gathering that featured a look at the advertising originated that year for Burnett's clients. The meeting always ended with a few words of wisdom from Leo.

First, a word about the man, Leo Burnett. Unassuming in appearance, he belied the Madison Avenue idea of an advertising man. Someone once said, "he always wore a freshly rumpled suit." His glasses were always slipping down, and he kept poking them back into place. But as ordinary as was his appearance, his written words, spoken in a quiet voice, became the verbal cornerstone of his fine advertising agency.

I'll never forget the remarks he made many years ago in discussing the pitfalls of advertising:

> Ideas take shape in the brain of man alone. Ideas alone allow man to survive and flourish. Man without ideas would still be living in caves and tearing at raw meat. Everything we call wealth—everything we call comfort—indeed everything we call civilization is a product of ideas.
>
> I am proud to be an advertising man. Of course, if you want to look at the whole procedure cynically, you will call it not persuasion, but manipulation. And manipulation is what it can become—without integrity.
>
> As the tools of persuasion grow ever more powerful, more subtle, and more sophisticated, we are increasingly faced with that great temptation—the temptation to tell it, not like it is, but how it might be, or even how it ain't.

These profound thoughts hold true today. The sophisticated tools are all available, and manipulation has too often become the order of the day. Our ability to persuade is now backed with such potent sight-and-sound weaponry that persuasion can very easily turn into manipulation.

But the newest generation of advertising men and women are still fighting the good fight for persuasion versus manipulation. Many of them are striving mightily to "tell it like it is—not how it ain't," as Leo put it.

I find this true as I speak to advertising people all over the world, in symposia in Finland, Sweden, Denmark, England; on the European continent; and throughout North and South America, Japan, and Australia.

It is my continuing observation, as I work with these young men and women, that their brightness includes a sense of ethical responsibility. The tools of persuasion are in capable and responsible hands.

And may I add this personal postscript: I feel that I have never worked a day in my life. True, I never missed a day at the office in all those years, and I traveled the world in my business, but it wasn't work. It was the pure excitement of invention and accomplishment, as I saw products move off the shelf, or services succeed, because of some small addition I had made to that effort. I hope that you, too, can feel the same way about your own work experience as the years go by.

I sincerely hope this book will help this new generation of men and women to sell good products and worthwhile services, persuasively, creatively, and efficiently.

APPENDIX ONE

Leo Burnett's Production Specification Sheets

Most large advertising agencies that do a great deal of commercial production for their clients ask the film production houses to fill out the agency's specification sheets before being considered for commercial production. This is done to standardize the requirements for the various accounts serviced by the agency and to help make uniform the competitive bidding that the agency requires in pricing out its production before the work is finally assigned.

Leo Burnett has several such forms. This appendix provides examples of three of them:

1. **Television Production Specification Sheet.** This is a two-page form that thoroughly outlines the areas of cost responsibilities in making up a production bid.
2. **Post Production Specification Sheet.**
3. **Additional Production Costs.** This sheet seeks to control additional costs beyond the written bid approval.

Although you may have different requirements, these well-designed forms will be useful in helping you remember the multitude of cost considerations involved in any TV commercial production.

LEO BURNETT U.S.A.
A DIVISION OF LEO BURNETT COMPANY, INC.
35 WEST WACKER DRIVE, CHICAGO, ILLINOIS 60601
(312) 220-5959

TELEVISION PRODUCTION
SPECIFICATION SHEET

Date _____

TO: PRODUCTION CENTER

Production Manager: _____   Job No. P – _____

Asst. Prod. Manager: _____   Client _____

Agency Producer: _____

Executive Producer: _____   Product _____

Senior Producer: _____   Category _____

STUDIO BID BASED ON:

Cost Plus Fixed Fee   ☐ Complete job   ☐ 35mm   ☐ 16mm   ☐ Video-Tape
Firm Bid   ☐ Shooting thru dailies ☐ SYNC   ☐ MOS
                             ☐ Director's Cut

TITLE	CODE NUMBER	LENGTH	ORIG.	IF NO. EXPLAIN
#1				
#2				
#3				
#4				
#5				
#6				
#7				
#8				

CASTING   Casting Director: _____

To be paid by: Agency _____   Studio _____
Casting days: Prep _____   Cast _____   Callbacks _____   Polaroids _____
VTR days: Edit _____   3/4" Dubs _____   Ship To _____
Commercial will Air: National _____   Regional _____   Wild Spot _____   Test _____

Unless otherwise instructed all talent to be employed at scale rates. Casting Director is responsible for checking all talent membership status and client product conflicts. Payment questions must be directed to agency producer. Do not contact SAG/SEG direct.

TALENT INFORMATION

SAG Talent Session paid by: Agency _____   Production Studio _____
SEG Talent Session paid by: Agency _____   Studio _____   Other _____

Commercial	#1	#2	#3	#4	#5	#6	#7	#8
S.A.G. On Camera								
Double Cast								
Voice Over								
S.E.G. Extra								
Hand Model								
Special Contract								

Studios are responsible for complete and accurate preparation of all SAG/SEG contracts and LBC Talent Reports. Polaroids of talent in costume must be attached to the contract. Talent Reports and completed contracts must be returned to the local Burnett Production office immediately after shoot.

SCHEDULE INFORMATION

LEO BURNETT U.S.A.
A DIVISION OF LEO BURNETT COMPANY, INC.
35 WEST WACKER DRIVE, CHICAGO, ILLINOIS 60601
(312) 220-5959

TELEVISION PRODUCTION   Page 2
SPECIFICATION SHEET

Job # P _____

CHECK LIST FOR BIDDING

Specific Requirements	Agency (A)	Production Studio (P)	
Special Security	_____	VTR w/playback w/o playback	_____
Location fees/permits	_____	Teleprompter	_____
Set sketches/construction	_____	Sync sound/playback	_____
Client product	_____	Live sound effects	_____
Color corrected packages	_____	Sync dailies	_____
Props/wardrobe	_____	Crane	_____
Stylist	_____	Helicopter	_____
Make-up	_____	Special Insurance	_____
Hairdresser	_____	Talent travel/per diem	_____
Home Economist	_____	Limo service	_____
Food purchase & prep	_____	Music/announcer tracks	_____
Choreographer	_____	AD Reports	_____
Welfare worker/teacher	_____	Stock or existing footage	_____
Technical advisor	_____	Production stills	_____
Hi-speed photography	_____	Other _____	_____

ADDITIONAL INFORMATION

All buying procedures as spelled out in the LBC Standard Provisions Contract and Cost Plus Fixed Fee policy are applicable to this production.

Communications Procedure: Studio must submit all material through the local Burnett production office _____

_____ (LBC-LA); _____ (LBC-NY)

_____ (LBC-CHI). This includes appropriate Cost Detail Bid sheets (same day verbal bid is given to Agency Producer), Additional Production Cost sheet (after cost has been approved by Agency Producer), AD reports and all billing information as well as appropriate talent contracts, polaroids and talent reports.

Additional Cost Reporting: Production overages must be approved in advance by obtaining Agency Producer's signature on the LBC "Additional Cost" form. Additional costs not approved in writing by the Agency Producer's signature will not be honored.

LEO BURNETT U.S.A.
A DIVISION OF LEO BURNETT COMPANY, INC.
35 WEST WACKER DRIVE, CHICAGO, ILLINOIS 60601
(312) 220-5959

POST PRODUCTION
SPECIFICATION SHEET

Date: _____

Agency Job #: _____

Client: _____

Product: _____

Editor: _____

Agency Producer: _____

Prod. Mgr.: _____

Ass't Prod. Mgr.: _____

Exec. Producer: _____

Senior Producer: _____

SCHEDULE

Shooting Date: _____

Begin Edit Date: _____

Rough Cut Date: _____

Finish Date: _____

Air Date: _____

CODE NUMBER	TITLE	LENGTH	CODE NUMBER	TITLE	LENGTH
#1			#7		
#2			#8		
#3			#9		
#4			#10		
#5			#11		
#6			#12		

BID BASED ON:

Edit Only; ____ Edit & Finish on Tape (____ APO; ____ Select Neg); ____ Edit & Finish on Film; ____ Edit & Finish Tape & Film

FOOTAGE PROVIDED   (__ Original, __ Pick-up*) * _____
16mm film   ___ Sync (__ Synced dailies to be provided)   ___ Videotape (___ 1" ___ 3/4" ___ 1/2")
35mm film   ___ MOS   ___ Other (specify) _____

SOUND ("A" = agency; "S" = studio; "E" = editor;)
___ Anncr tracks
___ Music (___ Original, ___ Stock, ___ Pick-up existing client music)
___ SFX (___ Recorded on Location; ___ Stock)
___ Scratch Mix ___ Mix (___ Stereo ___ Mono)
___ Mag Transfers _____

OPTICALS & ANIMATION ("A" = agency, "E" = editor;)
___ Artwork
___ Animation/Rotoscope/Special effects
___ Existing footage (logo, tag, product demo, etc.)
Comments: _____

VIDEOTAPE

Note: Edit company may schedule time, but all sessions to be booked in Burnett name. Agency Production Manager will issue purchase order.
___ Film to Tape xfer w/color correction
___ On-line editing   ___ off-line editing   ___ work-pix to 3/4" cassette
___ Electronic Opticals anticipated (DVE, ADO, Paintbox, character generator)
Comments: _____
_____

___ Tape to Film xfer (Agency to handle)

VIDEOTAPE FINISH CONTRACT REQUIREMENTS (+ # COPIES)

___ 1" Master (separate masters for each comm'l)

___ 1" Safety Master (___ Separate   ___ Tied)

___ 1" Generic Submaster Requirements: _____

___ Cassettes: ___ 3/4"   ___ 1/2" VHS   ___ 1/2" Beta

FILM FINISH CONTRACT REQUIREMENTS (+ # COPIES)
___ 35mm Optical Pix Neg (___ without titles)
___ 35mm Answer print
___ 35mm Protection IP
___ 35mm Release Print
___ 35mm Mixed Magnetic Track
___ Optical Track Neg (___ 35mm ___ 16mm)
___ 16mm Pix Neg
___ 16mm release prints (___ 5400k ___ 3200k)

Upon client approval, Agency will advise
shipping/forwarding requirements.

Ship Production Elements to: _____

Ship Printing Elements to: _____

Ship vtr master to: _____

Supplemental information:

Rev 5/89

Leo Burnett U.S.A.

ADDITIONAL PRODUCTION COSTS

Production Company shall advise Agency and obtain written approval before incurring costs beyond original bid. Agency Production Manager will issue a purchase order for the estimated amount.

Note Regarding Cost + Fixed Fee Jobs: regardless of anticipated savings in other categories, you must still get this approval. Although you will receive a purchase order for these overages, on C + FF no charges are to be invoiced against the PO. Rather, the overages are to be included and properly categorized on the final/actual AICP and included in the Production Company's final invoice. (See Standard Provisions Contract).

Production Company _____   Agency Job # _____
Address _____   Producer _____
Phone # _____   Production Mgr _____
Production Contact _____   Ass't PM _____

Client/Product _____   Comm'l Title _____

Changes per: ☐ Pre-pro meeting   ☐ Other _____

Overage Areas:

_____ Pre-pro/wrap   _____ Studio/Set Construction

_____ Crew   _____ Equipment Costs

_____ Location Expenses   _____ Stock/Processing

_____ Props, Wardrobe, Animals   _____ Editorial

                                        _____ Other: _____

Detailed Description:	Amount

Agency Producer Approval: _____ Date: _____

Please forward copies to Agency Producer and Agency Production Manager within 5 days.

2/86

APPENDIX TWO

Television Production Requirements and Procedures from D'Arcy Masius Benton & Bowles (DMB&B)

This appendix illustrates how a major advertising agency administers the business aspects of its television commercial production. This is a complete bidding procedures manual. It covers every area in which the agency becomes involved for its television clients. I am deeply grateful to DMB&B for allowing me to include this complete document in this book.

TABLE OF CONTENTS

TRAVEL MARKUP

INSURANCE

CREW & DIRECTORS FRINGES

TALENT

SUBCONTRACTED SERVICES

WEATHER DAYS, POSTPONEMENTS, CANCELLATIONS

THE SECOND BID

PRODUCTION DOCUMENTS

OVERAGES

ACTUAL SUPPORTABLE DOCUMENTATION

WARDROBE

D M B & B INSURANCE POLICY

THE SPEC SHEET

TRAVEL MARKUP

TRAVEL MARKUP CANNOT EXCEED 15% OF THE ESTIMATED TRAVEL AND PER DIEM COST. THIS IS NOT A FIXED FEE AND 15% IS PAID BASED ON ACTUAL COST ONLY.

WHEN ACTUAL DOCUMENTATION IS RECEIVED, OVERAGES OR UNDERAGES WILL BE RECONCILED.

A DETAILED BREAKDOWN OF TRAVEL (I.E. AIRFARES, HOTELS, CAR RENTALS, ETC.) MUST BE SUBMITTED WITH THE BID.

INSURANCE

A 2.5% FEE FOR INSURANCE MAY BE TAKEN ON DIRECT COSTS EXCLUDING PRODUCTION MARKUP AND DIRECTORS FEE. INSURANCE CANNOT BE MARKED UP. FOR FURTHER DETAILS , SEE D M B & B INSURANCE POLICY ATTACHMENT.

WE REQUIRE 5 MILLION LIABILITY INSURANCE FOR AUTOMOTIVE CLIENTS AND 2 MILLION LIABILITY INSURANCE FOR NON-AUTOMOTIVE CLIENTS, WITH PROVISIONS FOR THE FOLLOWING INSURANCE COVERAGES:

> EQUIPMENT, PROPS, SETS, WARDROBE AND FILM NEGATIVE INSURANCE

> THIRD PARTY PROPERTY DAMAGE INSURANCE

> UMBRELLA LIABILITY

> AUTOMOBILE LIABILITY WITH PUBLIC LIABILITY, SINGLE LIMIT

> WORKERS' COMPENSATION INSURANCE AS REQUIRED

PASS THROUGH EDITORIAL AND VEHICLE PREPARATION COST (SEE SUBCONTRACTED SERVICES) ARE TO BE COVERED; HOWEVER, OVERAGES AND ADDITIONAL EDITORIAL VERSIONS ARE NOT COVERED.

A CERTIFICATE OF INSURANCE MUST BE SUBMITTED AT THE TIME THE JOB IS AWARDED, LISTING D M B & B AS AN ADDITIONAL INSURED AND PROVIDE US WITH EVIDENCE.

INSURANCE IS NOT A FIXED FEE. IT IS 2.5% OF ACTUAL.

SPECIAL INSURANCE PREMIUMS WILL BE COVERED SEPARATELY AND IN ADDITION TO PRODUCTION INSURANCE.

CREW AND DIRECTORS FRINGES

DIRECTORS

DIRECTOR'S FEE SHOULD BE BROKEN OUT BY PREP DAYS AND PRODUCTION DAYS. DIRECTOR'S FEE <u>CANNOT</u> BE MARKED UP.

CREW

EXTERNAL PAYROLL COST WHICH ARE FICA, PAYROLL TAXES, WORKER'S COMPENSATION INSURANCE, PENSION & WELFARE, VACATION AND HOLIDAY ETC., CANNOT BE MARKED UP AND MUST BE BASED ON ACTUAL COST. HANDLING FEE ON ABOVE MUST BE BASED ON ACTUAL AND CANNOT BE MARKED UP. VERIFICATION OF OUTSIDE PAYROLL SERVICE WITH A COPY OF CREW'S WORK SHEETS MUST BE PROVIDED BY PRODUCTION HOUSE.

INDEPENDENT CONTRACTORS CANNOT INVOICE FOR FRINGES.

THIS COST MUST BE INCLUDED IN THE AICP TOTAL. (A SUGGESTION IS TO USE LINE 16 FOR THIS PURPOSE.)

TALENT

TALENT CONTRACTS ARE REQUIRED WITH PHOTOGRAPHS OF THE TALENT ATTACHED.

ON-CAMERA PERFORMERS ARE PAID BY THE AGENCY UNLESS OTHERWISE SPECIFIED.

EXTRAS ARE PAID BY THE PRODUCTION COMPANY AND MUST BE INCLUDED IN THE BID.

WHEN SHOOTING IN THE L. A. ZONE, CENTRAL CASTING (2600 WEST OLIVE DRIVE, BURBANK, CA 91505, TELEPHONE 818-569-5200.) SHOULD BE USED BECAUSE D M B & B RECEIVES A DISCOUNT AND WILL BILL DMB & B DIRECTLY.

AIR FARE AND PER DIEM FOR EXTRAS AND ON-CAMERA PERFORMERS MUST BE INCLUDED IN THE BID WITH THE CREW TRAVEL AND PER DIEM. (REFER TO TRAVEL MARKUP SECTION)

WHENEVER POSSIBLE, TRAVEL THE TALENT AFTER 12:00 P.M. AND PAY 1/2 DAY OR AFTER 6:00 P.M. AND PAY PER HOUR.

ASSOCIATION OF INDEPENDENT COMMERCIAL PRODUCERS

CONTINGENCY DAY GUIDELINE

A. In order to more accurately reflect the conditions and arrangements between production company and agency, it is submitted that what has heretofore been known as a "weather day", be now known as a "Contingency Day." A contingency day is defined as any day where a scheduled film or tape shooting has been prevented from occurring due to circumstances beyond the control of the production company.

B. These circumstances may include, but should not be limited to:

(1) *Weather conditions*: rain, fog, sleet, wind, hail or any adverse condition that is not consistent with the prescribed shooting conditions desired by the agency.

(2) *Non-performance of talent or animals* due to illness, physical impairment or death.

(3) *Injury or illness involving irreplaceable production members.*

(4) *"Breakdowns" not due to gross negligence on the part of the production company.*

Circumstances 3 & 4 are a common problem to advertising agencies and producers alike. A suggested solution is to place these liabilities upon the production company allowing the producers to charge an insurance factor of 1% to 2% of the gross production cost.

(5) *"Force Majeur"* (earthquake, riot, fire, flood, act of war, etc.)

C. The production company recognizes its obligation to minimize Contingency Day liabilities and will apply all union job cancellation regulations and conventional industry cancellation privileges.

D. The production company will quote the maximum exposure figure (a "not to exceed" figure) as a Contingency Day cost. This will be a *cost per* figure. However, this figure does not include the cost of raw stock and processing Saturday/Sunday/holiday premiums.

E. If a production is postponed due to a Contingency situation and provided that day can be re-scheduled to be contiguous with scheduled shooting day(s) in that calender week, the cost of that Contingency Day will consist of:

(1) All non-recoverable out-of-pocket costs.

(2) All directorial costs arrived at as follows:

(a) Full director's cost as bid if the shoot is postponed after Noon of the day prior to the shoot day.

(3) A service charge of no less than 15% on all the above amounts or $500,000, whichever is greater.

F. If a production is postponed because of a contingency situation and is rescheduled for a later date *not contiguous* with the originally scheduled shooting day(s), the cost will be:

(1) All non-recoverable out-of-pocket expenses.

(2) Full director's cost a bid.

(3) A service charge of no less than 15% on (1) & (2) or $500,000 whichever is grater.

G. If, and when, the job is resumed all "start up" costs (i.e. re-casting, rehiring crew, etc.) will be billed at cost plus a service charge of no less than 25%.

H. If, because of a Contingency Day situation, a production is extended beyond the hours originally budgeted, or if additional personnel and/or equipment is necessary, the cost will be:

(1) Out-of-pocket costs for those hours, personnel, equipment, etc.

(2) A service charge on the above items of no less than 15%.

CANCELLATION/POSTPONEMENT GUIDELINE

The basis for the AICP Guideline is to define and set a value for the production company's primary commodity which is the time and service of its directors as well as the production support in personnel and equipment that the production company provides.

If the production company blocks out a specific period of time with the agreement that it represents a firm commitment from the agency and/or client then obviously no further efforts are made to sell that time. If, within the framework of the guideline time, i.e., less than 5 days, more than 5 days, etc., the job is cancelled or postponed than it is highly unlikely that this time can be regained. It should be understood that this time represents the primary source of income.

It is the production company's obligation to make all reasonable efforts to re-book the cancelled/postponed time with another client. If the time is re-booked, then there is an obvious area for discussion on the director's cost and/or the markup. If a rebate is due against the director's cost and/or the markup the amount of the rebate would be dependent on the relative dollars involved in the cancelled/postponed job and the job that was replacing it. In this instance all out of pocket expenses would be reimbursed with a service charge of no less than 15%.

A. If notice of cancellation/postponement is given within 1-5 *working days* of the shoot, the agency will be liable to the production company for:

(1) All out of pocket costs.

(2) Full director's cost as bid.

(3) Full markup on the job as bid.

B. If notice of cancellation/postponement is given within 6-10 *working days* of the shoot, the agency will be liable to the production company for:

(1) All out of pocket costs.

(2) Full director's cost as bid.

(3) 50% of markup on the job as bid.

C. If notice of cancellation/postponement is given *prior to 10 working days* of the shoot, the agency will be liable to the production company for:

(1) All out of pocket costs.

(2) A service charge of no less than 15%.

(3) The director's cost and markup will be subject to negotiation.

SUBCONTRACTED SERVICES

VEHICLE PREPARATION WILL BE SUBCONTRACTED BY THE PRODUCTION COMPANY AS A PASS THROUGH PAYMENT(S) ONLY. BID AND BACK-UP WILL BE SENT DIRECTLY TO AGENCY.

EDITORIAL MAY BE SUBCONTRACTED THROUGH THE PRODUCTION COMPANY AS A PASS THROUGH PAYMENT(S) ONLY. THIS DECISION WILL BE MADE AT THE TIME OF AWARDING THE BID.

PAYMENTS FOR VEHICLE PREPARATION AND EDITORIAL <u>CANNOT</u> BE MARKED UP.

THE SECOND BID

THIS IS FOR COST PLUS FIXED FEE JOBS ONLY.

AFTER THE JOB HAS BEEN AWARDED AND A PREPRODUCTION MEETING WITH AGENCY AND PRODUCTION HOUSE HAS TAKEN PLACE, A SECOND AICP BID IS TO BE SUBMITTED TO THE AGENCY ALONG WITH A SHOOTING/TRAVEL CALENDAR.

AT THIS TIME THE PRODUCTION FEE BECOMES A FIXED FEE BASED ON THE SAME % AS IT WAS AT THE TIME OF AWARDING THE JOB.

THIS BID SHOULD REFLECT ACCURATE AND CURRENT COSTS BASED ON LOCATIONS, SHOOT DATES AND CREATIVE DECISIONS.

DETAILED BREAKDOWNS ARE REQUIRED FOR SECTION J (FILM STOCK, DEVELOPMENT AND PRINT), SECTION I, (EQUIPMENT RENTAL), ALL TALENT AND CREW TRAVEL, AND INSURANCE.

PRODUCTION DOCUMENTS

PRODUCTION CALENDARS, PRODUCTION SCHEDULES, SCRIPT NOTES,
PRODUCTION REPORTS AND DAILY CALL SHEETS MUST BE SUBMITTED
WITH THE ACTUAL BACKUP FOR EACH PRODUCTION OR AS
DETERMINED BY PRODUCER PRIOR TO EACH PRODUCTION.

OVERAGES

PRIOR OR DURING THE PRODUCTION ALL PROJECTED OVERAGES,
WHETHER REAL OR ESTIMATED, MUST BE SUBMITTED TO THE AGENCY
PRODUCER AND BUSINESS DEPARTMENT PRIOR TO SPENDING THE
MONEY TO INSURE PROPER APPROVALS AND PAYMENT.

ACTUAL SUPPORTABLE DOCUMENTATION

ACTUAL SUPPORTABLE DOCUMENTATION MUST BE SUBMITTED WITHIN
A REASONABLE TIME PERIOD AFTER THE SHOOT. THIS
DOCUMENTATION MUST BE ORGANIZED BY AICP LINE NUMBER AND
EASILY RECONCILED WITH THE ACTUAL AICP.

SPECIFICALLY, THE FOLLOWING:

* THE COST OF ASSEMBLING BACKUP AS REQUIRED BY
  THE AGENCY (NO MARKUP).

* WHENEVER POSSIBLE SUPPORT CREW SHOULD BE HIRED
  LOCALLY.

* CREW AND TALENT PER DIEM MUST INDICATE
  PERSON'S NAME, TITLE, FUNCTION, DATES AND
  AMOUNT PER DAY. PER DIEM CANNOT BE GIVEN FOR
  MEALS THAT ARE SERVED DURING SHOOTING.
  CALENDAR OF CREW PER DIEM MAY HELP CLARIFY
  THIS AND CREW MEALS.

* ALL HOTEL BILLS MUST BE SUBMITTED ITEMIZED BY
  NAME OF PERSON, ROOM NUMBER, ROOM CHARGE AND
  ITEMIZED INCIDENTALS.

* AIR FARE BILLS MUST INCLUDE NAMES, DATES,
  CLASS OF TRAVEL, DESTINATIONS AND AMOUNTS.
  THIS MUST BE A COPY OF THE TICKET

* LIMOUSINE SERVICE MUST BE APPROVED BY THE
  PRODUCER.

* TAXI RECEIPTS MUST INCLUDE NAMES, DATES,
  DESTINATIONS AND AMOUNTS

* REPAIRS TO PERSONAL VEHICLES ARE NOT ALLOWED.

* MOBILE PHONE USE MUST BE APPROVED BY THE
  PRODUCER.

* MOBILE PHONE CHARGES ARE TO BE ITEMIZED BY
  COST PER DAY AND COST PER MINUTE.

* ACTUAL PHONE COMPANY RECEIPTS ARE REQUIRED.

ACTUAL SUPPORTABLE DOCUMENTATION (CONT.)

* AGENCY AND CLIENT MEALS FOR ENTERTAINMENT ARE <u>NOT</u> ALLOWABLE.

* AGENCY AND CLIENT WORKING MEALS ARE ALLOWABLE AND REQUIRE ITEMIZED LIST OF NAMES AND BUSINESS DISCUSSED.

* PETTY CASH/EXPENSE ACCOUNTS SHOULD BE FOR MINOR CASH EXPENSES. EVERY EFFORT MUST BE MADE TO MINIMIZE THE USE.

* ALL INVOICES AND RECEIPTS MUST INDICATE WHAT WAS PURCHASED AND WHY OR WHAT IT WAS USED FOR. ALSO WHO PURCHASED IT.

* ALCOHOL, CIGARETTES, AND PERSONAL ITEMS ARE NOT ALLOWED.

* ALL CREDIT CARD PURCHASES MUST BE SUBMITTED IN THE FORM OF A RECEIPT NOT STATEMENT.

* MOST FAVORABLE DISCOUNT MUST ALWAYS BE TAKEN AND PASSED ALONG TO US.

* PRODUCTION HOUSE MUST SUPPLY ITEMIZED RATE CARDS FOR OWNED EQUIPMENT, FACILITIES AND VEHICLES.

* 50% OF LOST, DAMAGED OR REPAIRED PROPS, EQUIPMENT OR WARDROBE WILL BE PAID BY THE PRODUCTION COMPANY AND 50% WILL BE PAID BY THE AGENCY ON BEHALF OF OUR CLIENT, UP TO A MAXIMUM OF $1,250.00 PER OCCURRENCE OR ACTUAL, WHICH EVER IS LESS.

* PROPS AND WARDROBE PROCEDURES ARE TO RENT AS MUCH AS POSSIBLE. AGENCY WARDROBE AND PROP INVENTORY PROCEDURES MUST BE USED WHEN PURCHASES ARE MADE. AS MUCH WARDROBE/PROPS AS POSSIBLE SHOULD BE SOLD AT HALF PRICE. AFTER THE SHOOT IS COMPLETE, THE REMAINING WARDROBE/PROPS MUST BE TAGGED BY NUMBER IN CORRESPONDENCE WITH THE WARDROBE AND PROP INVENTORY SHEET AND SENT TO THE BUSINESS DEPARTMENT <u>WITH</u> A COPY OF THE <u>COMPLETE</u> INVENTORY SHEET. WHEN BACK-UP IS SUBMITTED RECEIPTS FOR WARDROBE/PROP PURCHASES MUST INDICATE THE TAG NUMBER BY EACH ITEM.

ACTUAL SUPPORTABLE DOCUMENTATION (CONT.)

* A 1" TAPE OF FINISHED SPOT FOR PRODUCTION
  COMPANY MUST BE APPROVED BY AGENCY PRODUCER
  AND HANDLED DIRECTLY WITH POST PRODUCTION
  FACILITY.

* PRODUCTION HOUSE MUST KEEP ALL ORIGINAL
  SUPPORTABLE DOCUMENTATION FOR THREE YEARS.

* SHIPPING/DELIVERY RECEIPTS MUST INDICATE DATE
  OF SHIPMENT, WHAT WAS SHIPPED, TO WHAT
  ADDRESS, WHO REQUESTED THE SHIPMENT, AND COST.

CLIENT: _____

PRODUCTION HOUSE: _____

D M B & B WARDROBE AND PROP INVENTORY

PURCHASER'S NAME: _____

TAG NO.	DATE OF PURCHASE	STORE PURCHASED FROM	DESCRIPTION (Itemized – include size)	PURCHASE COST (Itemized)	COST BILLED (Itemized)	LINE NO.	DISPOSITION (Sold with cost/ Returned for refund with amount/return to agency)

D M B & B INSURANCE POLICY

SUPPLIER INSURANCE REQUIREMENTS: THE SUPPLIER SHALL NOT COMMENCE WORK UNTIL IT HAS OBTAINED THE INSURANCE REQUIRED BELOW. ALL COVERAGES SHALL BE WITH INSURANCE COMPANIES LICENSED AND ADMITTED TO DO BUSINESS IN THE STATE(S) WHERE THE WORK IS TO BE PERFORMED. ALL COVERAGES SHALL BE WITH INSURANCE CARRIERS ACCEPTABLE TO D M B & B.

A. WORKERS' COMPENSATION INSURANCE: THE SUPPLIER SHALL PROCURE AND MAINTAIN DURING THE LIFE OF THE CONTRACT, WORKERS' COMPENSATION INSURANCE, INCLUDING EMPLOYERS' LIABILITY COVERAGE, IN ACCORDANCE WITH ALL APPLICABLE STATUTES OF THE STATE(S) WHERE THE WORK IS TO BE PERFORMED.

B. COMMERCIAL GENERAL LIABILITY INSURANCE: THE SUPPLIER SHALL PROCURE AND MAINTAIN DURING THE LIFE OF THE CONTRACT, COMMERCIAL GENERAL LIABILITY INSURANCE, ON AN "OCCURRENCE BASIS" WITH LIMITS OF LIABILITY NOT LESS THAN $1,000,000 PER OCCURRENCE AND $1,000,000 AGGREGATE COMBINED SINGLE LIMIT PERSONAL INJURY, BODILY INJURY AND PROPERTY DAMAGE. COVERAGE SHALL INCLUDE THE FOLLOWING EXTENSIONS: (A) CONTRACTUAL LIABILITY; (B) PRODUCTS AND COMPLETED OPERATIONS; (C) INDEPENDENT CONTRACTORS COVERAGE; (D) BROAD FORM GENERAL LIABILITY EXTENSIONS, OR EQUIVALENT.

C. MOTOR VEHICLE LIABILITY: THE SUPPLIER SHALL PROCURE AND MAINTAIN DURING THE LIFE OF THE CONTRACT, MOTOR VEHICLE LIABILITY INSURANCE, INCLUDING APPLICABLE NO-FAULT COVERAGE, WITH LIMITS OF LIABILITY NOT LESS THAN $1,000,000 PER OCCURRENCE COMBINED SINGLE LIMIT BODILY INJURY AND PROPERTY DAMAGE. COVERAGE SHALL INCLUDE ALL OWNED VEHICLES, ALL NON-OWNED VEHICLES AND ALL HIRED VEHICLES.

D. OWNER'S PROTECTIVE LIABILITY INSURANCE: THE SUPPLIER SHALL PROCURE AND MAINTAIN DURING THE LIFE OF THE CONTRACT, OWNER'S PROTECTIVE LIABILITY INSURANCE WITH THE LIMITS OF LIABILITY NOT LESS THAN $1,000,000 PER OCCURRENCE AND $1,000,000 AGGREGATE, COMBINED SINGLE LIMIT, BODILY INJURY AND PROPERTY DAMAGE. D M B & B SHALL BE "NAMED INSURED" ON SAID COVERAGE.

E. UMBRELLA LIABILITY INSURANCE: THE SUPPLIER SHALL PROCURE AND MAINTAIN DURING THE LIFE OF THE CONTRACT, AN UMBRELLA LIABILITY POLICY TO APPLY IN ADDITION TO LIABILITY INSURANCE COVERAGES SPECIFIED ABOVE. SUCH POLICY SHALL HAVE A COMBINED LIMIT OF LIABILITY FOR BODILY INJURY AND PROPERTY DAMAGE OF NOT LESS THAN $5,000,000 PER OCCURRENCE.

D M B & B INSURANCE POLICY (CONT.)

F.   <u>PROPERTY INSURANCE:</u> THE SUPPLIER SHALL PROCURE AND
     MAINTAIN DURING THE LIFE OF THE CONTRACT, ALL RISKS
     OF PHYSICAL LOSS OR DAMAGE INSURANCE (INCLUDING
     FLOOD AND EARTHQUAKE) ON ANY AND ALL PROPERTY OF D M
     B & B OR ITS CLIENTS IN THE POSSESSION OR CONTROL OF
     SUPPLIER INCLUDING ITS AGENTS, EMPLOYEES AND
     CONTRACTORS. SUCH INSURANCE WILL BE BASED ON THE
     REPLACEMENT COST VALUE OF SUCH PROPERTY WHICH WILL
     BE FURNISHED TO SUPPLIER IN ADVANCE OF THE
     COMMENCEMENT OF WORK. "PROPERTY" SHALL INCLUDE, BUT
     NOT BE LIMITED TO, EQUIPMENT, AUTOMOBILES, PROPS,
     SETS, WARDROBE AND VALUABLE PAPERS (FILM
     NEGATIVES). THE INSURANCE ON VALUABLE PAPERS SHALL
     INCLUDE THE ADDITIONAL PRODUCTION COSTS INCURRED TO
     REPLACE DAMAGED FILMS AND SUCH INSURANCE WILL
     CONTINUE IN FORCE UNTIL ALL VALUABLE PAPERS ARE
     RETURNED TO D M B & B.

G.   <u>ADDITIONAL INSURED:</u> COMMERCIAL GENERAL LIABILITY,
     MOTOR VEHICLE LIABILITY, UMBRELLA LIABILITY,
     PROPERTY AND LOSS OF INCOME INSURANCE SHALL INCLUDE
     AN ENDORSEMENT STATING THE FOLLOWING:

     "ADDITIONAL INSUREDS": D'ARCY MASIUS BENTON &
     BOWLES INCLUDING ANY SUBSIDIARY AND AFFILIATED
     CORPORATIONS, COMPANIES AND PARTNERSHIPS.

H.   <u>CANCELLATION NOTICE:</u> ALL INSURANCE IDENTIFIED IN
     PARAGRAPHS A THRU G SHALL INCLUDE AN ENDORSEMENT
     STATING THE FOLLOWING:

     "IT IS UNDERSTOOD AND AGREED THAT THIRTY (30) DAYS
     ADVANCE WRITTEN NOTICE OF CANCELLATION, NON-RENEWAL,
     AND/OR MATERIAL CHANGE IN COVERAGE WILL BE SENT TO:
     "....."

D M B & B INSURANCE POLICY (CONT.)

I.   **PROOF OF INSURANCE COVERAGE:** THE SUPPLIER SHALL PROVIDE D M B & B AT THE TIME CONTRACTS ARE RETURNED FOR EXECUTION, CERTIFICATES AND POLICIES AS LISTED BELOW:

   1.   THREE (3) COPIES OF CERTIFICATES OF INSURANCE FOR THESE COVERAGES IDENTIFIED IN PARAGRAPHS A, B, C, E, F, AND G ABOVE.

   2.   ORIGINAL POLICY, OR ORIGINAL BINDER PENDING ISSUANCE OF POLICY, FOR OWNER'S PROTECTIVE LIABILITY INSURANCE (SEE PARAGRAPH D ABOVE).

   3.   IF SO REQUESTED, CERTIFIED COPIES OF ALL POLICIES MENTIONED ABOVE WILL BE FURNISHED.

   4.   ALL CERTIFICATES OF INSURANCE FORWARDED TO D M B & B BY THE SUPPLIER SHALL INCLUDE A CLAUSE WHICH SHALL STATE THAT THE SUPPLIER SHALL DEFEND, INDEMNIFY AND HOLD D M B & B AND ITS CLIENTS HARMLESS FROM ANY AND ALL CLAIMS AND JUDGEMENTS TO WHICH D M B & B MAY BE SUBJECTED OR WHICH IT MAY SUFFER OR INCUR BY REASON OF A CONTRACT WITH THE PRIMARY INSURED NAMED IN THE CERTIFICATE.

J.   IF ANY OF THE ABOVE COVERAGES EXPIRE DURING THE TERM OF A CONTRACT, THE SUPPLIER SHALL DELIVER RENEWAL CERTIFICATES AND/OR POLICIES TO D M B & B AT LEAST TEN (10) DAYS PRIOR TO EXPIRATION DATE.

DMB&B

TV COMMERCIAL PRODUCTION
BID SPECIFICATION FORM

Client _____   Production Company _____

Agency Job # _____   Address _____

Approx. Shoot Date(s) _____   Telephone # _____

Agency Producer _____   Initial Contact Date _____

Agency Art Director _____   Prod. Co. Contact _____

Agency Writer _____   Director _____

Spot Titles	Length	Lift	Version
1.			
2.			
3.			
4.			
5.			
6.			

BID SPECS:

Bid Through:	Type of Bid:	Format:	Venue:
Dailies _____	Firm Bid _____	Live Action _____	Location _____
Edited VTR Master _____	Cost Plus/Fixed Fee _____	Animation _____	Interiors _____
Corrected Answer Print _____		Film _____	Exteriors _____
Other _____		35 mm _____	Studio _____
		16 mm _____	Sets _____
		Video Tape _____	Table Top _____
		1" _____	
		¾" _____	

Production

A · Agency P · Production Company E · Editor	A	P
Set Design		
Location Search		
Location Fees		
Stage Rental/Expenses		
Casting · Principals		
Casting · Extras		
Talent Travel/Per Diem		
Talent Payment · Principals		
· V/O		
· Extras		
Set Construction		
Props		
Wardrobe		
Client Product		
Color Corrected Packaging		
Home Economist		
Work Kitchen		
Make Up		
Hair		
Wardrobe Stylist		
Script Person		
Production Stills		
Weather Contingency		
Talent Reports, Union Forms, W-4's		
Technical Advisor		
Stock Footage Search		
Stock Footage Purchase		
Screening Of Dailies		
Video Assist		

	A	P	E
Screen Dailies (projection or flatbed)			
Mag X-FER			
Sync Dailies			
V/O Recording			
Original Music			
Stock Music			

Comments:

VEHICLE PREPARATION

VEHICLE PREPARATION BIDS MUST BE BASED ON SPEC SHEET SUPPLIED BY AGENCY PRODUCER AND BUSINESS MANAGER.

A CALENDAR SPECIFYING TRAVEL, PREPARATION, SHOOT AND DRIVING DAYS MUST BE SUBMITTED WITH THE BID.

REVISIONS TO THE CALENDAR OR THE PROJECT RESULTING IN INCREASED COSTS, MUST BE SUBMITTED IN WRITING BEFORE THE MONEY IS SPENT.

THE AGENCY PRODUCER MUST BE INFORMED OF OVERAGES DURING THE PROJECT THAT ARE OFFSET BY AN UNDERAGE IN ANOTHER AREA.

THE AGENCY PRODUCER AND AN ACCOUNT PERSON ARE THE MAIN CONTACT ON ALL JOBS AND MUST BE INFORMED OF ANY AND ALL CAR REQUIREMENTS INCLUDING VARIATIONS IN THE SCHEDULING OF CARS.

OVERTIME AND WEEKEND TIME SHOULD BE ESTIMATED AND BILLED ON AN HOURLY BASIS. MONDAY - FRIDAY RATES CAN BE DAILY BASED ON PRODUCTION COMPANY SCHEDULE.

ALL RATES ON EXTENDED JOBS CAN BE NEGOTIATED.

A DAILY LOG OF PEOPLE, AREA OF RESPONSIBILITY, EQUIPMENT AND HOURS MUST BE SUBMITTED WITH THE FINAL INVOICE. ALL OUT-OF-POCKET EXPENSES MUST BE ITEMIZED AND A COPY ATTACHED TO THE FINAL INVOICE.

TRANSPORTERS ARE BILLED AT A DAILY RATE.

MILEAGE IS BILLABLE AT $0.65 PER MILE.

FUEL CHARGES ARE NOT ACCEPTED.

DRIVER RATES ARE NEGOTIATED.

OVERAGES - THE ATTACHED OVERAGE FORM WILL FACILITATE OVERAGE AUTHORIZATION. A ONE-PAGE FAX SHEET IS USED TO NOTIFY THE AGENCY OF AN OVERAGE. THE SAME SHEET CAN BE FAXED BACK AUTHORIZING THE OVERAGE. OVERAGES MUST NOT BE INCURRED UNTIL PROPER APPROVALS FROM THE AGENCY HAVE BEEN OBTAINED.

VEHICLE PREPARATION (CONT.)

PREPARATION KITS - PREP KITS CONTAIN, BUT ARE NOT LIMITED TO, THE FOLLOWING ITEMS NECESSARY TO PREPARE A VEHICLE FOR INTERIOR, AS WELL AS EXTERIOR PHOTOGRAPHY.

> VACUUM
> WHEEL WEIGHT TOOL
> TIRE BRUSH
> CARPET BRUSH
> TIRE INFLATOR TOOL
> TIRE PRESSURE GAUGE
> WRENCHES FOR DOOR/SEAT REMOVAL
> SCREWDRIVER FOR LICENSE PLATE AND ETC.
> NITROGEN AIR NOZZLE
> PLIERS
> SIDE CUTTERS FOR TIRE DE-RUBBING
> RAZOR KNIFE
> FLASHLIGHT

EXPENDABLE SUPPLIES SHOULD BE PURCHASED FOR EACH PROJECT AND INVOICED ACCORDINGLY.

PER DIEM - IF MEALS/DRINKS ARE ON HOTEL BILL THEY MUST BE DEDUCTED FROM THAT DAY'S PER DIEM.

PHONE CALLS - ALL PERSONAL PHONE CALLS SHOULD BE PAID BY THE INDIVIDUAL. BUSINESS PHONE CALLS SHOULD BE HIGHLIGHTED ON THE PHONE STATEMENT AND INVOICED. (I.E. FROM HOTEL TO DMB & B OR CAR TRANSPORT COMPANY ETC.)

DAILY WORK LOG - PLEASE SEE ATTACHED EXAMPLE OF A DAILY WORK LOG. THESE LOGS ARE USED BY PROJECT FOREMEN AND ARE SENT AS SOON AS POSSIBLE TO AGENCY DURING THE SHOOT.

HANDLING FEE - THIS FEE IS ONLY CHARGED ON EQUIPMENT/VEHICLE RENTAL, AND SUBCONTRACTED SERVICES/EXPENSES. THE MARK-UP IS 15%.

TAXI'S, PARKING, ETC. - RECEIPTS MUST BE SUBMITTED WITH FINAL INVOICE.

VEHICLE PREPARATION SPEC SHEET

DATE: _____   JOB NUMBER: _____

CLIENT: _____

AGENCY BUSINESS MANAGER: _____

AGENCY PRODUCER: _____

SHOOT DATES: _____

NUMBER OF CARS: _____

NUMBER OF PRECISION DRIVERS: _____

NUMBER OF LOCATION DAYS: _____

LOCATION: _____

NUMBER OF STUDIO DAYS: _____

STUDIO LOCATION: _____

NUMBER OF TRAVEL DAYS: _____

NUMBER OF CAR PREP DAYS: _____

PRODUCTION COMPANY: _____

PRODUCTION COMPANY CONTACT: _____

PRODUCTION COMPANY PHONE: _____

AUTOMOTIVE PRODUCTION SERVICES

DAILY WORK LOG

Date _____   Location _____

Name _____ IN _____ OUT _____ Tot HRS _____

Work/Explanation _____
_____

Name _____ IN _____ OUT _____ Tot HRS _____

Work/Explanation _____
_____

Name _____ IN _____ OUT _____ Tot HRS _____

Work/Explanation _____
_____

Name _____ IN _____ OUT _____ Tot HRS _____

Work/Explanation _____
_____

Name _____ IN _____ OUT _____ Tot HRS _____

Work/Explanation _____
_____

Comments _____
_____
_____
_____

Picture Vehicles _____

Equipment Used _____
_____

Truck Number _____ _____ _____ _____ _____ _____ Mileage _____

Verification

_____   _____   _____
   Printed Name   Signature   Date

Notification of Cost Overages

Date: _____

Firm: _____

Contact: _____

File Number: _____

Description: _____

_____

_____

_____

Reason: _____

_____

_____

Materials/Service   Est   Overage

_____

_____

_____

Requestor: _____

Return Endorsement Dated: _____

Approved: _____

Please sign and return this document at your earliest possible convenience.

EDITORIAL

ESTIMATED COSTS AND ACTUAL COSTS MUST BE SUBMITTED ON AICE FORM. ALL SUB-CONTRACTED SERVICES COSTS MUST BE DOCUMENTED AND ATTACHED TO THE ACTUAL AICE.

EDITORIAL FEE REPRESENTS LABOR TO ACCOMMODATE REVISIONS/CHANGES THROUGH FINAL CLIENT APPROVAL. HOWEVER, THE SPECIFICATIONS OF THE PROJECT MUST NOT CHANGE.

IF SPECIFICATIONS CHANGE, AN ADDITIONAL FEE WILL BE INCURRED AND MUST BE SUBMITTED IN WRITING FOR APPROVAL FROM THE AGENCY.

CHANGES AFTER FINAL CLIENT APPROVAL WILL REQUIRE AN ADDITIONAL BID INCLUDING A FEE AND MUST BE SUBMITTED IN WRITING.

MISCELLANEOUS EXPENSES THAT CANNOT BE MARKED-UP INCLUDE THE FOLLOWING:

> AIR FARE
> PER DIEM
> HOTEL
> MESSENGERS/CAB/AIRFREIGHT
> IN HOUSE CASSETTES, TAPES,
> DATABASE BACK-UP CARTRIDGES

ACTUAL SUPPORTABLE DOCUMENTATION MUST BE SUBMITTED AS FOLLOWS:

* ALL HOTEL BILLS MUST BE SUBMITTED ITEMIZED BY NAME OF PERSON, ROOM NUMBER, ROOM CHARGE, AND ITEMIZED INCIDENTALS.

* AIRFARE BILLS MUST INCLUDE NAMES, DATES, CLASS OF TRAVEL, DESTINATIONS AND AMOUNTS.

* AGENCY AND CLIENT WORKING MEALS ARE ALLOWABLE AND REQUIRE AN ITEMIZED LIST OF NAMES AND BUSINESS DISCUSSED.

* PER DIEM IS $35 A DAY EXCEPT IN LOS ANGELES, TORONTO, AND NEW YORK WHERE IT WILL BE $50 A DAY. IF MEALS/DRINKS ARE ON HOTEL BILL THEY MUST BE DEDUCTED FROM THAT DAY'S PER DIEM.

* RECEIPTS FOR TAXIS, PARKING, ETC. MUST BE SUBMITTED WITH FINAL INVOICE.

MUSIC

A WRITTEN BID MUST BE RECEIVED BY THE BUSINESS DEPARTMENT ON THE DMB&B MUSIC BID FORM PRIOR TO DOING ANY WORK. WE CANNOT GUARANTEE PAYMENT WITHOUT THE WRITTEN BID.

FOR EACH SUBMISSION OF A DEMO TRACK/FINISHED COMPOSITION, YOU WILL RECEIVE A MUSIC RIGHTS AGREEMENT. KEEP IN MIND THIS TRANSFERS PUBLISHING RIGHTS TO DMB&B ON BEHALF OF OUR RESPECTIVE CLIENTS, IF WE BUY THE WORK.

INVOICES MUST BE SUBMITTED IN A TIMELY MANNER AFTER WORK IS APPROVED. DOCUMENTATION OF STUDIO TIME INCLUDING HOURS, COST PER HOUR, TAPE STOCK, ETC. MUST BE INCLUDED. MUSICIANS AND SINGERS CONTRACTS MUST BE ATTACHED ALONG WITH LEAD SHEETS FOR EACH ARRANGEMENT.

IF THERE ARE ANY OVERAGES AND/OR ADDITIONAL COSTS, THEY MUST BE APPROVED BY THE BUSINESS DEPARTMENT PRIOR TO INCURRING THE COST OR WE CANNOT GUARANTEE PAYMENT.

DMB&B

1725 N. Woodward Avenue • Bloomfield Hills, MI • (313) 258-8300

MUSIC BID FORM

Date _____   Agency Job Number _____

Agency _____   Agency Producer _____

Address _____   Telephone _____

_____   Agency Business Contact _____

Title(s) _____   Telephone _____

_____   Product _____

_____   No. of :60's _____   :30's _____   :15's _____

Leader Scale _____   Leader's Hours _____   Leader Base Pay _____

Contractor Scale _____   Contractor's Hours _____   Contractor Base Pay _____

Sidemen Scale _____   Sidemen Hours _____ No. of Side Units _____ Sidemen Base Pay _____

Instr. Arrangement Rate _____   Instr. Arrangements _____   Instr. Arrangers Base Pay _____

Vocal Arrangement Rate _____   Vocal Arrangements _____   Vocal Arrangers Base Pay _____

Copying Rate _____   Arrangements Copied _____   Copy Base Pay _____

Composer *(Check one)* ASCAP _____ BMI _____ None _____   Musicians Sub Total _____

TV P&W Total @ 10% _____

H&W Rate _____   H&W Total _____

MUSICIANS TOTAL _____

Solo Duo Scale _____   Solo Duo Multi Tracking _____   SD Sub Total _____

Number of Solo Singers _____   Number of Solo Spots _____   Solo Duo Base Pay _____

Group 3 to 5 Scale _____   G3 to 5 Multi Tracking _____   G3 to 5 Sub Total _____

Number of G3 to 5 Singers _____   Number of G3 to 5 Spots _____   Group 3 to 5 Base Pay _____

Group 6 to 8 Scale _____   G6 to 8 Multi Tracking _____   G6 to 8 Sub Total _____

Number of G6 to 8 Singers _____   Number of G6 to 8 Spots _____   Group 6 to 8 Base Pay _____

Group 9 Scale _____   G9 Multi Tracking _____   G9 Sub Total _____

Number of G9 Singers _____   Number of G9 Spots _____   Group 9 Base Pay _____

Contractor 3 to 8 Base Pay _____

Contractor 9 Base Pay _____

Singers Sub Total _____

H&R @ 11.5% _____

SINGERS TOTAL _____

TOTAL BASE PAY _____

TPI Handling & Payroll Taxes _____

Studio Costs _____

Outside Instrument Rental _____

Outside Equipment Rental _____

Cartage _____

Messenger Air Freight Charges _____

Miscellaneous: [   ]   Misc. Charges _____

JOB SUB TOTAL _____

TOTAL SESSION COSTS _____

Arranging Fee _____   Number of Spots Arranged _____   ARRANGING FEE TOTAL _____

Production Fee _____   Number of Spots Produced _____   PRODUCTION FEE TOTAL _____

Creative Fee _____   Number of Spots Created _____   CREATIVE FEE TOTAL _____

Submitted by: _____

Approved by: _____

TOTAL JOB COSTS _____

Publishing Notation: I have reviewed and am in agreement with terms set forth in the music rights agreement as attached.

_____   _____
NAME   DATE

_____
TITLE

Appendix Three

Association of Independent Commercial Producers (AICP) Cost Summary Forms

The AICP film/videotape production cost summary forms have become industry standards. The AICP continues to develop and revise its forms as crew and equipment requirements change with the intoduction of new computer-driven production techniques. This appendix shows a form developed by the AICP, with an addendum developed to help isolate and identify the costs involved in computerized production and finishing.

This particular AICP form is used by R/Greenberg Associates, which commissioned the design of this customized special-effects bid form as an addendum to the regular AICP form. The "Special Visual Effects" portion of the form (pp. 7–11) was developed by the Computer Bidding Company, a computer software company formed by Mark Androw and Todd Freese in Wilmette, Illinois. Mark Androw is an executive producer with the Chicago production company Chicago Story. Todd Freese is a producer and editor for Freese & Friends, also in Chicago.

The two Chicago production people started working together on computer programs for the production industry when the Apple Macintosh was introduced in 1984. They saw the wide applications that the Macintosh could provide to the production industry that had not been addressed by any other software developer.

Their first program, "The Bid Form," was developed for bidding TV commercials on a computerized AICP form. The program stores standard crew rates, overtime multipliers, fringe benefit amounts, raw stock costs, and all the standard cost elements that go into making a TV commercial. The user specifies the number of shoot days, the amount of overtime, and the particulars of the job, and the program does all the math.

The current version of the program, "Bid Form 7.0," has been endorsed by the AICP as the official AICP Macintosh bidding program. It is used by more than 125 production companies around the world.

After "The Bid Form" had achieved widespread use for live-action production companies, several special-effects production companies approached the Computer Bidding Company to adapt the bidding program for their businesses. Special-effects production has many areas not covered in the standard, six-page AICP bid form. Motion control, blue-screen photography, computer graphics, model making, and many other areas are utilized by the special-effects producers.

So at the urging of Lucasfilm, Dream Quest, and R/Greenberg Associates, the Computer Bidding Company developed a special-effects bid form to meet the needs of these companies. The specific needs of each of these companies are addressed in this new form.

The Computer Bidding Company has also developed a program for job cost accounting, called "Actualization." This is a useful tool for cost-plus jobs, where the production company must submit the actual production costs to the agency. An interface with a full accounting program is also in use by many production companies. Additional programs are available for sales reps for production companies.

FILM PRODUCTION COST SUMMARY

	Bid Date:		Actualization Date:	
Production Company:	R/Greeberg Associates		Agency:	
Address:	350 W. 39th St., NY 10018		Client:	
Telephone No:	(212)239-6767			
Production Contact:			Producer:	Tel:
Director:			Art Dir:	Tel:
Cameraman:			Writer:	Tel:
Set Designer:			Bus. Mgr:	Tel:
Editor:			Commercial Title:	No.
No. Pre Prod Days:	Days	Pre-Lite	1	
Build/Strike Days:	Days	Hours	2	
Studio Shoot Days:	Days	Hours	3	
No. Location Days:	Days	Hours	4	
Location Sites:			5	
			6	

SUMMARY OF ESTIMATED PRODUCTION COSTS		ESTIMATED	ACTUAL	
1. Pre-production and wrap costs	Totals A & C			
2. Shooting crew labor	Total B			
3. Location and travel expenses	Total D			
4. Props, wardrobe, animals	Total E			
5. Studio & Set Construction Costs	Total F, G & H			
6. Equipment costs	Total I			
7. Film stock & printing ft. 35 mm	Total J			
8. Miscellaneous	Total K			
9 Sub Total A to K				
10. Director/creative fees(Not included in Direct Costs)	Total L			
11. Insurance				
12 Sub Total: Direct Costs:				
13. Production Fee				
14. Talent Costs and expenses	Totals M & N			
15. Editorial and finishing per:	Total O			
16 Special Effects Total				
17 Grand Total(Including Director's Fee)				
18. Contingency				

Comments:

PAGE 1

	CREW	ESTIMATED (A: PRE-PRODUCTION/WRAP)				ACTUAL					ESTIMATED (B: SHOOTING CREW)				ACTUAL			
		DAY	RATE	1.5	2	TOTAL	DAY	RATE	O/T	TOTAL		DAY	RATE	1.5	2	TOTAL	DAY	RATE	O/T	TOTAL
1	Proudcer										51									
2	Asst Director:										52									
3	Cameraman:										53									
4	Camera Operator:										54									
5	Asst Cameraman:										55									
6	Outside Prop:										56									
7											57									
8	Inside Prop:										58									
9											59									
10											60									
11	Gaffer:										61									
12	Best Boy:										62									
13											63									
14											64									
15											65									
16	Key Grip:										66									
17	Grip:										67									
18	Dolly Grip:										68									
19	Crane Grip:										69									
20	Mixer:										70									
21	Boom Man:										71									
22	Recordist:										72									
23	Playback:										73									
24	Make-up:										74									
25	Hair:										75									
26	Stylist:										76									
27	Wardrobe:										77									
28	Script:										78									
29	Home Ec.:										79									
30	Asst. Home Ec:										80									
31	VTR Man:										81									
32	EFX Man:										82									
33	Scenic:										83									
34	Telepr. Operator:										84									
35	Generator Man:										85									
36	Still Man:										86									
37	Loc. Scout:										87									
38	P.A.:										88									
39	Coord/Prod Mgr:										89									
40	Nurse:										90									
41	Craft Service:										91									
42	Fireman:										92									
43	Policeman:										93									
44	Wlfr:/Tchr:										94									
45	Teamster:										95									
46											96									
47											97									
48											98									
49											99									
50											100									

SUB TOTAL A

PT/P& W

TOTAL A

SUB TOTAL B

PT/P&W

TOTAL B

PAGE 2

PRE-PRODUCTION & WRAP/MATERIALS & EXPENSES			ESTIMATED	ACTUAL
101	Auto Rentals No. of Cars	x Amount per Car		
102	Air Fares: No. of People	x Amount per fare		
103	Per Diems: No. of People	x Amount per day		
104	Still Camera Rental & Film			
105	Messengers			
106	Trucking			
107	Deliveries & Taxis			
108	Home Economist Supplies			
109	Telephone & Cable			
110	Casting Call/Prep Casting Call Backs			
111	Casting Facilities			
112	Working Meals			
113				
		Sub Total C		

LOCATION EXPENSES			ESTIMATED	ACTUAL
114	Location Fees			
115	Permits			
116	Car Rentals			
117	Bus Rentals			
118	Camper, Dressing Room Vehicles			
119	Parking, Tolls & Gas			
120	Trucking			
121	Other Vehicles			
122	Other Vehicles			
123	Customs			
124	Air freight/Excess Baggage			
125	Air Fares: No. of people	Cost Per Fare		
126	Per Diems: No. of man days	Amount per day		
127	Air Fares: No. of people	Cost Per Fare		
128	Per Diems: No. of man days	Amount per day		
129	Breakfast No. of man days	Amount per person		
130	Lunch No. of man days	Amount per person		
131	Dinner No. of man days	Amount per person		
132	Guards			
133	Limousines(Celebrity Service)			
134	Cabs and Other Transportation			
135	Kit Rental			
136	Art Work			
137	Gratuities			
138				
139				
		Sub Total D		

PROPS AND WARDROBE & ANIMALS		ESTIMATED	ACTUAL
140	Prop Rental		
141	Prop Purchase		
142	Wardrobe Rental		
143	Wardrobe Purchase		
144	Picture Vehicles		
145	Animals & Handlers		
146	Wigs & Mustaches		
147	Color Correction		
148			
	Sub Total E		

PAGE 3

STUDIO RENTAL & EXPENSES-STAGE	ESTIMATED				ACTUAL		
	Days	Rate	Total		Days	Rate	Total
151 Rental for Build Days							
152 Rental for Build O.T. Hours							
153 Rental for Pre-Lite Days							
154 Rental for Pre-Lite O.T. Hours							
155 Rental for Shoot Days							
156 Rental for Shoot O.T. Hours							
157 Rental for Strike Days							
158 Rental for Strike O.T. Hours							
159 Generator & Operator							
160 Set Guards							
161 Total Power Charge & Bulbs							
162 Misc. Studio Charges(Cartage, Phone, Coffee)							
163 Meals for Crew & Talent(Lunch, Dinner)							
164 Craft Service							
165							
166							
167							
Sub Total F							

SET CONSTRUCTION	ESTIMATED				ACTUAL			
	Days	Rate	O/T Hrs	Total	Days	Rate	O/T $	Total
168 Set Designers Name:								
169 Carpenters								
170 Grips								
171 Outside Props								
172 Inside Props								
173 Scenics								
174 Electricians								
175 Teamsters								
176 Men for Strike								
177 P.A.'s								
178								
179								
180								
Sub Total G								
PT/P &W								
TOTAL G								

SET CONSTRUCTION MATERIALS	ESTIMATED	ACTUAL
181 Props(Set Dressing Purchase)		
182 Props(Set Dressing Rental)		
183 Lumber		
184 Paint		
185 Hardware		
186 Special Effects		
187 Special Outside Construction		
188 Trucking		
189 Messengers/Deliveries		
190 Kit Rental		
191		
192		
Sub Total H		

PAGE 4

EQUIPMENT RENTAL		Days	Rate	ESTIMATED	ACTUAL
193	Camera Rental				
194	Sound Rental				
195	Lighting Rental				
196	Grip Rental				
197	Generator Rental				
198	Crane/Cherry Picker Rental				
199	VTR Rental With Playback X Without Playback				
200	Walkie Talkies, Bull Horns				
201	Dolly Rental				
202	Camera Car				
203	Helicopter				
204	Production Supplies				
205	Teleprompter				
206					
207					
208					
209					
210					
	Sub Total I				

STOCK   35 MM

FILM RAW STOCK DEVELOP & PRINT		ESTIMATED FOOTAGE	$/FT	TOTAL	ACTUAL FOOTAGE	$/FT.	TOTAL
211	Purchase of Raw Stock: Footage		.49				
212	Developing footage amount		.18				
213	Printing Footage amount		.32				
214	Transfer to Mag.		.12				
215	Sync/Screen Dailies						
216	Prep for video transfer						
	Sub Total J						

MISCELLANEOUS COSTS		ESTIMATED	ACTUAL
217	Petty Cash		
218	Air Shipping/Special Carriers		
219	Phones and Cables		
220	Accountable Cash Expenditures Under $15 Each		
221	External Billing Costs(Computer Accounting, etc.)		
222	Special Insurance		
223	DGA P & W		
224			
225			
226			
	Sub Total K		

DIRECTOR/CREATIVE FEES		ESTIMATED	ACTUAL
227	Prep		
228	Travel		
229	Shoot Days		
230	Post-Production		
231			
232			
233			
	Sub Total L		

PAGE 5

TALENT		No.	Rate	Days	Travel	1.5 OT	2X OT	ESTIMATED	No.	Days	ACTUAL
234	O/C Principals										
235	O/C Principals										
236	O/C Principals										
237	O/C Principals										
238	O/C Principals										
239	O/C Principals										
240	O/C Principals										
241	O/C Principals										
242	O/C Principals										
243	O/C Principals										
244											
245											
246											
247	General Extras										
248	General Extras										
249	General Extras										
250	General Extras										
251	General Extras										
252	General Extras										
253											
254											
255											
256	Hand Model										
257											
258	Voice Over										
259	Fitting Fees S.A.G.										
260	Fitting Fees S.E.G.										
261											
262	Audtion Fees S.A.G.										
263	Audtion Fees S.E.G.										
264											
265											
	Sub Total										
266	Payroll & P/W Taxes										
267	Wardrobe Allowence No of talent & garments					fee per garment					
268											
	Sub Total										
269	Other										
270	Mark-up										
						Sub Total M					

TALENT EXPENSES				ESTIMATED	ACTUAL
271	Per diem:	No. of man days	amount per day		
272	Air Fares:	No. of people	amount per fare		
273	Cabs and other transportation				
274	Mark-up				
275					
276					
			Sub Total N		

PAGE 6

EDITORIAL COMPLETION	Quantity	Units	Rate	ESTIMATED	ACTUAL
277 Editor		Days			
278 Editing Room		Days			
279 Assistant Editor		Days			
280 Conforming		Hours			
281 Projection					
282 Artwork for Supers					
283 Shooting Artwork					
284 Stock Footage					
285 Still Photos					
286 Optical					
287 Animation					
288 Stock Music					
289 Original Music					
290 Sound Effects					
291 Dubbing Studio		Hours			
292 Record Narration		Hours			
293 Transfer to cassette					
294 Mix		Hours			
295 Optical Tracks		foot			
296 Answer Prints		foot			
297 Interpositive/Dupe Neg		foot			
298 Contract Items					
VIDEOTAPE FINISHING					
299 Off-Line Editing		Hours			
300 Film To Tape Transfer		Hours			
301 "Pin Registered" Trans/Composite		Hours			
302 On-Line Editing		Hours			
303 Additional VTR's		Hours			
304 ADO/Kaleidoscope		Hours			
305 Paint Box/Harry		Hours			
306 Abekas DDR		Hours			
307 Workprint to Cassette		Spot			
308 D1 Tape		Spot			
309 Tape		Spot			
310 Master & Safetys		Spot			
311 Cassettes		Spot			
312 Post Production Supervisor		Days			
313 Working Meals					
314 Shipping					
315					
316					
317					
318					
319					
320					
321					
322					
323					
324					
325					
326 Misc					
327 P & W					
328	SUB TOTAL EDITORIAL COSTS				
329 Editorial Handling Fee					
			Sub Total O		

PAGE 7
SPECIAL VISUAL EFFECTS

	CREW	ESTIMATED					ACTUAL			
		DAYS	RATE	OT 1	OT 2	TOTAL	DAYS	RATE	O/T $	TOTAL
330	FX Producer									
331	Production Manager									
332	Coordinator									
333	Dir. of Photography									
334	Asst. Camera									
335	Electrician									
336	Grip									
337	Rigger									
338	Model Wrangler									
339	Technical Director									
340	Computer Programmer									
341	SPFX Supervisor									
342										
343										
344										
345										
346										
347	M.C. Operator									
348	Production Assistant									
		SUB TOTAL P					SUB TOTAL P			
		PT/P& W					PT/P& W			
		TOTAL P					TOTAL P			

STAGE COSTS		Quanity	$/Unit	ESTIMATED	ACTUAL
349	Stage Prep				
350	Prep O.T.				
351	Stage Shoot				
352	Shoot O.T.				
353	Stage Strike				
354	Strike O.T.				
355	Total Power Charges				
356	Misc Stage Costs				
			Sub Total Q		

EQUIPMENT/RIGS/PROPS		Days	Rate	ESTIMATED	ACTUAL
357	Motion Control Camera				
358	Motion Control System				
359	Motion Graphics System				
360	Matte Camera System				
361	Lighting/Grip Equipment				
362	Generator				
363	VTR				
364	Motion Control Dolly/Track				
365	Production Supplies				
366	Special Rigs				
367	Rear Screen Projector				
368	Props				
369					
370					
			Sub Total R		

PAGE 8

PRODUCTION SUPPLIES		Quanity	Units	$/Unit	ESTIMATED	ACTUAL
371	Craft Services		Days			
372	Production Meals		Days			
373	Working Meals		Days			
374	Telephone, Telex, FAX		Weeks			
375	Couriers, Shipping		Weeks			
				Sub Total S		

MODEL/SPECIAL EFX CONSTRUCTION		Quanity	Units	$/Unit	ESTIMATED	ACTUAL
376	Model maker		Days			
377	Model Wrangler		Days			
378	Model Supplies		Allow			
379						
380						
381	Other		Allow			
				Sub Total T		

				ESTIMATED				ACTUAL		
ART DEPARTMENT		Quanity	Units	$/Unit	OT Hrs	TOTAL	DAYS	RATE	O/T $	TOTAL
382	Art Director		Days							
383	Artist/Animator		Days							
384	Assistant		Days							
385	Ink & Paint		Days							
386	Art Support/Strip-Up		Days							
387	Rotoscope		Days							
388	Photos/Stats		Days							
389	Art supplies		Days							
390	Typset		Days							
391	Storyboards		Days							
392	Research & Development		Days							
393										
394										
395										
396	Other		Allow							
				PT/PW			PT/PW			
				Sub Total U			Sub Total U			

ANIMATION		Days	Units	Rate	ESTIMATED	ACTUAL
397			Days			
398			Days			
399			Days			
400			Days			
401			Days			
402			Days			
403			Days			
404			Days			
405			Days			
406			Days			
				Sub Total V		

PAGE 9

FILM/PROCESSING	Footage	Cost/ft.	ESTIMATED	ACTUAL
407 Color Stock				
408 Process & Print				
409 Lab Rush Orders				
410 Registered Prints				
411 B/W Raw Stock				
412 B/W Prints				
413 Stock Footage				
		Sub Total W		

COMPUTER GENERATED IMAGERY	Quanity	Units	$/Unit	ESTIMATED	ACTUAL
414 Producer		Days			
415 Director		Days			
416 Animator 1		Days			
417 Animator 2		Weeks			
418 Technical Director					
419 Scanner Operator					
420 Animation Workstation					
421 Image Processing Workstation					
422 Input Output Scanners					
423 Rendering Workstation					
424 Research and Development					
425 Computer Output to Video					
426 Computer Output from Video					
427					
428					
429		Weeks			
			Sub Total X		

CGI INTERGRATION	Quanity	Units	$/Unit	ESTIMATED	ACTUAL
430 Live Action Matching		Days			
431 Motion Control Matching		Days			
432		Days			
			Sub Total Y		

PAGE 10

DIGITAL/VIDEO GRAPHICS	Quantity	Units	Rate	ESTIMATED	ACTUAL
433 Supervisor/Layout		hours			
434 Digital Video Suite(unsupervised)		hours			
435 Digital Video Suite(unsupervised O.T.)		hours			
436 Digital Video Suite(supervised)		hours			
437 Digital Video Suite(unsupervised O.T.)		hours			
438 Additional Abekas		hours			
439 Additional D1- DVTR		hours			
440 Additional D2- DVTR		hours			
441 GCG Kaleddoscope(per channel)					
442 Digital Paint System		hours			
443 Digital Paint System(Rotoscope)		hours			
444 Digital Conform		hours			
445 Special Color Correction					
446 Digital Noise Reduction		hours			
447 D-1 to 1" Video		hours			
448 D-1 to 3/4" Video		hours			
449 Audio Relay		hours			
450 Digital Video to Recording					
451 Conversion to PAL or SEACAM		hours			
452					
453					
454					
455					
456					
457					
458					
459					
			Sub Total Z		

DIGITAL/VIDEO GRAPHICS MATERIALS	Quantity	Units	Rate	ESTIMATED	ACTUAL
460 1/2" Cassettes		Cassettes			
461 1" Tape 30 minutes		Rolls			
462 1" Dubs		Spots			
463 3/4" Cassettes		Cassettes			
464 D-1 Cassettes (76 minutes)		Cassettes			
465 D-1 Cassettes(34 minutes)		Cassettes			
466 D-1 Cassettes(12 minutes)		Cassettes			
467					
468					
469					
470					
			Sub Total AA		

TRAVEL	Persons	Units	$/Unit	ESTIMATED	ACTUAL
471 Round Trip Airfares		Fares			
472 Per Diems		Days			
473 Lodging		Nights			
474 Auto Rentals, Cabs		Days			
			Sub Total AB		

PAGE 11

MISCELLANOUS		ESTIMATED	ACTUAL
475	Messengers		
476	Taxis/Cabs		
477	Shipping		
478	Working Meals		
479	Other		
480			
481			
	Sub Total AC		

ADDITIONAL		Quanity	Units	$/Unit	ESTIMATED	ACTUAL
482						
483						
484						
485						
486						
487						
488						
489						
490						
491						
492						
				Sub Total AD		

DIRECTOR/CREATIVE FEES		ESTIMATED	ACTUAL
493	Prep		
494	Shoot Days		
495	Post Production		
	PT/PW		
	Sub -Total AE		

496	Special Effects Sub-Total	(Except Digital Video Graphics & Materials)		
497	Mark-Up on Above	35%		
498	Director/Creative Fees	Sub Total AE		
499	Digital Video Graphics & Materials	Sub Total Z & AA		
500	Total Effects			

Computer Bidding Company

October 13, 1992

The Computer Bidding Company is a computer software company formed by Mark Androw and Todd Freese.

The 2 Chicago production people starting working together on computer programs for the production industry when the Apple Macintosh was introduced in 1984. They saw the wide applications that the Macintosh could provide to the production industry that had not been addressed by any other software developer.

Their first program **THE BID FORM** was developed for bidding TV commercials on a computerized AICP form. The program stores standard crew rates, overtime multipliers, fringe benefit amounts, raw stock costs and all the standard cost elements that go into making a TV commercial. The user specifies the number of shoot days, the amount of overtime and the particulars of the job and the program does all the math.

The current version of the program **BID FORM 7.0** has been endorsed by the AICP as the official AICP Macintosh bidding program. It is used by over 125 production companies around the world.

After **THE BID FORM** had achieved widespread use for live-action production companies several special effects production companies approached The Computer Bidding Company to adapt the bidding program for their businesses. Special effects production has many areas not covered in the standard 6 page AICP Bid Form. Motion control, blue screen photography, computer graphics, model making and many other areas are utilized by the special effects producers.

So at the urging of Lucasfilm, Dream Quest, and R/Greenberg Associates the Computer Bidding Company developed a special effects bid form to meet the needs of these companies. The specific needs of each of these

522 Eighth Street   Wilmette, IL 60091   (312) 642-3173

producers has the form vary slightly from company to company the this new form meets the requirements of these specialized companies.

The Computer Bidding Company has also developed programs for Job Cost accounting , called **ACTUALIZATION** This is an useful tool for Cost Plus jobs, where the production company must submit the actual production costs to the agency. An interface with a full accounting program is also in use by many production companies.

Additional program are available for sales reps for production companies and scheduling programs.

Mark Androw is an Executive Producer with the Chicago production company, Chicago Story. Todd Freese is a producer and editor for Freese & Friends, also in Chicago.

APPENDIX FOUR

Rules and Regulations Governing the Employment of Minors in the Entertainment Industry (Casting Directors, Producers, Directors, Assistant Directors, and all others who employ, supervise, or work with minors)

Gereral Information

The following rules, pertaining to the hiring of juveniles in commercial production, apply specifically to all production originated in Los Angeles County, California.

A. PERMITS

1. Minors may not work without an ENTERTAINMENT WORK PERMIT, and may not lawfully be employed by an individual or organization which does not have a PERMIT TO EMPLOY MINORS in the Entertainment Industry.

2. For work in motion pictures, television, or other forms of entertainment the ENTERTAINMENT WORK PERMIT in Southern California is issued by the State Division of Labor Law Enforcement, 107 South Broadway, Los Angeles 90012 . . . . The work permit must be inspected and endorsed by the Teacher-Welfare Worker and returned to the minor before the end of the day.

3. The PERMIT TO EMPLOY MINORS is issued by the Labor Commissioner on condition that the employer comply with the requirements of the law and the regulations embodied in this booklet.

4. The "Responsibility of the Employer" is placed in the individual or organization to whom the PERMIT TO EMPLOY MINORS is issued and in the producer, director, unit manager, assistant director, or other employee delegated authority by the permittee.

B. TEACHER-WELFARE WORKER

1. The TEACHER-WELFARE WORKER is a teacher who holds proper California State Teaching Credentials, who is experienced

in welfare supervision, who has been certified and assigned by the Work Permits Office of the Los Angeles United School District.

2. The employer in motion pictures, television, and the legitimate theater shall provide a Teacher-Welfare Worker wherever minors are employed, i.e., each set, individual group, or separate company in any one day. In an emergency, with the permission of the Work Permits Office when no other teacher is available, one teacher may cover two different sets but must be paid a full day's pay by each Production company. When the public schools are in session, a Teacher-Welfare Worker must be provided for each group of ten or fraction thereof; on weekends, school holidays, or vacations for each group of twenty or fraction thereof. Special arrangements may be made for the number of Teacher-Welfare Workers with groups of minors numbering one hundred fifty (150) or more.

3. All Teacher-Welfare Workers in Southern California, including Resident Teachers, must be secured through the Work Permits Office of the Los Angeles United School District . . . . The establishment and maintenance of lists of legally certificated Teacher-Welfare Workers shall be done in accordance with a contract between the Los Angeles United School District and the Association of Motion Picture and Television Producers.

C. SCHOOL REQUIREMENTS FOR MINORS

1. All minors who have not been graduated from a recognized high school must be taught at least three hours on school days, between the hours of 8:00 a.m. and 4:00 p.m. No period of less than 20 minutes duration may be accepted as school time.

2. Married minors must have work permits. A Teacher-Welfare Worker is necessary. Married minors are not required to attend school at any work place unless enrolled in regular school.

3. A minor must be taught continuously at the studio or other work place during a "long run" picture, television series, or any production that would extend for a length of time that would handicap a youngster educationally or emotionally if he were to alternate his schooling for short periods between school and work. This applies where a minor may be working only 2 or 3 days a week.

4. A "long run" picture or television "series" may be defined as a run or series which lasts more than half the weeks in a semester, or for a length of time that would seriously handicap a minor if he returned to his regular school intermittently. During a "long run" or "series" the minor must continue his schooling at the place of employment unless there is a 30-day break, in which case he may return to his regular school.

5. If a "long run" or "series" is finished more than 30 days before the end of the term or semester, then a minor may be returned to his regular school. However, if 30 days or less remain, the minor must

remain in school at his place of employment for the remainder of the school year or semester.

6. Minors must not be taught while being transported to or from local locations.

7. A minor may be schooled only on the production on which he is employed.

8. Minors whose schooling is provided by the employer shall be taught on the studio lot, theater, or place of employment. A suitable place shall be provided at the place of employment or location. The child may not be taught in his own home or the home of the teacher without special permission from the Work Permits Office.

9. Minors shall not be called out of full-time school, either public or private, for any type of work in the Entertainment Industry or photography, recording, publicity, fittings, or interviews without special permission from the Work Permits Office, which shall be granted under emergency conditions only.

10. Minors who are employed in the Entertainment Industry follow the school calendar of the public school district. The parochial or private school calendar may be followed, by special permission of the Work Permits Office, when only parochial or private school children are involved.

D. SCHOOL FACILITIES

1. School facilities such as a school house or classroom, trailer school house, nursery space, parents' waiting room, etc., with equipment and supplies shall be provided by all employers. Convenient and comfortable arrangements on stages, locations, or any place of employment must closely approximate the basic requirements for classrooms; especially in provision for lighting, heating, and desk and chair facilities.

2. Buses and cars are not adequate facilities unless used exclusively for the children during school time. A moving car or bus should never be used.

E. TRAVEL TIME FOR MINORS

1. Companies traveling from studios to a location or from a location to a studio, shall count one half of the total travel time as part of the working day. Total travel time shall not exceed 4 hours per day.

2. Minors on location must leave location no later than the end of their working day; and not be held for transportation; for example, on a 7:00 a.m. call minors must leave location no later than 4:00 p.m., if 1 hour lunch has been given.

3. When a company on distant location has to travel daily between living quarters and the place where it is actually working, the time spent

traveling will not count as work, providing the company does not spend more than 45 minutes traveling each way and furnishes the necessary transportation. This is a general rule and subject to reasonable changes either way by the Teacher-Welfare Worker with the company. Working and transportation conditions, age of minors, etc., will influence the final decision.

F. WORKING HOURS OF MINORS

The hours minors may be permitted at the place of employment are limited according to the age of the minor and are distributed as follows:

1. Babies who have reached the age of 15 days but have not reached the age of 6 months may be permitted to remain at the place of employment for a total of two hours. The day's work shall not exceed 20 minutes and under no conditions shall the baby be exposed to bright lights for more than 30 seconds at any one time.

a. Infants under 6 months may be at the place of employment for a maximum of two hours between the hours of 9:00 a.m. and 4:30 p.m.
b. When babies under 6 weeks of age are used, a nurse and Teacher-Welfare Worker must be provided for each 3 babies or fraction thereof. When infants from age 6 weeks to 6 months are used, one nurse and one Teacher-Welfare Worker must be provided for each 10 babies or fraction thereof.
c. Employer must furnish transportation for babies less than 6 months of age.

2. Minors who have reached the age of 6 months and who have not attained the age of 2 years may be permitted at the place of employment for four hours, two hours work, and two hours rest and recreation.

a. Each minor under 2 years of age must be accompanied by an adult, either a parent or guardian.
b. It is recommended that the employer furnish transportation for babies 6 months of age to 2 years of age, and for any minor under certain conditions as determined by the Division of Labor Law Enforcement.

3. Minors who have reached the age of 2 years but who have not attained the age of 6 years may be permitted at the place of employment for six hours, three hours at work and three hours at rest and recreation, or school. A suitable place for minors to rest and play must be provided, otherwise the rules are the same as for babies under 2 years of age.

4. Minors who have reached the age of 6 years may be permitted at the place of employment for eight hours, four hours at work and four hours school, rest, and recreation. On days school is not in session, working hours may be increased to six hours at the discretion of the Teacher-Welfare Worker.

5. The working day for minors shall end not later than 6:30 p.m. If emergency* requests are granted for minors to work after 6:30 p.m., the following schedule should be followed. Each request must be considered individually by the Division of Labor Law Enforcement.

- 8 years & younger—6:30 p.m.
- 9 years—8:00 p.m.
- 10 through 12 years—9:00 p.m.
- 13 through 17 years—10:00 p.m.

6. Any request for minors to work between 10:00 p.m. and 12:00 p.m. must be made in writing, by the employer, to the Division of Labor Law Enforcement. Written consent of the Division must be obtained before the minor may work. At least 48 hours advance notice of such request should be given to allow adequate time for investigation. If permission is granted, the Division of Labor Law Enforcement will immediately notify the Work Permits Office by telephone.

7. Twelve hours must elapse between the minor's time of dismissal and the time of call on following day. If the minor's regular school starts less than twelve hours after his dismissal time, he must be schooled the following day at the employer's place of business.

G. SUMMARY OF WORKING HOURS OF MINORS

Age	School or Recreation	At Work	Total on Set
15 to 180 days, incl.	1 hr. 40 min.	20 min.	2 hrs.
6 months to 24 months, incl.	2 hrs.	2 hrs.	4 hrs.
2 to 5 years, incl.	3 hrs.	3 hrs.	6 hrs.
	(Total of 6 hrs. on set where nursery is provided —otherwise same as under 2 years of age.)		
6 to 18 years	4 hrs.	4 hrs.	8 hrs.
	(3 hrs. school, 1 hr. recreation)		

---

* Example: Night exteriors shot as exteriors, live television, or theatrical productions presented after 6:30 p.m.

H. Meal Periods for Minors

1. With the exception of infants under 6 months of age, all of the hours on the lot are exclusive of meal periods which must be of at least ½ hour and no more than 1 hour duration.

2. Minors must be sent to lunch no earlier than 11:30 a.m. and no later than 1:00 p.m. Minors must be sent to dinner no earlier than 4:30 p.m. and no later than 6:30 p.m. However, in no case may the minor be on call at place of employment for a period longer than 5½ hours without a meal break.

I. Early Morning Calls

Minors under 14 years of age should not be asked to report for work before 7:00 a.m.

J. School Time for Minors

The required 3 hours of school time for minors must be provided between the hours of 8:00 a.m. and 4:00 p.m. No period of less than 20 minutes duration may be accepted as school time.

1. Employers must provide a Teacher-Welfare Worker on each call for minors under 18 years of age. Where more than 10 minors are sent to work on the same set one teacher must be provided for each group of 10 or fraction thereof. On Saturdays, Sundays, holidays, or on school vacation periods a Teacher-Welfare Worker must be provided for each group of 20 minors or fraction thereof. Companies taking minors from California to work on location in another State shall take a regular certified Teacher-Welfare Worker.

2. When more than one baby is to be used, one nurse and one Teacher-Welfare Worker must be provided for each 3 babies or fraction thereof under 6 weeks of age, and one nurse and one Teacher-Welfare Worker must be provided for each 10 babies over 6 weeks of age and less than 6 months.

3. Teacher-Welfare Workers must be secured from the Work Permits Office. The employer or his agent must order the Teacher-Welfare Worker by calling 687-4831. For anticipated emergency Teacher-Welfare Worker calls after 4:30 p.m. or for week-ends, call the Work Permits Office between 4:00 p.m. and 4:30 p.m. of the day before the teacher is needed for a list of teachers who are available. This list becomes invalid when the Los Angeles United School District Office reopens at 8:00 a.m.

* * *

B. When Minor Works

1. All minors under 18 years of age must be tutored and supervised at the place of employment. The supervisor is known as a Teacher-Welfare Worker.

2. Parents must instruct the minor to report to the Teacher-Welfare Worker immediately upon reaching the place of employment.

3. Parents must be familiar with the requirements printed on the reverse side of the permit—this information is very important.

4. At all times, including weekends and vacations, the Teacher-Welfare Worker acts as a welfare worker whose duty is to safeguard the minor. Presence of the Teacher-Welfare Worker does not relieve parents of the responsibility of caring for their own children.

5. Parent or guardian must be present at all times while a minor is working. The parent is responsible during the lunch hour and any time the minor is not working. When school is in session, the Teacher-Welfare Worker has primary responsibility.

6. Only minors called for work are allowed on the set—parents are not permitted to bring other children without the special permission of the employer and the Teacher-Welfare Worker.

7. An acceptable Guardian must be at least 18 years of age, have the written permission of the parents to act as a guardian, and show sufficient maturity to be approved by the employer and Teacher-Welfare Worker.

8. When a parent is working at the minor's place of employment but not at the scene of employment, there must be a guardian with the minor.

*   *   *

9. No minor shall be called during school hours, for interviews, screen tests, or for any other purpose except when 3 hours or school are provided at the place of employment. School must be provided also when children are given "weather permitting" calls if and when these calls interfere with regular school attendance. Pupils may be granted permission to leave school with parent or guardian in emergency situations. This permission must be secured for the Work Permits Office.

Appendix Five

New American Federation of Musicians (AFM) Report Form

The Joint Policy Committee on Broadcast Talent Union Relations of the Association of National Advertisers (ANA) and the American Association of Advertising Agencies (AAAA) has reached an agreement with the American Federation of Musicians (AFM) to use the report form shown in this appendix.

This form is to accompany billing from music production companies, following recording sessions for commercials. The pay structure (as of 1992) is incorporated on the report forms. This form is required when any and all payments provided under the AFM Commercials Contract are made to musicians.

A.N.A.-A.A.A.A.
JOINT POLICY COMMITTEE ON BROADCAST TALENT UNION RELATIONS

ASSOCIATION OF NATIONAL ADVERTISERS, INC.
155 East 44th Street, New York, N.Y. 10017

AMERICAN ASSOCIATION OF ADVERTISING AGENCIES, INC.
666 Third Avenue, New York, N.Y. 10017

NEW AMERICAN FEDERATION OF MUSICIANS (AFM) REPORT FORM

As agreed in our negotiations with AFM last Spring, the AFM Report Form (Form B) has been revised; a copy is attached.

AFM is in the process of sending copies of the new Report Form to their Locals and signatories. As soon as this Report Form is available for use, agencies should insist that music production companies use it.

The revised Form will be simple to complete. All appropriate information must be inserted or checked. Among other things, please note that:

- *Employee's name* column requires the listing of instrument(s);

- *Wages* column provides for separate listing of wages and cartage. As in the past, there is a box to be checked when wages being paid are overscale;

- In the *Pension Contribution* column, be sure Pension is calculated only on *scale wages*, even if a musician is overscale;

- The *Employer of Record* is the company that is issuing checks to the musicians. In almost all cases the Employer of Record will be a payroll service;

- The new Form provides for the separate listing of the name of the Signatory of Record for the session and for use. The *Signatory of Record* is the party AFM will hold responsible for proper compliance with the AFM Commercials Agreement. You may want the music production company to be the Signatory of Record for the session, even though your agency may be willing to be the Signatory of Record for use purposes.

This Form, or a substitute form containing the same data, is required when any and all payments provided under the AFM Commercials Contract are made to musicians.

A.N.A.-A.A.A.A.
JOINT POLICY COMMITTEE ON BROADCAST TALENT UNION RELATIONS

ASSOCIATION OF NATIONAL ADVERTISERS, INC.
155 East 44th Street, New York, N.Y. 10017

AMERICAN ASSOCIATION OF ADVERTISING AGENCIES, INC.
666 Third Avenue, New York, N.Y. 10017

INCREASE IN AMERICAN FEDERATION OF MUSICIANS RATES

Effective 5/1/92, AFM rates increase as follows:

# OF MUSICIANS	SESSION		USE, REUSE, NEW USE & DUBBING	
	FROM	TO	FROM	TO
1	$156.00	$160.00	$117.00	$120.00
2-4	84.30	86.45	63.25	64.85
5 & over	78.00	80.00	58.50	60.00

Increases apply to commercial music tracks produced on or after 5/1/92 AND apply, regardless of the original recording date, to dubbing or new use fees due for music tracks incorporated into new commercials which first air on or after 5/1/92.

All other rates remain unchanged.

AMERICAN FEDERATION OF MUSICIANS REPORT FORM
TELEVISION AND RADIO COMMERCIAL ANNOUNCEMENTS   RP № 056002

DATE: _____

ADVERTISER: _____

PRODUCT: _____

ADVERTISING AGENCY: _____

AGENCY REP.: _____

AGENCY ADDRESS: _____

_____

AGENCY REP. PHONE: _____

ORIGINAL SESSION   AFM Local No. _____

Recording Date: _____   No. of Musicians: _____

Recording Studio: _____

City: _____   State: _____

Hours of Employment: _____

Music Prod. Co. Name: _____

RE-USE, DUBBING, NEW USE OR OTHER

Original Report Form No.: _____

Original Recording Date: _____

(a) LOWEST No. OF REPORTED HRS W'KD: _____

(b) No. OF ANNOUNCEMENTS CLAIMED: _____

One announcement may be claimed for every 20 minutes reported in (a) above, subject to a maximum of 8 announcements for synthesizer-only sessions.

IDENTIFICATION Titles and Code Nos. (Include track length for original sessions only.) When identification changes give prior and new.

Original (or Prior) Identification	TRK LGTH	New Identification
A. _____	_____	_____
B. _____	_____	_____
C. _____	_____	_____
D. _____	_____	_____
E. _____	_____	_____
F. _____	_____	_____
G. _____	_____	_____

First Air Date: _____

Cycle Dates Being Paid: _____

Check 1 and only 1 from each of these three columns.

Payment Type	Medium	Rates
___ Original Session	___ TV	___ National
___ Initial Use	___ Radio (13 weeks)	___ Foreign
___ Re-Use	___ Radio (8 weeks)	___ Regional (Nat'l Adv)
___ New Use	___ Non-Broadcast	___ Regional (Reg. Adv)
___ Dubbing	___ Other	___ Local (Nat'l Adv)
___ Dubbing (Longer/ Shorter Version)		___ Local (Local Adv)
___ Other		Indicate region or local area in MEMO box

Additional Info	Check here if
___ Short Term Use	___ Commercial made for cable only
___ Info Changes	___ PSA status confirmed by AFM
___ Mech. Edit	___ Session performed solely on synthesizer
___ Sideline Session	
___ Other	MEMO

EMPLOYER OF RECORD (e.g. Payroll Service) _____

SIGNATORY OF RECORD:

For Session Payments _____   Address _____

For All Other Payments _____   Address _____

The terms and conditions of the engagement covered by this Report Form include the terms and conditions of the AFM Commercial Announcements Agreement in effect at the time of such engagement.

Signatory of Record's Signature _____   Leader's Signature _____

Print Name of Signer _____   Phone _____   Leader's Phone _____

LOCAL UNION NO. CARD NO.	EMPLOYEE'S NAME (AS ON SOCIAL SECURITY CARD) LAST FIRST INITIAL (Instrument(s))	SOCIAL SECURITY NUMBER	HRS WK'D	NO. OF DBL PER SESS.	SPOT ID BY LETTER ABOVE	ID OF SPOT PER DBL	WAGES (1) CARTAGE	PENSION CONTRI- BUTION	H & W WHERE APPLIC- ABLE
--------	(LDR)								

--------	(ARR)								
--------	(ORC)								
--------	(COPY)								

(1) Insert X if wages being paid are overscale.

FOR FUND USE ONLY:

TOTAL H&W CONTRIBUTIONS

TOTAL PENSION CONTRIBUTIONS

FORM B-8 REV 1-90

Distribution of the 6 copies of this Report Form is as follows:

1. Original (first) page is to be sent to:

   AFM-EP Fund
   304 East 44th Street
   New York, NY 10017

   with Pension contribution check made payable to the AFM-EP Fund.

2. One copy is to be retained by the Music Production Company.

3. One copy to the Advertising Agency where applicable.

4. The remaining 3 copies are to be sent to the applicable AFM Local with the musicians' checks.

   The AFM Local will:

   - retain one copy
   - send one copy to the American Federation of Musicians, 1501 Broadway, Suite 600, New York, NY 10036
   - send one copy to the leader

Pension Contribution

	TV	Radio
Commercials produced on and after 2/7/79	9.0%	9.0%
Commercials produced on and after 2/7/82	10.0%	9.5%

Health and Welfare Payments

1. Original Session Only:

   $12.00 for each original service performed up to a maximum of two services

2. All Scale Wage Payments

   An amount equal to 2% of all scale wages (session, dubbing, new use and re-use fees) being paid under the AFM Commercials Announcements Agreement.

See Section X, Health & Welfare Payments, of the AFM Commercials Announcements Agreement for information regarding distribution of Health & Welfare payments.

AMERICAN FEDERATION OF MUSICIANS REPORT FORM
TELEVISION AND RADIO COMMERCIAL ANNOUNCEMENTS
CONTINUATION SHEET

Recording Date: _____

Leader's Name: _____

Report Form # _____

Page _____ of _____

LOCAL UNION NO. CARD NO.	EMPLOYEE'S NAME (AS ON SOCIAL SECURITY CARD) LAST FIRST INITIAL (Instrument(s))	SOCIAL SECURITY NUMBER	HRS WK'D	NO. OF DBL PER SESS.	SPOT ID BY LETTER ABOVE	ID OF SPOT PER DBL	WAGES (1) CARTAGE	PENSION CONTRI- BUTION	H & W WHERE APPLIC- ABLE
	(ARR)								
	(ORC)								
	(COPY)								

(1) Insert X if wages being paid are overscale.

FOR FUND USE ONLY:

TOTAL H&W CONTRIBUTIONS

TOTAL PENSION CONTRIBUTIONS

FORM B & H&W 1-92

Appendix Six

Production House Costs and Comparative Commercial Gross Average Costs Including Agency Commission*

The cost of commercial production continues to rise, due to increases in both union pay scales and construction and materials costs. This appendix provides a 10-year look at these costs, with a percentage assigned to the increase in the five years between 1986 and 1991.

The final page of the appendix shows the cost increase in production by product category. The only dramatic cost reduction is in commercials for consumer service/retail stores. The largest percentage increase is in the cost to produce commercials for computers and office equipment. Among the types of commercials produced, the largest cost increase involves interview/testimonial commercials. This is largely due to the use of film rather than videotape as a production tool in this type of commercial.

---

* Source: American Association of Advertising Agencies

Production House Costs

	1981	1986	1991	Percentage Change, 1986–1991
CREW (Cost per day)				
Producer	250	500	700	40%
Assistant Director	350	600	700	17
Director of Photography	600	2,500	2,500	—
Camera Operator	300	500	1,000	100
Assistant Cameraman	250	375	450	20
Outside Prop	250	375	450	20
Inside Prop	250	375	450	20
Electrician	250	375	450	20
Best Boy	200	350	425	21
Grip	250	375	450	20
Mixer	275	375	450	20
Boom Man	200	350	375	7
Recordist	250	450	450	—
Make-up	250	375	500	33
Hair	250	375	500	33
Stylist	250	375	500	33
Wardrobe Attendant	175	250	300	20
Script Clerk	225	375	450	20
Home Economist	250	500	700	40
VTR Man	200	300	425	42
Location/Contact Scout	200	300	400	33
Coordinator	150	250	375	50
Nurse/Teacher	200	300	350	17
Utility	100	150	150	—
PRODUCTION & WRAP MATERIALS EXPENSES				
Still Camera Rental & Film	200	175	250	43%
Messengers	100	150	250	67
Trucking	150	300	300	—
Telephone & Cable	75	150	250	67
Casting	325	400	500	25
LOCATION EXPENSES				
Location Fees	1,000	1,500	3,000	100%
Camper Dressing Rooms	225	600	500	−17
Parking, Tolls, & Gas	200	300	300	—
Trucking	225	350	350	—
Breakfast	100	250	350	40
Lunch	325	600	800	33
Guards	100	250	350	40

PRODUCTION HOUSE COSTS

	1981	1986	1991	Percentage Change, 1986–1991
SET CONSTRUCTION				
Set Designer	450	600	800	33%
Carpenters	65	150	250	67
Grips	65	150	250	67
Outside Props	100	300	450	50
Inside Props	150	150	350	133
Scenics	150	150	600	300
STUDIO RENTAL & EXPENSES—STAGE				
Rental for Build Days	450	450	900	100%
Rental for Pre-Light Days	450	700	1,800	157
Rental for Shoot Days	550	700	1,800	157
Total Power Charge & Bulbs	100	275	650	136
Misc. Studio Charges (cartage, coffee, phone)	125	300	450	33
Meals for Crew & Talent (lunch & dinner)	75	250	350	40
EQUIPMENT RENTAL				
Camera Rental	775	1,750	2,100	20%
Sound Rental	250	350	475	35
Lighting Rental	800	1,750	3,000	71
Grip Rental	275	900	1,500	67
Generator Rental	300	300	500	66
Crane/Cherry Picker Rental	300	800	1,200	50
VTR Rental	225	250	450	80
FILM—RAW STOCK/DEVELOP & PRINT				
Developing footage amount	0.66	0.82	0.99	21%
Transfer to mag	150	280		
Sync/Screen Dailies	160	233	250	7
TRAVEL & LIVING				
Air Fare (N.Y. to L.A.)	425	1,020	1,203	18%
Hotel	95	135	175	30
DIRECTOR'S FEE				
Per Shoot Day	3,500	9,000	10,000	11%

Production House Costs

	1981	1986	1991	Percentage Change, 1986–1991
TALENT				
O/C Principals	275	333	461	38%
General Extras	197	232	236	2
Hand Model	274	307	450	47
EDITING				
Final Mix	120	245	400/Hr.	63%
Negative Prep/Conform	20	35	35	—
Film to Tape w/ Color Correction	400	430	480	12
On-Line Edit	405	435	480	10
Editor's Fee per Hour	65	100	150	50
D2 Edit			505/Hr.	
Kaleidoscope (1st channel w/ edit)			385/Hr.	
Kaleidoscope (per additional channel)			250/Hr.	
Abekas—A62			300/Hr.	
Character Generator			150/Hr.	
Additional VTR (1" or D2)			150/Hr.	
Additional VTR (Beta Sp.)			100/Hr.	
Additional VTR (3/4")			75/Hr.	
Retrack-Reslash			500 each	
TELECINE				
Color Correct. Transfer to 1"			480/Hr.	
Color Correct. Transfer to D2			505/Hr.	
Best Light Transfer			250/Hr.	
MOTION CONTROL				
IMC 3565 2-D Video Motion Control			250/Hr. + VTRs	
ELECTRONIC GRAPHICS				
Quantel Paintbox			250/Hr.	
Quantel Harry Digital Editor			400/Hr.	
Abekas A53-D			225/Hr.	
DF-X Composium (in Abekas A-60)			325/Hr.	

MUSIC

Musicians Payment/Session				
1 musician	112	148	220	49%
2–4 musicians	61	80	120	50
5+ musicians	56	74	120	62
Musicians Payment/Dub/Residual				
1 musician				
2–4 musicians	84	111	156	41
	45	60	84.30	41

NATIONAL ADVERTISERS (Total Gross Cost Averages—Including Agency Commission)

Displayed by Product Category	Number of Commercials in Database	1989 National Advertisers ($000)	Number of Commercials in Database	1990 National Advertisers ($000)	Percentage Change
Automobiles/trucks/motorcycles	125	$272	179	$310	14%
Automotive accessories/supplies	28	188	40	182	–3
Beauty/fashion/cosmetics	40	218	45	247	13
Gifts/toys/hobbies/recreation	56	219	80	173	–21
Furniture/appliances/AV products	26	125	26	137	10
Apparel/clothing	4	129	7	164	27
Banking/financial/insurance	88	316	45	393	24
Consumer services/retail stores	71	256	20	161	–37
Corporate image/media promotion	52	289	42	306	6
Travel/vacation destination	30	309	25	356	15
Beer/wine	69	342	40	502	47
Soft drinks/snacks	114	277	124	265	–4
Retail & fast-food restaurants	188	143	186	172	20
Packaged food	477	142	449	176	24
Household products	136	182	125	166	–9
Drugs/toiletries	199	130	221	139	7
Office equipment/computers	32	219	10	331	51
Other products	35	162	32	195	20

Displayed by Commercial Type	Number of Commercials in Database	1989 National Advertisers ($000)	Number of Commercials in Database	1990 National Advertisers ($000)	Percentage Change
Monolog	194	$111	136	$138	24%
Interview/testimonial	73	99	114	155	57
Tabletop/ECU products, food	151	102	79	127	25
Multi-story line/vignettes	263	275	406	268	-3
Song & dance	27	334	38	307	-8
Animation	138	187	154	182	-3
Special effects	88	311	80	281	-10
Single situation—product performance	129	193	161	205	6
Single situation—voiceover	339	206	259	244	18
Single situation—dialog	367	200	269	173	-14

Displayed by Specific Length*	Number of Commercials in Database	1989 National Advertisers ($000)	Number of Commercials in Database	1990 National Advertisers ($000)	Percentage Change
:15's	172	$ 95	132	$ 95	0%
:30's	917	222	985	228	3
:45's	32	217	31	225	4
:60's	35	519	25	505	-3

*Multiple, different length packages are not included.

GLOSSARY OF PRODUCTION TERMS

Rather than divide the glossary into separate sections for film, videotape, and computer terms, I have opted to combine them in one alphabetical list. Whereas the film and videotape terms have been around a long while, the computer and its digital abilities continue to generate new terms and descriptions. Included here are definitions of some of the terms for the equipment and production procedures involved in this expanding high-tech area.

Novices to TV commercial production should not be put off by the technical terms used by professionals in the field. Unfortunately, some editors and computer experts use esoteric jargon to describe what is happening in the finishing suite. Whenever that happens, be sure to stop them and ask for a plain-English translation.

A and B rolls The placing of edited scenes on separate negative rolls when a commercial is shot, edited, and finished on film and there are no special optical effects between each scene. In making the composite negative, A and B are rolled together; on the A roll are odd-numbered scenes, and the even-numbered scenes are on the B roll. The scenes are so spaced that they fit together in the correct numerical order. A and B printing saves time and expense and allows the film editor to work with either the original film negative or an early "dupe" (duplicate) negative.

Academy leader A threading film lead-in for the film projector, numbered in a standard way, set by the Society of Motion Picture and Television Engineers (SMPTE). The numbers appear in descending order from 10 to 2. There is no 1; instead, a pulse sound is heard before the actual commercial picture and sound track.

AFTRA/SAG Unions that govern the use of actors in commercials. Videotape and radio commercials are governed by AFTRA (American Federation of Television and Radio Artists); filmed commercials are governed by SAG (Screen Actors Guild).

Analog A direct representation of picture information, which is subject to degradation when copied. In other words, each generation copied from the original is less clear, lacking the original's high quality. (See *digital*.)

Animatic A series of still pictures or drawings that demonstrate the commercial's hoped-for final look and action, often replacing the storyboard, in order to present the creative idea in real time.

American Society of Composers, Authors and Publishers (ASCAP)
The organization that controls and supervises the payment of royalties and use fees for music composed for and played in TV commercials.

Animation camera A special film camera, usually mounted on a post or column, with the lens pointing straight down at the animation stand. The camera is equipped to shoot one frame at a time and can be moved up and down on the post. With related accessories, it can rotate through 360 degrees and may be used for projecting matching scenes and effects. With a special motor, stop-motion effects can be made; with special magazines, the animation camera can be used for optical effects; and with special inserts, it can be used for matte shots. To a large extent, the film animation camera has been replaced by new computer equipment.

Animator (film) An artist who draws characters in motion; the drafts-man who carries out the concepts of the director of animation and gives the graphic characters a personality. Animators work with computers as well as in traditional cel drawings.

Apple box Wooden boxes used on the shooting stage for various purposes. For example, if the camera is too high to be viewed while standing on the floor, the camera person will ask for an apple box and stand on it to look through the lens. (In Australia, apple boxes are called *man makers*.)

Artificial intelligence A developing technology that allows the com-puter to make seemingly intuitive decisions.

ASCAP See American Society of Composers, Authors and Publishers.

Aspect ratio The relative dimensions of the TV viewing screen. The standard aspect ratio in the United States is 1 high by 1.33 wide. The prosposed screen ratio for HDTV is 9 high by 16 wide.

Bar sheet A complete written record of an animation, in terms of single-frame relationships to a sound track. These sheets show the exact length of each syllable and each word, each action, music, effects, and any other sound in the sound track. It is from the bar sheets that the film animator plans the drawn animation.

Barn door See Scrims, gobos, and barn doors.

Button The short closing musical phrase that "buttons up" and ends a music track.

Camera (film/videotape)   Different film cameras are used for several different negative film sizes, running normally at 24 frames of film per second. These film sizes range from the amateur 8mm to 16mm, 35mm, and 70mm. The most commonly used professional camera for commercial use is 35mm. The film cameras expose the negative, which must then be removed and developed at a film laboratory.

A videotape camera, in contrast, absorbs the light values of a scene and converts them to a corresponding series of electrical impulses. The video camera is not loaded with videotape the way a film camera is loaded with film. The video camera sends its electrical impulses to a videotape machine, which can be in any tape format: 1/2-inch, 3/4-inch, 1-inch, or 2-inch. The video camera can also bypass the videotape machine and be conducted directly to transmission.

CGI   See *Computer-generated imagery*.

Cel   An abbreviation for celluloid. The clear plastic sheet on which an animator draws a frame to be used in animation. If it is full animation, 24 different cels will be drawn for each second of screen time. In some instances, animation is drawn in twos, meaning each cel represents two frames of film instead of one.

Chrominance signal   The part of the total video signal that contains the color information.

Click track   A mechanical beat (similar to that of a metronome) that is recorded and played through earphones for musicians during a recording session. The speed of the click is calculated by the frames of film it represents (e.g., an 8-frame click is 3 beats per second at 24 frames of film per second).

Close-up   Photographing objects (or people) at close range. Listed as "CU" on the video side of the script; variations include ECU (Extreme Close-up) and MCU (Medium Close-up).

Color phase   The proper timing relationship with a color signal. Color is considered to be "in phase" when the hue is reproduced correctly on the video monitor.

Compatible color   A TV broadcast system that produces a color signal that can be received by either a black-and-white or a color TV set.

Composite track   The final mix of a sound track, including all elements of sound effects, voice, and music and "dubbed down" to their final balance.

Composite video signal   A video signal containing both picture and in-sync sound information.

Compositing   The combining of disparate visual material, in various layers, within a computer. Thus, live-action photography, computer-generated images, and traditional cel animation can be combined and manipulated by using a variety of computerized tools, including digital disk recorders and computer animation systems.

Computer-generated imagery (CGI) (Also *computer graphic imaging*.) Animation in which action is generated in a computer by a combination of artist and engineer. (See Chapter 11.)

Conforming   Preparing the negative materials, based on the marked-up work-print (or computer-generated work-print) for the final film or tape mix.

Cut   The director's command to the camera person to end a scene. Also used to describe editing (cutting the film or tape) and as an optical direction (e.g., straight-cut video material goes directly from one scene to the next without a dissolve or any other optical device).

Dailies (Also *rushes*.)   The print of scenes shot on each film shooting day, usually viewed the next day.

DAT   See *Digital Audio Tape*.

Demo   Short for "demonstration." Usually refers to a tape sample of a musician's, production company's, or voiceover announcer's work.

Depth of field   The distance between the closest object in focus and the farthest object in focus within a scene, as viewed by a particular lens. Depth of field varies with the amount of light in the scene: The more light, the deeper the field. Depth of field can vary with the quality and focal length (in millimeters) of the lens or with the f-stop setting.

Digital   The operative word in today's computerized editing and finishing. By transferring audio, video, and other signal information into the computer binary language made up of 0's and 1's, the material is not subject to signal errors and can be copied repeatedly without loss of quality. (See *analog*.)

D1   "D" stands for "digital video," in which film or videotape is fed into a computer. D1 is like a 35mm negative: All the information, including all the colors, is kept in its original form. D1 is needed to do special effects.

D2   Like a 35mm film print, D2 is used for editorial work where the artistic element is in the editing of the original filming. (See *D1*.)

D3   Similar to D2, but on a smaller tape format. It is wise to check with your editorial house for further advice, because new equipment is continually being developed. (See *D1*.)

Digital Audio Tape (DAT)   A smaller audio tape size, which is virtually noise-free and pure, because it has been digitized.

Dissolve   A short double-exposure between two scenes, in which the first scene is replaced slowly by the second scene. A cross-dissolve can be short or long, depending on the editor's (or director's) instructions.

Dolly   The four-wheel, movable platform on which the motion picture camera is mounted. A dolly-pusher moves the complete dolly, containing the camera and camera person, in all agreed-upon moves during the actual filming.

Edge numbers   See *Key numbers*.

Editorial Decision List (EDL)   A list of the various takes from which the final edit will be made; usually printed out from a computer.

Electronic news gathering (ENG)   The use of video cameras and related gear to collect news stories for TV airing.

Erase head   An electromagnet that erases an existing signal from an audio tape or videotape, allowing a new signal to be recorded. Videotape can be erased and re-used; film cannot be.

Fade   "Fade up" means coming from black and fading up into a scene. "Fade down" is fading out of a scene into black.

Finder   The viewing lens through which you can see what the camera sees.

F-stop   The calibration which allows more or less light to reach the film through the camera lens. The number of the F-stop determines the aperture of the lens.

Gaffer's tape   A 3-inch, heavy-duty tape, similar to electrician's tape. It is used for every purpose imaginable during production—from covering exposed electrical wiring on the stage floor to holding all sorts of things together during the shooting of a scene. No production should be without gaffer's tape.

Generation   Each successive step in duplicating a picture or sound on tape, resulting in a gradual loss of image or audio quality. (See *digital*.)

Gobo   See *Scrims, gobos, and barn doors*.

Heads out   Film wound onto a core or reel with the beginning of the film on the outside of the reel, ready to be played or viewed. (See *Tails out*.)

High hat   The lowest platform on which to place a camera, about six inches above the floor.

Inches per second (IPS)   The speed that magnetic sound tape travels. Amateur speed for sound recording is either 3-3/4 or 7-1/2 IPS. The professional speed is either 15 or 30 IPS. The faster the tape recording and playback speed, the higher the fidelity of the sound.

Infomercial   A contraction of "information" and "commercial." An in-fomercial is usually 30 minutes in length and thinly hides its commercial message in a program format.

In sync   The condition in which picture action matches perfectly with the sound track. If, on the other hand, the actor's mouth movements do not match the sound of his voice, the film is "out of sync," and the track must be moved until it matches the picture. ("Sync" is an abbreviation for "synchronous.")

Interlock   The locking together together of the separated picture and sound track in film production. When film is shot with on-camera sound, the sound and picture elements are recorded separately. Videotape is automatically in sync and interlocked, because both sound and picture share the same magnetic tape.

IPS   See *Inches per second*.

Key numbers (Also *edge numbers*.)   All film negative stock has this series of numbers along its edge. In tape parlance, a similar identifying system can be achieved by adding "time code" to the videotape. Either system allows the editor to catalog all the film and tape elements for later use.

Layering   Using the off-line capabilities of the digital computer, various layers of foregrounds, backgrounds, and visuals in between can be built within a single frame of film, all with first-generation clarity.

Library music   A source for music in the public domain, which can be used by paying a nominal, one-time licensing fee to the music publisher. These pieces of music can be found in the libraries of recording studios, film companies, and radio and TV stations.

Lip sync   Spoken lines recorded simultaneously with filming of the action. Usually, the script will make this reference (OC for On Camera) at the beginning of the scene.

Loop   A large circle of film or tape used in dubbing sessions. If you want to re-voice an actor's reading, you "loop it." The actor stands in a recording studio watching the projected film loop on the screen, which keeps repeating until the actor has matched his or her voice to the movement of the lips on the screen.

Minicam (Also *microcam*.)   Lightweight, often self-contained, portable video camera for ENG taping.

Monitor   A TV set without a tuner, used to directly display the sound and picture from a camera, from a videotape recorder, or from a special-effects generator.

Morphing   The computer's ability to make continuous alterations (metamorphoses) in shape and form. This effect has been heavily used in computer-edited commercials using Computer Graphic Imaging (CGI). (See Chapter 14.)

MOS   A silent take. The term derives from a European director who thought he was saying, "This scene will be without sound." But he actually said, "This scene will be mitout sound."

National Television Systems Committee (NTSC)   The NTSC standard for television in the United States dictated that transmission of the TV signal would be at 525 lines, a coarser picture than that seen in other countries around the world.

Nonlinear editing   See *Random access/nonlinear editing*.

Ones, twos, threes   In drawn animation, the number of different drawings used. If a new drawing or variation is done for every frame, it is being animated "in ones." This is the smoothest type of animated action. If the drawing changes every two frames, it is "in twos." If the drawing changes every third frame, "in threes," the action will be jumpy. "In threes" is usually shot only for effect.

Optical window A small segment of the picture frame into which another scene is positioned while the major film or tape action continues. Optical windows are often used in the final scene of a commercial while addresses and product logos appear on the rest of the screen.

Opticals Any effect added to the original film: dissolves, wipes, titles, blow-ups, reductions, zooms, etc. Opticals are usually added in the final compositing room, where the film has already been transferred to tape.

Out of sync See *In sync*.

Overcrank See *Undercrank*.

PAL See *Phase Alternating Line*.

Phase The relative timing of a signal in relation to another signal. If both signals occur at the same instant, they are "in phase." If they do not, they are "out of phase."

Phase Alternating Line (PAL) The transmission standard for European TV transmission at 625 lines, guaranteeing a higher definition picture than in the United States. The PAL system is also used in other parts of the world.

Primary colors The three primary colors (red, green, and blue) are used in color TV. No two of the three can be combined to produce the third.

Random access/nonlinear editing When visuals and sounds (from film, videotape, or sound tape) are transferred into the computer, they can be instantly retrieved in any order (random access) and rearranged in any way (nonlinear editing), without disturbing the original material.

Resolution A measure of the greatest amount of detail seen in an image. The higher the resolution, the clearer and more detailed the image.

Rotoscope A method of adding animation to a live-action scene. Previously, rotoscoping was a tedious frame-by-frame optical process. The computer has made rotoscoping much simpler and quicker to accomplish.

Rough-cut The first edit of a commercial. The various scenes are cut into their proper order, but the scene lengths are still "rough."

SAG See *AFTRA/SAG*.

Scratch-off   An animation technique in which a portion of the first complete drawing is erased with each successive frame of exposed film. The opposite effect, a "scratch-on," is obtained by reversing the film.

Scrims, gobos, and barn doors   Various additions to the lights that illuminate the set. A scrim (also *silk*) is a thin piece of translucent cloth used to diffuse and soften the light. Gobos and barn doors are physical elements, usually mounted on separate stands, that can block out certain portions of the light source at the direction of the camera operator. They can be moved about, up and down.

Sequentiel à Couleur Memoire **(SECAM)**   625-line transmission system used in France and many Eastern European countries. The phrase means "sequential color and memory."

16mm   An intermediate film size developed by the military during the second world war. Originally considered to be "amateur film," the newest 16mm negatives have exceptional fine grain qualities and join 35mm film in professional use. (See *35mm*.)

Standards conversion   The process of changing the various signals (NTSC, PAL, and SECAM) from one system to another. Inherent problems include errors resulting from the different frame rates and soft or jittery motion.

Sticks and legs   Tripods on which the camera is mounted in a stationary position. (If you want the camera to move about, don't use sticks—mount the camera on a movable dolly.)

Stock footage   Previously shot scenes of all kinds, found in stock footage libraries. The initial charge is for making an examination print or tape of the footage requested, plus a per-foot charge for the footage that is actually used in a commercial. Stock footage includes historic newsreel footage, scenic locations in all types of weather, as well as every imaginable type of sports or stunts.

Storyboard   A series of either art frames or photos which depict the planned-for action of a commercial. Usually presented on large cardboard backing for easy viewing by a group. The traditional way to present the look of a proposed commercial.

Strobing   Because film normally goes through the camera in a series of 24 still pictures per second, sometimes the filmed action "strobes," or seems to jump and flicker. In the case of a turning wheel, it may even seem to be turning backward instead of forward. The camera operator can sometimes solve this problem by changing the angle of photography or varying the speed of the film through the camera to more than 24 frames per second.

Tails out   Film wound onto a core or reel with the end of the film on the outside of the reel. (See *Heads out*.)

Take   Each new filming of a scene. The number of the take is recorded on the clap-board so the editor can identify it later. Also refers to an actor's surprised reaction, as in "double-take."

35mm   A professional 35mm film negative stock. Originally developed by Eastman Kodak, it continues to represent the ultimate in motion picture photography. New emulsions are continually being developed, pushing the boundaries of image-making capabilities.

Threes   See *Ones, twos, threes*.

Time code   See *Key numbers*.

Twos   See *Ones, twos, threes*.

Ultimatte   A high-quality video matting system that uses various colors for inserting one image into another. The term is often used in the generic to refer to other blue-screen or green-screen matting techniques.

Undercrank   To slow down the film through the camera to 16 frames per second or less. When the scene is played back at its normal speed of 24 frames per second, the action is fast and jerky, resembling old-time movie action. If you wish the action to be slowed down, reverse the procedure and **overcrank** (i.e., shoot the film at more than 24 frames per second).

Video   The visual portion of TV broadcast. The word *video* is also applied to both the picture and sound portion of the video signal.

Videocassette   A self-contained video module, about the size of a book, played on a specially designed videotape recorder. It houses two reels (supply and take-up), with the tape running between them but connected to both.

Video cassette recorder (VCR)   Playback through which videotape cassettes can be filled with sound and picture information from a TV set or a camera and then played back at will.

Virtual reality   A complicated graphics and optics system, in which a person can "walk through" a three-dimensional computer graphics environment. All the "virtually real" elements exist only in the computer and are displayed only to a person wearing headgear linked to the computer system.

Voiceover   An announcer's or actor's voice heard in the sound track without that person being seen on film. On a script, such voices are listed as "VO."

Wild motor   A device attached to a camera to film in extreme slow motion by running the film negative past the lens at 48, 72, or 144 frames per second, and even more. If the idea is to see corn flakes floating down into a bowl, the camera speed will probably be at least 144 frames per second. If, on the other hand, the idea is to show a golf club hitting a golf ball in an extreme close-up (ECU), the special motor will involve a "pull-down" camera that rushes the film through at speeds of up to 1,000 or more frames per second. Such cameras can race through a 400-foot roll of negative film in a few seconds, but the resultant slow motion may last the entire 30 seconds of commercial time.

Index